To the Pure . . .

A STUDY OF OBSCENITY
AND THE CENSOR

To the Pure . . .

A STUDY OF OBSCENITY AND THE CENSOR

BY MORRIS L. ERNST
AND WILLIAM SEAGLE

THE VIKING PRESS

NEW YORK   MCMXXVIII

THIS BOOK IS DEDICATED

to

THE PERPLEXED BOOKSELLERS

*who, under the unknown rules
of literary decency, cannot insure
themselves against imprisonment,
even by reading all the volumes
on their shelves*

INTRODUCTION

WHAT is obscenity? Is it more than an empty word? The human race is easily enslaved by a combination of letters and readily tyrannized by a phrase. Taboos have often been evoked by the creation of labels, and most labels are only confessions of ignorance. Even scientists snatch at a Greek or Latin polysyllable to describe a state of facts which they do not fully understand. One of the prime uses of speech is to overpower the unknown and many words have no reality behind them. By such tokens people have been brought to believe that there is such a concept as The Obscene.

The mere existence of vice societies, public prosecutions, unfortunate authors, and guilty publishers creates the impression that there must be such a fact as obscenity. Where there is smoke there must be fire.

But few words are as fluid and vague in content as the six deadly adjectives—*obscene, lewd, lascivious, filthy, indecent* and *disgusting*—which are the basis of the censorship. No two persons agree on these definitions. We shall see that judges differ to such an extent that courts divide by narrow margins, thus justifying the ironic complaint of infallible government by the odd man. Juries disagree with judges and the cynicisms and enthusiasms of lawyers bear a relation to the size of the retaining fees. Authors have to adapt their ideas to an unknown measure and jails invite those who cannot guess the contemporary meaning of obscenity. What are the standards and tests which determine the obscene? Is it only a matter of fashion? What effect does obscenity have on society? Can lewdness be regulated by statute? What is the function of the obscenity laws in modern society? What is their history?

There is probably not a single group of statutes which is more important than the obscenity laws. Society is concerned peculiarly with them because they involve the spread of thought and wisdom. The *res* is knowledge, at best a scant commodity, and whereas property has always been the subject of protection, ideas have always been the object of suppression. The importance of these laws is not lessened because the average man feels them only indirectly and cannot appraise their real influences. Like all other forms of censorship they allow wide areas of dissent but only on subjects that do not matter. By indirection they set the limits of freedom wherever the censor's pattern of the universe is challenged. The frontiers behind which men are outlaws constantly shift, for this sex censorship is only active when the prestige of the censor's institution can no longer command the respect it once did. Dissent is given wide latitude only until it threatens to become effective. The vehemence of the suppression of so-called obscenity is always a sign of weakness. Whenever Jupiter appeals to thunder we know that he has erred. The obscenity laws set the whole tone of our society, and in all their ramifications represent a myopic counteractant to democracy. More than is generally supposed they interfere with freedom of opinion. The suppression of any single book is comparatively negligible when the general effects on literature are understood. Their ambiguity is the ultimate evidence of their viciousness.

A great deal has been written about the obscenity laws but mostly by hurried journalists who have been interested in only one or another of their aspects, usually the literary ones. The few jurists who have given them their attention have confined their observations to technical legal quandaries. The individual biographies of vice crusaders are valuable but are generally too much confined to their subjects. It is obvious that many volumes might be filled with the histories of book, movie, play, or newspaper censorship. Indeed, they have! But the problem of the obscenity laws can, however, never be understood with any real insight until it is treated as a whole. We have chosen for our inquiry books—first, because they allow this to be done most conveniently, and second, because they are the dominant conveyers of ideas. Music, painting and sculpture are relatively non-ideational, and the press possesses very special immunities. While, however, we are primarily interested in the interpretation of literary obscenity, the exposition should also illumine other forms. Where the possible differentials are removed, the book, play, motion picture, and the press may be considered upon the same basis.

While we are chiefly interested in obscenity as a contemporary phenomenon, in the contradictions of practice as they reveal themselves in objects, agents, means, and legal or extra-legal supports, a considerable acquaintance with the historical background not only of the obscenity laws but of political and ecclesiastical censorship is essential to understand the continuing unity of purpose behind all forms of suppression. The theoretic and philosophic aspects which give meaning to our apprehensions can be derived only from the past. Again, while we are primarily interested in the American situation, of necessity we must dwell also upon the British. The factor of common language links the contemporary problems, and a common heritage makes the history of the English obscenity laws, indeed, more important than the American. The book thus has an Anglo-Saxon cast rather than an American. It has also been necessary to bring in modern Continental countries to carry the argument to a logical conclusion.

Often it is declared that we are living in enlightened times which have considerably moderated the old rigidity of the sex censorship. But whenever we have been lulled into the belief that the worst ravages of the obscenity laws are over, we suddenly find them again applied, as witness the Boston Book Party of 1927, which will remain memorable for a long time. We are no longer living, it is true, in mid-Victorianism, but we still are very far from liberation. The optimism which prevails in many quarters is still often rudely shattered. Our delusion at times arises from the failure to take into account the extent to which the hysterical campaigns for pure literature in the past have inhibited us, so that for the most part we tend now to respect the obscenity laws automatically.

It may be amusing for the reader before opening the first chapter to write out his own present definition of Obscenity. Try to translate it into words other than the five famous synonyms. Then apply such definition to books, plays, movies and music. See if it satisfies! And then after reading this study compare those tests with the legal standards of organized society. Such a subjective approach to this inquiry may create a fuller appreciation of the fact that obscenity is only a superstition of the day—the modern counterpart of ancient witchcraft.

CONTENTS

xi

To the Pure . . .

A STUDY OF OBSCENITY
AND THE CENSOR

I

THE BATTLE OVER BOOKS

*To the pure all things are pure: but to them that
are defiled and unbelieving is nothing pure. . . .*
—THE EPISTLE OF PAUL TO TITUS. Chapter 1,
verse 15.

THERE is no accurate gauge for those influences of censorship which arise before the time when the author turns
over his manuscript to the publisher. While the pen is in
the writer's hand, his own individual censor is inextricably
merged with the taboos of his environment. The accident
of each personal law of suppression colors all writings. No
doubt some venal writers, like autoists, try to reach the
speed limit. For them no rule is effective. If the statute
permitted 100 volts of sex stimulation, the minimum used
by them would be 99-44/100.

But after the moods, thoughts, and emotions are translated into words, we can clearly trace the difficult course
which the book must travel. At the very start, society
possesses censors in the publishers themselves. Their tastes
and fears discard many a work. Dr. Joseph Collins, a
well-known physician, author, and psychologist, remarked
recently that one handicap to literature is the cowardice of
publishers, unwilling to risk jail for their ideals. The result is that only the least vulnerable works come to the attention of the district attorney. Publishers, representing
more capital than the author, are naturally more timid. Many

1

of them provide, in the forms used for their readers' reports on manuscripts, a clause: "Is there anything in the book that would make it liable to prosecution by the Society for the Suppression of Vice? If so, please designate such pages." It is easy to understand the desire of the publisher to avoid court action, for he is not in business for pleasure nor even primarily to enlarge the bounds of freedom. When he says "Business is business," he means it is not morality. Wisely enough he goes to the district attorney to get advice in advance of printing, hoping to avoid the destruction of thousands of dollars' worth of paper and ink.

But the prosecutor is also in a deplorable dilemma. If he is decent and courteous he reads the book and gives an informal opinion. Thereupon the publisher, if dissatisfied, protests vigorously against censorship in advance, and the public is outraged that one man, not even a literary critic, can proscribe the circulation of new ideas. If, on the contrary, the prosecutor adheres to his technical functions, he may refuse to pass on the manuscript on the ground that the crime arises only at the time of "sale," "mailing," or "transporting." In such a situation the publisher protests that he should not be put to the unnecessary burden of printing before ascertaining the prosecutor's ultimate interpretation of obscenity. It is a clear case of "Be damned if you do and be damned if you don't." The public interprets it as repugnant one-man censorship in advance, or as inexcusable and unconscionable penalty for an undefined crime. But these are only the preliminaries—the game of matching wits known as legal action still lies ahead.

OBSCENITY IN ACTION

ONE way or another the binding is put on the book and it is offered for sale. Charges are filed against the volume. These complaints are often indirect and mysterious. In some instances individual citizens write letters protesting against a filthy book. In a few jurisdictions action is taken by public officers on their own sole initiative. For example, the customs officials—acting under the tariff act—are their own readers for smut; and in Boston the police are the first official critics of literary decency. But in most cases the "obscenity" is discovered by the societies organized for the purpose of finding it. In the offices of vice societies sit secretaries, clerks, and stenographers avidly looking for more business. Their activity can only be appraised by results, and results are only obtained by the filing of public charges. Naturally during periods of public lethargy these crusaders go out on independent searches for violators of the law. The business must be kept up to last year's record. A pure literature is inconceivable and the absence of complaints may be used by the financial supporters as an excuse for discontinuance of contributions.

Again the prosecutor is in a sorry plight. Is the prominence of the signature on a letter an indication of a possible crime? Or should the matter be presented to the Grand Jury only if a quantity of protests pour in? And finally, even though the quantity and quality of protest commend an indictment of the work, must not the prosecutor withdraw to his own study, sit as a critic, and with blue pencil hunt for indecency? By the time the legal complaint is filed, no matter what its origin, the officers, stenographers, and clerks of the vice societies, and even the prosecutors, have been exposed to the corrupting influences of the provocative paragraphs. We must assume that familiarity produces a satisfactory sexual anti-toxin.

The day of trial comes on. The district attorney in charge has no inordinate fear of sex. Usually he is "one of the boys" and tells his own smoking-room stories at his political club when announcing his impending battle. The press favors him. The trial is good publicity, because the papers spread forth columns of near-smut under the rule of privilege, while the editorial pages inveigh against the corrupting influences of books, entirely overlooking the similar effects which newspapers may produce.

The jurors, having brought in a verdict in a case of income-tax fraud or highway robbery, now turn their attention to literature, the intellectual rights of the adult, and the protection of all those men and women not on the jury. There sit the twelve good men and true. They await fresh, exciting testimony. Few jurors try to get excused. They all want to hear the "dirt." The district attorney knows that his battle is half won if he picks the right jury. Here is a subject essentially involved with emotional background. Impaneling the jury recalls one of the early lessons of lawyers defending a rape case: "Fill the jury with libertines on the theory that we men must stand together." In this case, staid parents are better jurors for his purpose than gay bachelors. If a juror says he was born near Boston, that city of literary prudery, the prosecutor is elated while consternation enters the camp of the defense. Every experienced prosecutor will challenge a man who runs a small stationery store, a soda-water clerk, or an artist who has studied or traveled abroad. When a juror states that he is an architect, a dealer in corsets, or a reader of many books, the defendant's representatives seldom exercise their rights of challenge. The prosecutor's game is to secure substantial citizens who never read books. And this is not difficult. Persons who belong to the book-buying public usually possess sufficient wealth or political influence to keep their names off jury panels. The reading-matter of jurors is a delightful subject. In the recent case against *Replenishing Jessica*, three jurors said they never read because of bad eyesight; eight others had never heard of such best-sellers as *Elmer Gantry, Oil,* or Ludwig's *Napoleon*; only one of the twelve had read *An American Tragedy,* and he had "stopped in the middle, it was too long." One honest male declared he never read, "but my wife does the reading for the family."

In several recent cases such as that against "Hatrack" in *The American Mercury,* readers of journals of liberal thought have been excused from jury service by the district attorney. To subscribe to *The Nation* or *The Survey* has become a disqualification. All this is good practice. A liberal in any field of thought is likely to be open-minded on obscenity.

The attorney for the defendant is no freer from this approach, although too often he is apologetic in his demeanor. He is afraid that the folks back home will know that he likes a dirty story. He is inclined to exclude from the jury all readers of the tabloid press. This reasoning is based on the theory that the man who gets his private kick from the newspaper details of the current sexual divorce trial favors public suppression of obscenity. Likewise the juror who reads all the testimony of the woman heretofore just a private harlot, but now a popular murderess, knows his obscenity, and is the acme of righteousness when considering the welfare of others. In the jury-box he is shocked by a word such as "bastard," which he uses liberally in the street, and for once prefers the euphemism "illegitimate child." But, unfortunately for the defense, there are never enough challenges left to bar all readers of the sex-crime Daily Thrillers. It searches in vain for æsthetes.

To the twelve men finally unassailed is left the decision. It is so tempting to pose as a moral example for all men that the case is half won by the People before it begins. After convicting *What Happens,* by John Herrman, in New York City in 1927, several jurors came up and shook hands with the defeated author. The jurors were in a good humor for they had retained the exhibits, the copies of the condemned book. "And why did you vote against my book?" queried the author. The masculine answer was direct and typical, more honest than can usually be expected. "You see, that book wouldn't hurt me. I wasn't scared by the mention of masturbation. But then I felt it might hurt some other people. As for me, I get my kick out of riding down in the crowded subway." Such is the obscenity of the trial forum.

The trial itself is usually a bore. The defendants fail to look like desperate criminals. The evidence before the jurors is relatively unimportant. The prosecutor reads isolated portions of the book, a phrase here, a word there. Unrelated to the thought, removed from its context, any sentence may be distorted. But that is one of the tricks of trials at law. Neither side wants justice. Victory is the sole objective. Of course, in most jurisdictions, the publisher or author may read the rest of the book. But there is a penalty. The jury is anxious to end its case. To read through an entire volume, aloud, at one sitting, is tiresome. Jury antagonism is easily aroused by boredom, and the first duty of the defense is entertainment. On the other hand, to read only parts of the book is seized upon by the prosecutor in his summation as a sign of cowardice. But the attorney for the book drags into evidence any item no matter how irrelevant that may prejudice the jury his way. Even in the higher courts able counsel, such as those who defended Dreiser's *The "Genius,"* ended an argument with a wholly immaterial peroration of great length describing in heart-rending phrases the American soldiers then dying on the battlefields of France. The lawyer's task cannot be easily limited even though the book is usually the sole legal evidence. It is not proper, under the present rules of the arena, to let the author tell his motive for writing the book; it is not admissible to have literary critics testify as to the author's style or other æsthetic values, and the author may not read passages of other obscene books freely circulating at that very time in the same community. No judge will allow the jury to be entertained by the shocking passages of famous classics. And it is not relevant to prove that a book is true. For disturbing as it may seem to many, truth is no defense. And above all no plaintiff takes the stand to testify to the injury the book has caused.

The juror has been entertained but he does not yet know what it is all about. The judge must explain to him the rules of law to be applied in the case. When the judge asks the jury to decide if the book will create "sexual desire" or "libidinous thoughts," their confusion is complete. Ordinarily a juror in his box is too respectful of the judge to ask: "What do you mean by libidinous? Please tell us who has been hurt by the book? Do you mean me, for example, Judge?"

In contrast to such confusion, we find that terrifying reformation which enters every human soul when touched

by even an edge of ermine. As a juror he is judge of his
peers! It is a satisfying emotion to lay down a lordly moral
dictum on this subject of obscenity. All those who play a
rôle in the game of censor gladly assume the weaknesses of
their fellow men, with no doubt as to their own incorrupt-
ibility. Thus the jurors enjoy taking a stand for the ascetic
ideal no matter how inconsistent that may be with their rou-
tine swapping of excrementary jokes in Pullman smokers.

Under such influences the jurors withdraw to secret de-
liberations on the criminal extent of the sexual stimulation
in the culprit book. The exhibit is carried with them into
the jury room. In some cases they are locked up for hours
until they are able to decide that the book will excite "libidinous thoughts." In fact, we expect the jurors to analyze
all the evidence unemotionally in order to find out if their
emotions have been aroused. While the jury is deliberating
the defendant's lawyers and the district attorneys in charge
assemble in the corridors of the court house and, under the
influence of the debated subject, swap jokes dealing with
connubial infidelity and the details of homosexual legal
proceedings. Court decisions of shocking sexual frankness
are so in demand that such volumes in the legal libraries are
rebound many times as often as case books containing decisions on less erotic subjects. This is not surprising. Why
should we expect prosecutors to be subnormal on this subject of general interest?

After the verdict is submitted, the judge takes the matter
in hand. In these higher realms of appeal we find equally
striking disagreements as to tests, definitions, and emotional
reactions.

The defendant's lawyer tries to shift the case from judges
who are elders in churches to those "regular guys" who

play poker at the big round table at the district political club. By and large, the judges, somewhat immunized against public flattery or condemnation, are more tolerant or brave than the jurors. But the New York Society for the Suppression of Vice points out that at least one unnamed magistrate was part owner of an obscene stage production, and that others were antagonistic to the suppression of obscenity.

Our most learned judges have been unable to agree in many cases. At no stage of the entire proceedings is there certainty. In no other type of criminal trial is there the same necessity for the legal adversaries to play upon the prejudices and whims of the jurors. In no other field of law does the temperament of the presiding judge reach such importance. And as will soon be evident there is no definition in the entire law that so clearly violates the fundamental principle that a criminal charge must be clear, precise, and definite in all its terms and details.

THE VICE SOCIETIES

THE public's acquaintance with an attack on a book begins only at the time when an arrest is made or an indictment filed. But long before that dramatic moment, the machinery of suppression has been in action. Investigations, decoy letters, and secret meetings have preceded the official duties of the prosecuting authorities.

Vice societies are no anomaly in our social and political life. In America, especially, public opinion has become organized by groups. We have come to believe in mob momentum and group moralities. Our American political party system has developed alongside of the Knights of Labor,

the Ku Klux Klan, the Knights of Columbus, thousands of
fraternal orders, the Anti-Saloon League, the Women's
Christian Temperance Union, and all other prohibition societies. There is the closest analogy, indeed, between the
prohibition and the vice societies, and their evolution was
contemporaneous. The suppression of both liquor and literature has required special agents and stealth.

Publishers on occasion submit manuscripts in advance of
publication to these vice societies. Many State's attorneys
take up so-called obscenity cases with the greatest reluc-
tance, overcome only by fear of the political power of the
purity leagues. In fact the New England society went to
such lengths in its extra-legal duress in *The American Mercury* case that a Boston court enjoined it from continuing
certain threatening practices against the book dealers.
Though these societies have abandoned their right of search
and seizure they still act at times as probation officers for
the courts. The convicted book dealer, reporting weekly
at that office which contains one of the best-known collec-
tions of lewd writing in America, the office of the New
York Vice Society, presents an ironic picture.

In the fall of the year 1873 in the City of New York there
met a group of prominent gentlemen among whom were
such wealthy citizens as William E. Dodge, Jr., Morris K.
Jesup, J. Pierpont Morgan, and Robert R. McBurney. The
meeting took place in the rooms of the Young Men's Christian Association under the inspiration of a young man by
the name of Anthony Comstock, who not many years before
had emerged from the backwoods of Connecticut to lead
the crusade against indecent literature, and who before he
died was to make his fame felt in every part of the English-speaking world, and to add, indeed, a new noun to the

language. The result of this momentous gathering was the organization of the New York Society for the Suppression of Vice under a special Act of the sovereign Legislature of the State of New York. It gave the Society a monopoly of vice, and its agents the rights of search, seizure and arrest which had always been thought to belong exclusively to the publicly constituted police authorities. The Society was actually more important than the obscenity laws. It represented a new departure in the administration of the criminal law. The idea was to spread quickly, and within a few years the Western Society for the Suppression of Vice in Cincinnati and the New England Watch and Ward Society in Boston were organized. In little more than a decade the National Vigilance Association, the spiritual successor of similar English societies, was to be organized in London for the same purposes.

Even though these vice crusaders start with the single aim of attacking the lewd in literature, the zeal of the game soon expands their fields of operation. No manifestations are exempt. Museums, art galleries, dance halls, gambling, stag parties are all subject to attack. In fact, outside of the press, which is immune because more powerful than the crusaders, we find these organizations alert for any new form of emotional entertainment. Books are only saved at times because dancing has supplanted them as a peril to our civilization. If a limit of 2.75 per cent of sex stimulation were established the vice hunters would not be content. As is often the case, men of kindly temper and honest zeal become void of mercy when any moral heresy is suspected.

But the struggle is continual. Localities vary in their attitudes so that we have local options even in original sin. The very effort of suppression creates some of the demand.

Forbidden fruits have unique flavors and the bounds of suppression create the new limits of desire. The condemned areas of today become the profitable market places of tomorrow. At times suppression is a violent boomerang. An amusing proof of this point accompanied the closing of *The Captive,* a serious play concerning the relations of two women. On the night of suppression, ten-year-old newsboys sold extras at the theatre door. They shouted to the thousands who previously had never heard of the subject of the play that the "Lesbian Show was off the Boards." The vice-crusaders admit such a tendency to act as involuntary accomplice. In its 1926 report, the New York Society says:

"The unwarranted and mischievous publicity which the daily prints enjoy giving to such procedures against books does immeasurable damage in several directions, unless the damage be offset eventually by a judgment against the book in court."

With wise strategy the annual reports of all the vice societies omit the titles of books which have been attacked, whether acquitted or suppressed. This lesson was learned by Anthony Comstock long before the Boston Book Massacre of 1927.

The Boston episode is worthy of passing comment as illustrative of obscenity-hunting in action. Books of all varieties were banned by a reign of terror, not of law. Fiction and biography were made contraband by police fiat without even a hearing in court. It was a stupid eruption, serving as proof that suppression is not wholly efficient. That city, through a process of anonymously circulated slips of paper bearing names of doubtful books, was the best advertiser of more than one hundred titles. Many volumes previously buried were revived by police mention. Publishers and authors who could not afford to buy advertising space in the press received thousands of dollars' worth of publicity without a penny of cost. The duress on the local book dealers created a mail-order business which the citadel of elegance could not destroy. No one has ever discovered the formula by which books were selected for the high honor of suppression.

No bookseller or police captain produced a complete list, but every dealer knew just what books were on it. No member of the Watch and Ward Society or the District Attorney's Office wanted to admit responsibility for the additional sale of thousands of volumes through free advertising. The public followed the proclaiming of the bans with an avidity only equaled by the attention paid in Wall Street to the ticker on a day of rising markets. The methods used in the Boston Book Party were so clumsy as to invite general public disapproval.

THE HYPOCRISY OF THE GAME

CENSORSHIP in action has little to commend it. Suppression is a sordid, unhappy sport. The legal chicanery brings out the worst in every one concerned. It is bad enough to expand the ego by judicial robes, but then at least there is a kind of responsiveness to vague but valid public tendencies. To act the rôle of censor develops a lack of honesty more anti-social than any amount of sexual excess. The perfect censor does not exist. The American jury of peers does not qualify, because each man is subject to his own invisible censor.

Suppressors are found in all classes and places. Look at the men who stood at the Flatiron Building corner in New

York City frankly waiting to see girls' thighs on a gusty day. Watch the men who read the details of adultery divorce trials. Keep in mind the men who sit in the front rows of bare-legged revues. Recall those men who belong to vice societies but enjoy showing, of course in a scientific manner, postal cards of homosexual acts. And then again those who are tight-lipped, inhibited, emotionally dwarfed. These are the censors. Examples of public hypocrisy are too multitudinous to permit a detailed inventory. This has ever been the case where men have set themselves up as judges of morality, taste or knowledge.

Each person should be humbled by the mere process of dealing with his own personal censor. It is not strange that the human race has always taken delight in the revelations of dishonesty of public censors. And crusading against the vague obscene cannot be separated from hypocrisy. A lack of mental integrity pervades the champions of literary decency. All this is well exemplified by a fable to be drawn from the records of the New York Society for the Suppression of Vice.

A half century after its initial meeting in the rooms of the Young Men's Christian Association, it celebrated its Fiftieth Anniversary. It was fitting and proper that a Founders' Committee be organized to commemorate these long years of good work. What more natural than that the minds of the Committee should turn to the President of the United States for the Honorary Chairmanship? The work of the society was surely important enough to merit acceptance. The President of the United States, it will be recalled, was at that time the Honorable Warren Gamaliel Harding. The agreeable occupant of the White House, indeed, bowed to the honor, and under the date of May 18, 1923, wrote to the general Chairman of the Committee:

THE WHITE HOUSE
WASHINGTON

May 18, 1923.

My dear Governor Whitman:

I have received your invitation, on behalf of the Founders Committee of the New York Society for the Suppression of Vice, to accept the Honorary Chairmanship of the Committee. My own sentiments so strongly coincide with the purposes of your organization that, with the reservation that I shall doubtless be unable to perform any very useful or definite services, I am glad to accept. The work of the organization has engaged my interest and sympathy for many years and has my best wishes for the future.

Sincerely yours,
(*Signed*) WARREN G. HARDING.

Hon. Charles S. Whitman,
New York City.

Four years later the New York Society for the Suppression of Vice attempted to suppress a certain book called *The President's Daughter,* which claims to be the love story of the unmarried mother of the only child of the same Warren Gamaliel Harding, twenty-ninth President of the United States. An insert in the book, published in 1927, reads:

SIX BURLY MEN

(and Mr. Sumner)

This First Edition of *The President's Daughter* has been trodden upon by interests which do not want to see this mother's true story given to the world. On June 10th six

burly New York policemen and John S. Sumner, agent for
the Society for the Suppression of Vice, armed with a
"Warrant of Search and Seizure," entered the printing
plant where the making of the book was in process. They
seized and carried off the plates and printed sheets. On
June 29th, in a magistrate's court, the case was dismissed.
The seized plates and printed sheets have been returned
to the publishers.

Obscenity in action, the forces operating behind the court
scenes, and the hypocrisy of the environment well justify
the paraphrase: "To the Pure All Things are Impure."

II

THE VEHICLES OF INFECTION

I should say that there is a very wide distinction be-
tween what is read and what is seen. In a novel
one may read that "Eliza stripped off her dressing
gown and stepped into her bath" without any harm;
but I think that if that were presented on the stage
it would be shocking.—SIR WILLIAM GILBERT before the British Stage Censorship Committee of
1909.

ONE cannot consider the censorship of books by itself. In
the first place, a play is simply a literary production until it is
performed. At the very outset it is necessary to institute
comparisons not only to show the differences which may be
advanced to justify the separate treatment of books but to
dispose of them if they are not substantial enough. To do
this, however, is to demonstrate not only the inconsistencies
of theory, practice, and standards, but ultimately to make
clear the futility which underlies the whole sex censorship.
In other words, we are contributing to its *reductio ad ab-*
surdum at the same time that we are removing the differentials.

Many a vice crusader has declared that obscenity is to
be treated as a crime in precisely the same fashion as arson,
burglary, bigamy, and other heinous offenses. A reasonable man would expect, then, that the campaign against its
malignant influences would be conducted with equal intensity upon all fronts. *"Écrasez l'infame!"* might well be re-

17

vived as a battle cry.   But the discovery is soon made that
there is specialization in obscenity both actually and theo-
retically.   A group which wants to maintain a rigid censorship of salacious books is often quite oblivious of equally
salacious plays.   The censorship of the movies is considered
from an entirely different angle than the problem of tabloids.
The arts may be allotropic but as vehicles of infection they
are differentiated.   A subject as it changes its form has to
run a gauntlet of censorship which is bitterer and fiercer at
some points than at others.   There is, thus, no unity, no harmony, no common purpose.

It is a lamentable state of affairs.   A muffled Rabelaisian
laughter may be heard in the Latin quarters, the back-alley
stage entrances, the cinema lots, and the city rooms.   The
villains are accorded quite separate privileges.   All forms
of censorship are brought into contumely and contempt
when there are found to be different standards of decency
governing different art forms.   Is the word more potent than
the smear of paint, the shadow on the screen, the burst of
sound?   Is verbal magic more persuasive in a play than in
a book, and in a book than in a newspaper?   Does each
medium have a varying capacity for excitability?   Are there
really distinctions which justify diversity of treatment?

As the most convenient form of procedure we need only
imagine a character who has been denied access to obscenity in any one art—say literature.   This perverted individual has no desire to resort to the manifold sources of life
to satisfy his craving for indecency but prefers the reflections of life which are music, sculpture, the play, the motion
picture, the press.   We need only follow him from concert
hall to art gallery, to the theatre, to the movie, to the corner
news-stand, to discover that the impediments in his way are

not always the same. Where æsthetic values do not dictate varying standards of obscenity, social considerations may enter which allow a greater freedom in one sphere than in another. These operating in the background control our adventurer, and we may reflect upon them as he proceeds in his unholy quest.

THE SANCTUARIES OF ART

AMONG all the arts, our inquisitive fellow will discover that the ones which are least molested are music, painting and sculpture. Despite the erotic nature of a good deal of concert music, we do not attempt to establish a censorship over its performance. It is only as a provincial eccentricity that Judge Ben Lindsey reports a bill in the Colorado Legislature to censor music that "arouses the passions." The Church at one time in its history regarded music as too erotic to be performed in its edifices of worship, and only later came to accept the organ. Among primitive tribes drums are beaten at mating periods for the purpose of sex stimulation, and probably certain instruments are taboo for children and others played only before married men. But in this respect we have grown so civilized that only extremists among moralists want to prohibit jazz, although in such a crusade they might have the support of many music lovers. Dancing is regulated, but only to guard against the moral dangers which might arise from this contact of the sexes.

Thus the sexual kick which is denied in a rather lightly charged book or play may be obtained from the manipulation of percussion instruments. The piano which is enshrined in the parlor of every middle-class home may be the cause of more mischief than a hundred thousand copies of *Women in Love.* One may imagine, as Arnold Bennett does, the perplexities of a parent who tries to prevent a Lothario from seducing his daughter by playing *Tristan und Isolde.* Music to the average man is the most mysterious of all the arts, and the one whose technical values he least understands. It is too abstract for him to begin to connect it immediately with morals. Its value as sound alone saves it from interference. "It is," said the morally minded Doctor Johnson, "the only sensual pleasure without vice."

A little more unwelcome attention is paid to the art gallery than to the concert hall. When the Carnegie Trust gave the Pittsburgh Art Gallery Sir William Orpen's *Myself and Venus,* representing the painter in a studio with a large reproduction of the Venus de Milo, the title was modestly changed to *Portrait of the Artist.* The pother about the cubist and expressionist nudes in the exhibition at the Metropolitan is still fresh in memory, but on the whole the raids on art galleries which were such a prominent feature of the great Comstock days are largely a thing of the past. Whoever is denied illustrations of the nude in books may find them in the museum. It is only when *Venus Disrobed for the Bath,* or *Phryne Before Her Judges,* or *Perseus and Andromeda,* or *La Répose,* or *Asphyxia* are given wide circulation upon picture post cards that the secretaries of the vice societies grow alarmed. It is the indignity of the public display of untrammeled sculpture which is behind such outcries as that of Boston over Power's *Greek Bacchante,* or of Chicago over Polasek's *Sower,* or New York over MacMonnies's *Civic Virtue.*

The representational character of painting and sculpture has made for the slightly greater alertness than is shown towards music. One wonders if the abstractionist tendencies of modern painting have any connection with a subconscious desire to escape the clutches of the moralist. There appears to be little contagion in cold marble and bronze: only Pygmalion fell in love with the Galatea his own fingers had fashioned. If the Greeks introduced the fig-leaf in a period of late Puritanism, we must remember that sculpture was the art of greatest social importance among them, and hence its dangers to the impressionable were more sternly regarded. In the painter's work there is no moral, and the claims of art for art's sake are more readily admitted. But if it is supposed, as is often done, that there are limitations to his art which make it less easy for him to be obscene than the writer, then one has only to look at the drawings of George Gross. The whole "dirty" picture post card business is a standing refutation of the contention. If there is such a thing as "pornography," painting and sculpture can produce more vivid samples than literature. In the last analysis it is the seclusion and inaccessibility of the art galleries which is their protection. We rely upon the reassuring probability that they will not be visited too often except by those already hopelessly lost.

THE OBSCENE AFTER 8:30 P. M.

BUT the art which from the earliest times has been supposed to constitute a special incitement and a special problem is the drama. The censorship of the theatre has always been more stringent than that of the plastic arts, from the days of Greece and Rome to the present. Indeed, according to one derivation, the very word "obscene" came from the Latin *obscena,* meaning that which may not be seen upon the stage. Goethe, who made light of vicious books, wanted to keep the immature from the theatre, and the scandalous Voltaire, the author of *Candide* and *La Pucelle,* suffering an attack of modesty, condemned Corneille for introducing in *Théodora* a prostitute upon the stage. "For reasons not quite clear to me," says W. L. George, a prejudiced novelist, "a play is supposed to be more dangerous than a picture or a book—a strange idea, given that these dangerous plays seldom run longer than a fortnight." On the other hand, dramatic critics from Aristotle down to Alexander Woollcott have often thought differently.

Long after censorship of books before publication had been abandoned upon the Continent, the censorship of plays before production persisted, exercised either by special censors, magistrates, or *police de mœurs.* Such a previous censorship existed in France till 1906, and still obtains in some European countries. In England, the Lord Chamberlain is still the bane of British playwrights despite parliamentary investigating committees and protests to the King from the embattled ranks, resenting this special tutelage from which the English novelist has been free for over two centuries. In New York, where we have no Lord Chamberlain to license plays for us before they are produced, the subsequent criminal prosecutions assume a vigor, prominence and vindictiveness to which books are rarely subjected. The hullabaloo over *Sex, The Captive, A Good Bad Woman, The Virgin Man* or *Maya* makes the demurrers against *An American Tragedy, Replenishing Jessica* and even *Elmer Gantry* mild in comparison. We would tolerate no Book Jury to pass on manuscripts with too much sex appeal, but we put up with a Play Jury. Up to last year this emphasis upon the stage in America was simply a matter of tendency. The New York State Legislature then proceeded, however, to pass the monstrous Wales Act, under which a theatre owner who has rented his house for the production of a play which may subsequently be adjudged "obscene" may have it padlocked for an entire year. The burden of making the wrong guess is thus put upon the innocent owner of theatre property. This is virtually a previous censorship which is in a way worse than the Lord Chamberlain's. After all, censorship by an officer of His Majesty's household is to be preferred perhaps to censorship by landlords under the whip of a Commissioner of Licences. In Boston, the Mayor grants licences for the theatrical season. But a Board consisting of the Mayor, the Police Commissioner, and the Chief Justice of the Municipal Court may by a majority vote suspend a licence at their pleasure. The story goes that a former Boston mayor used to go regularly to New York to see plays which were under suspicion there, and then as a result of his researches banned them before they so much as reached Boston!

There is certainly a great practical difficulty in the censorship of the stage. A book may be censored with far more convenience; when the secretary of a vice society has affixed his imprimatur to the proofs, he knows that the book will reach the reader in precisely that form. But it is not so easy to control stage business, costuming, and asides, by means of which actor and producer may transform a scene which is comparatively innocent in the author's dialogue into indecency to shock the censor. He cannot control the leer, the wink, the snicker, the nudge in the ribs, the inflection of the voice. The embarrassment is felt most acutely when the censor attempts to supervise such more popular forms of entertainment as the music hall and vaudeville. It has been the same from the days when the pious Maria

Theresa attempted in vain to supervise the extemporaneous
Lustspiele of the people's theatre, in which the actor made
up his lines as he went along, to the futile efforts of the
Lord Chamberlain to curb the music halls. But the fact that
the demand for a more stringent stage censorship has persisted despite the obstacles in its way only testifies the more
to its presumed urgency.

Undoubtedly the æsthetic canons of literature and the
drama invoke variations in response. The psychological
reactions to word, speech, gesture, and color are not the
same. The play is not only a direct representation like
painting and sculpture but a living representation. The effect of mob psychology is felt when the play is performed
to a full house. The book is read in private, and its
obscenity is for the eye and the senses of the reader
alone, and public decency is as little outraged when he scans
the words at his reading table as when he undresses in his
bedroom. It is the public performance of the play which
supposedly makes it a greater affront, since the preliminaries
to seduction and adultery are actually introduced before the
spectator.

But is the æsthetic of the obscene, if we may use the
phrase, really so different in book and play that a more
severe censorship of the one than of the other is justified?
Such a subtle trifler as G. K. Chesterton makes the distinction that an immoral book may be closed with a snap but
that it is necessary to crawl over half-a-dozen knees to escape
from an immoral play. The only advice which can be given
to such a sensitive and temperamental person is to follow
the example of long-legged men and get aisle seats. Perhaps the emotions of the play are, after all, more fugitive
than those aroused by the permanent possession of a book.

The very fact of the public performance of a play may serve to guard the adolescent in the audience against the immediate indulgence which is possible in the privacy of one's room, dissipating the impulse towards secret vice by the time home is reached. Although the play is declared to be a much more powerful stimulant, the performance of an immoral play has never yet led to the rape of the women in the audience. After all, the use of asterisks for a few lines is in every way as suggestive as the lowering of the curtain for a few minutes to indicate a lapse of virtue.

In truth the factors which have focused attention upon the play are mostly historical, and there is no poorer excuse for a censorship than history. The Puritans concentrated upon the stage and left books comparatively alone. Not only Jeremy Collier but a long line of Puritan pamphleteers such as Northbrooke, Stephen Gosson, and Philip Stubbes attacked its immoralities and lewdness. The closing of the theatres was often a sanitary measure to prevent the spread of plague, and the institution of the Master of the Revels which was established by the eighth Henry, from which the office of the present Lord Chamberlain has derived its jurisdiction over the drama, arose from the necessities of the royal household in those times, and from the public interest in the restraint of vagrancy and vagabondage which was then tied up with the actor's profession. The objection of the Puritans was less to plays than to the theatres, which were almost houses of ill fame, to so large an extent were they devoted to the opportunities of drinking and the importunities of prostitution.

The confusion has arisen from the failure always to distinguish between the theatre as an art and the theatre as life. It is recognized, however, by the dramatists who

from Shakespeare and Calderón to Schnitzler and Molnar
have been fascinated by the play within the play. Considered as an art form the play need be subject only to the
laws of art, and there is no greater need for its censorship
than for that of the book. But considered as part of life,
the play is subject to the laws of life, among which are the
duly enacted statutes of the country. If the theatre attracts prostitution, then surely it is no sanctuary; the
law operates there as well as in the street, and one might
as well abolish the highway as the theatre. If there is cursing and swearing in a play, then there are laws against profanity. If there is nudity upon the stage, then, as Shaw
pointed out to Sir William Gilbert's example of Eliza and
her bath, there is simply a violation of a very definite law
against indecent exposure. These are the only laws which
a playwright should need to observe as long as we see fit to
keep them on the statute books.

But now let us assume that a play has been suppressed as a
result of a greater vigilance. It reappears in another vehicle
of infection. When the Lord Chamberlain refuses a licence
to a play, it is performed at so-called private subscription
performances over which he has no control. As these usually
take place on Sunday, which is the only day a theatre is to
be had, the obscenity is for the Lord's Day. But more!—
The fact that the Lord Chamberlain has refused a licence for
a play to be performed does not at all prevent its publication.
The play has also a separate existence as a book, and upon
this career it now enters and spreads its poison. What may
not be had in the theatre is to be had in the bookshop. Of
examples of English banned plays which have been made
available in book form Shaw's *Mrs. Warren's Profession*
is, perhaps, best known; but one may also mention such

comparatively recent works as Zangwill's *The Next Religion,* Christopher St. John's *The Coronation,* and most recently, Dr. Marie Stopes's *Vestia,* which the Lord Chamberlain considered a little too ardent a defense of a woman's right to love. Thus the fear of Lord Chesterfield, expressed when the censorship of the Lord Chamberlain was established, that it would lead ultimately to the abrogation of the freedom of the press, has not been fulfilled. Inconsistency has been preferred as the lesser evil.

In New York much of the same lamentable state of affairs prevails. The police, heroically wading into the temples of art, raided and closed Asch's *The God of Vengeance.* But no prosecution has been brought against the publishers of this presumably disgusting play. The whole of American civilization seemed imperiled when *The Captive* was on the boards, and the theatre had to close its doors. Yet it can be rented for twenty-five cents at any circulating library. *Maya* is available in book form to the New Yorker who may have missed it in its brief two-weeks' run. Indeed, now one may comfortably read the plays in the sanctity of the home on many an evening instead of one. Moreover, the inhabitants of Kansas, Iowa, Montana, who could not come to Babylon because of the distance and expense, will be only the more likely to read the banned plays because of the advertisement which suppression gives.

THE CENSORED ART

OUR adventurer in the movie palace may have a far harder time in his unholy quest for the salacious. The product which is offered to him on the silver screen is the only censored art in the strict sense of the term which is to be had in America. A movie producer is not subjected to criminal prosecutions but his films are censored in advance. It is the only example of an admitted previous censorship in the land of the free. The American who has revolted against every other licensing of the arts has tolerated this. The Supreme Court of the United States in 1915 upheld the regulation, against the invocation of the First Amendment, holding that the moving picture was not essentially a medium for the communication of ideas, and not so much an art as an industry. It may well have been influenced by the general spirit of repression and censorship which prevailed in wartime. It did not even take the precaution to exempt news or educational films, and the printed matter in others. Boards of censorship have been set up now in seven American states: Florida, Kansas, Maryland, New York, Ohio, Pennsylvania, and Virginia. Six concerted efforts have been made to secure the establishment of a Federal movie censorship in the United States. One is less surprised at the existence of a preventive movie censorship in England, where the drama is the plaything of the Lord Chamberlain. It prevails all over the world—in Canada, Australia, India, Italy, Germany, Czecho-Slovakia, Poland, Sweden, Japan.

It is almost inevitable that every art is subjected to a censorship in its infancy. We are unfamiliar with its possibilities and naturally it takes a long time to overcome our suspicions and allay our fears. It was thus when printing was invented, and the same history is now repeated in the movies. There are a great many people who would grow apoplectic if a censorship of the theatre were suggested but who are ready to find all sorts of justifications for a censorship of the movies. We may dismiss the reasons that are often heard

for guarding against a greater degree of sex appeal in the
movie than in the drama: that a movie palace is so much
darker than a legitimate theatre, that it affords a better opportunity for holding hands, that a movie is continuous
from 1 to 11 P. M. so that the perverted can see it twice for
the same price, or that the constant musical accompaniment
increases the power of its episodes. It is idle to deny, however, that the current run of pictures is such that the greater
public concern over them can at least be understood. The
censorship is based rather upon the assumed low character
of the masses of movie patrons than upon the greater capacity for demoralization which is inherent in the movie as an
art form. It may be true as psychologists maintain that the
visual appeal which the movie supplies is even stronger than
the living representation of the drama, but the difference is
important only in relation to low mentality. "I don't care
what the papers write about me," said Boss Tweed when
he offered Thomas Nast a half million dollars to cease cari-
caturing him; "my constituents can't read but they can
understand pictures." And the fact is that the more than fifteen million people who go to the movies every day in the
United States alone largely belong to this class. The figures
of the National Research Council show that the average
mental age of the American is fourteen years, and in this
is supposed to lie the much-talked-of menace of the movies.
It is interesting, however, that precisely the same argument
was made by the secretary of the New York Society for the
Suppression of Vice some years ago when he pleaded for a
more effective censorship of books. It amounts to the same
thing as urging that since our population is feeble-minded we
take steps to make them even more feeble-minded. It is
also pointed out that the movie's one-night or one-week

stand makes censorship through subsequent criminal prosecution impractical, and makes a previous censorship imperative. But first we must admit that censorship is necessary
at all.

It is not surprising to find that the same literary critics
who as a class grow terribly indignant when a literary
magazine is barred from the mails or a book is attacked by
the Vice Society, often show themselves quite apathetic to
movie censorship, and regard the vagaries of Will Hays
and the minions of censorship under him as so many harmless jocosities. They are more than inclined to agree with
the Supreme Court of the United States that the movies
are indeed not an art but an industry, thus furnishing one
of the few instances in which professionally jealous critics
have acknowledged jurists to be judges of art or artlessness.
One recalls the tirades of such men as James Huneker and
Burton Rascoe against the movies about a decade ago. Often, indeed, it must be admitted to be almost in bad taste to
invoke the great traditional principles of Anglo-Saxon
freedom against the deletion of a few heaves, pants and
sighs, or the reduction in the length of a kiss in a picture
which is such a distortion of life that it has no claims to
existence as an entirety. But the movies are as capable
of good and noble things as the novel and the drama, and
in recent years they have proved their possibilities more and
more. Already we have a great number of pictures which
may well lay claim to the title of "screen classics": *The
Cabinet of Dr. Caligari, The Golem, The Last Laugh,
Variety, Potemkin* are a few of those which plead eloquently
against the censorship of the movies.

There is a school which believes that you cannot censor
nonsense. But it would be as reasonable to justify the cen-

sorship of Dreiser, H. G. Wells, and Sinclair Lewis because
we have Marie Corellis, Harold Bell Wrights, Eddie Guests,
and Elinor Glyns.   Indeed, if quantitative considerations
are raised, books are such a minor vehicle of infection that
we might as well cease to pay any attention to them.   We
will be told of the best sellers whose editions run into the
hundreds of thousands and which penetrate every part of
the country.   It is very impressive to say that a book has
sold 100,000 or 250,000 copies.   But we would still insist
that the followers of Dreiser, Wells, and Lewis are to be
accounted but a handful to the millions who read the Corellis, Wrights, Guests, and Glyns.   They will hardly compare to the fifteen million movie patrons.   There are few
books, however, that become best sellers.   If a novel sells
a few thousand copies a publisher is not ungrateful.   He
complains that there are whole states in the union which
have not more than a single real bookshop within their
borders.   We are constantly told that we as a nation are
more interested in automobiles than in literature.   Even
with a best seller, a little figuring will show that it means
very little that a book is selling over a hundred thousand
copies.   When the potential reading population is taken as
a basis, the result need not depress a member of a Clean
Books League.

Such reflections as these might well occupy our adventurer as he moves to his seat under the expert guidance of
a page boy who has been trained to Service.   However, he
would see that he was being subjected to still another code
of decorum and being victimized by still one more standard of comparison.   Organization and high finance and invention have abolished the old inflexibility.   The work of
an author now undergoes many mutations.   A successful

novel is serialized, dramatized, movieized. We may even
live to see the day when authors of economic, legal, and
philosophical treatises will sell at least the titles of their
works to the movies. When a book reaches the movies, it is
subjected to perhaps the most crucial tests of obscenity, and
the scandal of it is that it permits such direct comparisons.
The indecent classics themselves are transferred to the
screen, but only after they have undergone purification.
When *The Scarlet Letter* was adapted for the screen, the
adultery of Hester Prynne, permitted between the
covers of the book in the library, alarmed a board of
motion picture censorship, which insisted that a marriage
be performed at some point in the story to cure the sin in
celluloid. *Carmen* on the opera stage is one thing but her
long and passionate kiss has been cut to five feet, in the
movies. A woman sewing a layette may be all right in a
book but another moral problem is involved when the same
scene is presented in a movie. *Rain* held the stage in New
York and the towns on the road for several years without
shaking the foundations of Church and State, but the virtuous Will Hays for a time prohibited its adaptation for
the movies. There is a tale that his consent was subsequently secured by guile when Gloria Swanson, seated next
to him at a luncheon, sweetly asked if she might do a series
of short stories by one Somerset Maugham called *The
Trembling of a Leaf,* among which was a certain one called
"Miss Thompson."

Actually our adventurer would often find more sex appeal permitted in the movies than in a novel or the drama.
While the movie censorship insists upon the respect for
established morality, within these limits it trades in an un-
healthy sex sentimentalism. But often far more is prom-

ised than is ever performed. The fraud of sensational titles is most common in the movies. The canons of the movie art, requiring a greater pressure of love to the foot of celluloid than a page of a book, turn a *Madame Du Barry* into *Passion* and an *Admirable Crichton* into *Male and Female*.

THE FREEDOM OF THE PRESS

THE restless soul whom we have faithfully been following has been deprived of the printed word in the book. Tired of seeking substitutions, he makes for the news-stand at the next corner. Now, indeed, he can get rid of his repression. The thrill which he can derive from a wicked book, play, or movie is negligible in comparison. We are very watchful to keep from popular channels the indecencies of *The Arabian Nights,* Rabelais, and Boccaccio, which can be secured only at the price of several dollars, but a few cents will buy a copy of a daily newspaper which is often filled with enough details of sexual crimes and perversions to shock the secretary of a vice society out of his sedate senses. The grist of every day's news has its vast quantity, but at times cases occur which become so prominent that they agitate the minds of whole nations. A scandalous trial often lasts months, and sometimes drags over years, and leaves far more lasting effects than lurid novels. The readers of the reports are counted in the hundreds of thousands of each edition, a figure not achieved by even the few best sellers among books. The tales they tell are no fictions but grim realities which are more likely to lead the susceptible into imitation. Nor is it to be supposed that they are written in a style which is not as persuasive as the novels. Nowadays, the most skillful writers of the day are engaged in daily journalism, and many a novel is far less fascinating than the pages of a newspaper.

Not so long ago one of the great metropolitan papers employed no less than a novelist, an historian, a pseudo-philosopher, and a minister of religion to report a celebrated murder trial for its readers. They pander to the natural appetite that may be traced back to the Acta Diurna which, in manuscript form posted in public places, gave to the Romans the scandals of their day, wherein the poisoning of the Emperor Claudius by his wife Agrippina, to insure the succession of Nero, must have been the foremost. The Elizabethan tragedies based upon contemporary murders set a fashion which has been continued to our day. Only nowadays the reports of the press need no rewriting. There is a tale which concerns a great American novelist who took the newspaper account of an actual sexual crime as the basis of his tragedy. The reviewers praised particularly the remarkable realism of a series of letters in the novel which were supposed to have passed between the lover and his mistress. The truth was that the letters had not only been copied almost verbatim from the newspaper columns but had been made up by the reporter to tide over the public craving for news of the case in the dull days when nothing happened on the assignment!

The studies of the press made by Mathews, Speed, Garth, and Riis in this country and in England in the last two decades exhibit clearly the tendency to demoralization in the growing emphasis placed upon crime news, but we hardly need the proof. It is only necessary to recall the sexual details of the Hall-Mills, the Rhinelander, the "Peaches" Browning, the Aimee Semple McPherson, and the Snyder cases in this country and the Russel, "Mr. A", and Colonel

Denniston cases in England to be more than convinced that the worst books cannot compete with them in their effects. From the tabloids not too much is to be expected, but the venerable full-sized papers, too, have apparently adopted the new motto: "All the news that's unfit to print." Their headlines have been perhaps not quite so sensational, but competition made them print all the testimony in the "Peaches" Browning case, word for word, with none of the succulent details omitted. The solid *New York Times,* which once refused an advertisement of Pascal's *The Marriage Bed* as too suggestive, did not abstain entirely; and the New York *World,* which once led a crusade upon the art magazines, showed its sense of practicality none the less in following these cases faithfully.

That section of the periodical press which is composed of the art and sex magazines has a circulation which no novel ever achieves. The magazine *Physical Culture* alone has 400,000 readers. It is estimated that 150,000 copies of the sex magazines are sold monthly on the New York newsstands alone. A reliable correspondent has found that in a small town in Ohio of 25,000 population not less than 1800 copies of the same types of magazines were sold monthly. Thus the consumption of Main Street appears to be almost three times that of the metropolis per capita. The late Secretary of the Watch and Ward Society once estimated that the sex magazines had a total combined circulation in the country of 55,560,000 a year. As the average copy is read by four persons this means no less than 222,240,000 yearly readings!

It needs no alarmist to see that such figures are staggering. Qualitatively and quantitatively the daily and periodical press presents the hardest dilemma. Indeed, a Federal

Board of Magazine Censorship has been proposed in the
United States, and campaigns are initiated against the art
and sex magazines at rare intervals to still public clamor,
but no attempts are made to muzzle the daily newspapers.
They escape censorship entirely, although in theory of law
they are permitted no greater latitude. A year after the
unsuccessful attempt to bar Upton Sinclair's *The Jungle*
from the mails, the same action was sought against the
New York papers which ran the lurid testimony of Evelyn
Thaw in abundant detail. With engaging frankness the
official opinion admitted that this matter was probably worse
than many passages in *The Jungle* but went on to say that it
would have to refuse to intervene in order to avoid antag-
onizing the powerful daily press! In our own day we have
witnessed the complete failure of efforts to bar the New
York *Graphic,* which has triumphed over municipal edicts
and criminal prosecution.

It is its importance as a bulwark of liberty that exempts
the daily newspaper. Public policy demands that it shall
remain free despite its frequent salacity. Charges of that
sort might too easily be made merely a pretext for stifling
the cherished freedom of the press which the Anglo-Saxon
has won only after so many sanguinary battles. When the
phrase "the freedom of the press" is intoned, the worst
reactionary feels a shiver of dread. The managers of the
tabloid press in particular shrewdly realize this. They
trade in the sacred name of political liberty, which insures
the passage of their wares. The freedom of the press has
become converted into the freedom of the tabloids.

If the censorship of the movies is necessary to save their
patrons from themselves, then surely the readers of the
tabloids no less require special protection. "In a polite age,"

said Oliver Goldsmith, "almost every person becomes a reader and receives more instruction from the press than the pulpit." Such are the penalties of simple literacy.

Two years ago in England, Parliament tried a desperate remedy which had long been urged as a solution. The English, it is to be remembered, have led the world in purity. A law was passed which forbids newspapers to publish in any matrimonial action any more than the names and addresses of the parties, a bare statement of the charges, the points of law involved, the summing up of the judge and the verdict of the jury. Thus cases involving the pillars of society which might have filled many a screaming edition have been reduced to insignificant paragraphs. The Stillmans must have looked across the Atlantic in envy. The inevitable is happening in England. The basis of morality is not so much the solid satisfactions of virtue as the fear of being found out. At once suits for divorce shot up on the calendars. No scandal, no unwelcome publicity, were any longer involved. The law was an especial boon to a famous actress known on both sides of the waters. She brought a divorce action after the new law went into effect, and, as she was known to the public only by her stage name, and the law allowed only the publication of her real name in the little news item, hardly anyone knew that she had been divorced at all.

Perhaps in the almost perfect state of the future a unified and centralized National Board of Each and Every Kind of Censorship will eliminate the divergencies that now exist between the vehicles of infection. Then all the gates will be barred and all itineraries will be vain. Then no form of obscenity will be available. But now it is as if we had liquor prohibition laws which forbade us to drink whiskey from one kind of a bottle but not from another.

III

THE ENIGMAS OF LITERARY DECENCY

*Every attempt to restrict literature is open to a re-
ductio ad absurdum. There are always the com-
positors.*—HAVELOCK ELLIS.

IF the comparison of books, plays, the movies, and the
newspapers exhibits so many paradoxes, a greater single-
ness of purpose might be expected to prevail in the struggle
against any one vehicle of infection. The nature of obscenity is so enigmatic, however, that when we turn to books
alone no greater simplicity is to be discovered. Again,
æsthetic, social, and historical considerations intrude and
dictate varying attitudes toward books of different kinds
and often toward the same book. In the banning of books,
moreover, there exists the greatest discord, which it is impossible to harmonize upon any legitimate basis. The lifting of bans once imposed leads to further questioning.
One need not proceed very far to perceive that the inquiry
involves the ultimate elucidation of three puzzles, to wit:

(1) Where is an obscene book not obscene?
(2) When is an obscene book not obscene?
(3) Why is an obscene book not obscene?

At this point we need not go into the history of the evolution of criminal obscenity. Our present problem is the

statics of obscenity. Nor need we examine now the supposed judicial tests which are employed in the interpretation of the present laws. We omit also such demands for
censorship as represent personal eccentricity, taking only
cases where society has officially intervened in some form
either invoking, or threatening to invoke, the laws of criminal obscenity. We wish now merely to relate the strange
results which have been achieved under them. To make
the most favorable assumptions for the vice secretaries we
confine our examples entirely to Anglo-Saxon lands where
the ideals of civilization may be presumed to be much the
same. In selecting London, Boston, and New York for
standards of comparison, we have the advantage of dealing
with the leading book markets of the English-speaking publishing world.

The sale and distribution of obscene literature is now
finally established as a crime at the Common Law of England. The law of Massachusetts is the statute contained
in General Laws, Chapter 272, Section 28, which bans books
"containing obscene, indecent, or impure language, or manifestly tending to corrupt the morals of youth." The law
of New York is the famous Section 1141 of the Penal
Law which, as all those who have to do with the arts have
come to know, condemns all books which are "obscene, lewd,
lascivious, filthy, indecent, or disgusting." The laws are declared to be so simple that a jury of ordinary men can
understand them. A reasonable man might seek to account for the differences of standards and practice from
the varying phraseology of the statutes. In effect, however, they penalize any book which offends against any sense
of the deadly adjectives, and no very great reconciliation
upon this basis is possible. Unlike other statutes, the ob-

scenity laws are administered with very little emphasis upon fine verbal distinctions. Moral fervor interferes with judicial nicety.

THE TEMPORAL ASPECTS OF OBSCENITY

As the present obscenity laws date from late Victorianism, it is permissible to begin with some instructive Victorian parables.

In the year 1866 in England a poet by the name of Algernon Charles Swinburne published a book, *Poems and Ballads,* in which he sang of "quivering flanks," "splendid supple thighs," "hot sweet throats," and "the hot wan wine of love." He expressed the hope that the gods would "Come down and redeem us from virtue." The poems are now highly respectable but the obscenity of such lewd alliteration and immoral sentiment was quite palpable in 1866, and a great public clamor arose which led the publisher to withdraw the book after a threat of criminal prosecution.

In the year 1855 a poet by the name of Walt Whitman published *Leaves of Grass* and shocked American Puritanism and English Victorianism. There was a great deal of talk about the viciousness of the poems but it was not till 1881, twenty-six years after the first edition, that the obscenity of the book became so obvious that the Boston district attorney threatened criminal prosecution unless it was expurgated. Although Whitman had once said: "Damn all expurgated books, the dirtiest book of all is the expurgated book," he consented to revise some lines in "I Sing the Body Electric," "A Woman Waits for Me," and "Spontaneous Me." But the district attorney, representing the spirit of his time, had a more inclusive list of twenty-two

obviously obscene items, including all of "A Woman Waits
for Me," "The Dalliance of the Eagle," and "To a Common
Prostitute." So the publisher withdrew the book, and a
Philadelphia publisher took the plates over a little later, and
issued the edition as originally written. As a result of the
excitement caused by the attempted suppression, Whitman
earned enough in royalties to buy his Camden home.

In the year 1888 there commenced in England the long
battle against Henry Vizetelly, who was responsible as publisher for English translations of Zola's too naturalistic
novels. He had lived for many years in France, where he
had developed un-English ideas of the obscene, and he was
said to be a "radical publisher." It is true that he published
such wicked French authors as Flaubert, Goncourt, Gautier,
Murger, Maupassant, Daudet, and Paul Bourget, but he
had also done more than any other man to popularize Long-
fellow in England! A debate on the "pernicious literature"
which Vizetelly was sponsoring was opened in the House
of Commons by Samuel Smith, M.P. Would the British
public stand for such a scene as in *La Terre* where the dairy-
maid brings the bull to the cow at the farm of La Borderie?
When Vizetelly was prosecuted, he was regarded as so much
worse than a murderer and a thief that he could not get
counsel to defend him. He had to plead guilty, and although an old man of seventy, and suffering from a stric-
ture, he was sent to jail for three months. He died soon
after as a result. The cream of the jest is that the condemned versions of the Zola novels had been expurgated.
An expurgated Zola outraged the Victorians in 1888.

The Zola prosecution is the literary *cause célèbre* under
the English obscenity laws. A decade later it was a book
which is now universally recognized as a contribution to

science of the first order that made Victorian society lose
its senses. The prosecution of Havelock Ellis's *The Psychology of Sex* in 1898 rivaled in stupidity and vindictiveness the earlier outbreak. It was not Ellis, eager and ready
to defend his work, who was arrested, but a bookseller by
the name of George Bedborough who was worrying the
authorities as secretary of a "Legitimization League" and as
editor of *The Adult Review*. (The offensiveness of the
titles alone can well be imagined.) Although a defense
fund was raised, Bedborough refused to play the rôle of
possible martyr, and made a deal with the prosecution for a
suspended sentence. Thus the issue of the immunity of the
work of a man of science was not even presented. Now
Ellis is considered almost a sage, and a Boston publishing
house has put its imprint on a reverential biography of his
life.

In the year 1896 in New York, there was serious talk
of suppressing Hamlin Garland's *The Rose of Dutcher's
Cooly*. The New York *Critic* wrote: "We are bound to
say after reading both books that *Rose of Dutcher's Cooly*
leaves a more disagreeable taste in the mouth than *Jude the
Obscure*. Mr. Garland's word 'sex-maniac' is barbaric
enough, but the continual dwelling (we had almost said
gloating) on the thing is far worse." Now Hamlin Garland is quoted in the official reports of the New York Society for the Suppression of Vice as disgusted with the
sex-obsession of modern literature.

In the year 1897 in New York, d'Annunzio's *The
Triumph of Death* was prosecuted—but the jury refused to
convict.

In the year 1908, Boston fell upon and convicted the
publisher of Elinor Glyn's *Three Weeks*. It was much too

hot and sulphurous in its passion for 1908. The very same secretary of the New England Watch and Ward Society who secured this conviction sheepishly confessed to an interviewer in 1925: "I know you wouldn't make a fool of me, Mister, but I have been rereading *Three Weeks* recently. Do you know I couldn't get a conviction against that book nowadays. I wouldn't dare take it into court."

In the same year, a week before Christmas, in England, after a terrible hullabaloo, the publisher of Hubert Wales's *The Yoke* was dragged to Bow Street at the instigation of the Vigilance Association, compelled to plead guilty to publishing obscene literature, and escaped jail only by agreeing to have all the remaining copies destroyed.

In the year 1928 there came to light another bit of Victorian literary history. When thirty years ago W. Somerset Maugham had written a novel called *Mrs. Craddock,* it was refused by the publishers as too bold. When it was finally published by William Heinemann, it was carefully expurgated. Now, it is republished in America by Doubleday Doran, who advertise the fact that it has been a suppressed book. "Censored," begins the ad; "An Inside Story of Publishing"!

The healing power of time apparently applies to "obscene" books also. Many of them, indeed, are now required high-school reading. But it is one of the futilities of history that it is never entirely convincing. We are inclined to be charitable and to say that almost anything was possible in the comic interlude that was the dim and distant Victorian Age. The progressive change in the standards of literary decency is observable even in that period which on the whole had achieved a great uniformity of attitude. But Victorian parables do not satisfy the mind entirely. Why not let by-

gones be bygones? Why drag skeletons of literary prudery
from the closet where they have been mouldering for decades?—Is there any less relentlessness toward books in
our own time? The temporal nature of obscenity is illustrated today even more startlingly.

It is not many years ago that *Trilby, Hagar Revelly,
Homo Sapiens, The Rise and Fall of Susan Lenox,* Kreym-
borg's *Edna, a Girl of the Streets,* and Dreiser's *The "Genius"* were attacked and raided.

Very little time, indeed, elapsed between the withdrawal
and the republication of *The "Genius."* In 1916, it was suppressed in New York. In 1923, it was published openly in
New York with a jacket which announced that it had been
suppressed at the instigation of the Society for the Suppression of Vice.

A close examination of the works of George Moore reveals, perhaps, the neatest case in point. In 1917, Moore
had a conversation with John Balderston on censorship which
when published included a story comparing the novelist's
dread of the evil consequences of books to "the belief of the
old woman that if she *spat* into the sea she would bring
about an inundation." In 1923, when the same conversation
was reprinted in *Avowals,* it appeared in what was undoubtedly its original form. Now Moore was set down as re-
marking: "You know the story of the old woman who
was afraid to *relieve herself* into the sea lest she bring about
an inundation." How long will it take for the removal of
the euphemism?

THE SPATIAL ASPECTS OF OBSCENITY

A REFERENCE to comparative standards is always more damaging than a reference to changing standards in similar societies. The accidents of geography may determine the fate of books! Time and space are related, however obliquely. Whenever a book is suppressed in one Anglo-Saxon land one wonders that it is left unmolested in another. Why did England in late Victorianism concentrate upon Swinburne's *Poems and Ballads* while American Puritanism singled out *Leaves of Grass* as the focus of its wrath? Whitman had perhaps more defenders in England than America. Is it simply that a prophet is without honor in his own country? Why did the novels of Zola send their publisher to jail in England when there was no criminal prosecution in America? Why at almost the same time did England select *The Yoke,* and America *Three Weeks?* Is the spatial aspect of obscenity the result simply of the need for a sacrificial victim at any one time whereby decency may be vindicated till the next time?

Consider the scandal of discrepancies in modern censorship between England and America. London and New York each thinks that it is more civilized when it comes to policing books. Many an English author has deposed that interference with books nowadays in England is not to be compared with the ludicrous contretemps which occur among the Americans. Many an American author has returned the compliment. While we may not be able to agree with the mother country upon a naval policy, the *entente cordiale* against impure literature might well be much more close. Here are the two great English-speaking nations. The last edition of *The Encyclopædia Brittanica* was dedicated

jointly and severally to His Majesty King George V, and
His Excellency Woodrow Wilson, the President of the
United States. But there is no agreement as to the books
which are lewd, lascivious, indecent and obscene.

For a long time the pet bugaboo of English letters was
George Moore. While he was also attacked in America,
the books chosen for this unwelcome attention were not the
same. In England *A Mummer's Wife* shocked all the right-
thinking. In America, *Memoirs of My Dead Life* was
bowdlerized. The case of George Moore comes closest to
representing Anglo-Saxon harmony.

D. H. Lawrence is now the especial martyr of the English. His *The Rainbow* was chosen for prosecution in England while circulating freely in America. On the other hand,
his *Women in Love* left British prudery unmoved while it
stirred the New York Society for the Suppression of Vice
to action—quite unsuccessful despite the supporting crusade of Justice Ford, who was shocked to discover the book
in his unmarried daughter's hands. Thus a book which
failed to move British authority to prosecution led to the
founding of the Clean Books League in New York.

In England, Arnold Bennett's *The Pretty Lady* was
threatened with suppression and only an immediately aggres-
sive resistance saved the day. In America, there was not
even a murmur when it appeared.

In England W. L. George's *A Bed of Roses* makes the
guardians of public morals very uncomfortable but it has
been let alone in America.

When Sherwood Anderson published *Many Marriages,*
the scene wherein the hero strips naked before his wife as
a symbol that he is done with dissimulation led in America
merely to many travesties and a good deal of banter. When

the book was published in London in 1923, it was at once haled into the British courts.

Less than a year ago the British authorities proved that the obscenity laws in England are still very much to be respected. The book was *The Cantab,* a novel of undergraduate life in Cambridge by Shane Leslie. When it was banned by his bishop, the author, who was a Catholic, offered to withdraw the book. A criminal prosecution followed none the less. Leslie says he planned suicide when a lady told him that the French critics called the book "dull but not indecent." Later he saw the humor of the situation, and destroyed the epitaph he had proposed:

> Here lies an author fallen in his ruts;
> Dull but not indecent; had no guts.

The obscenity laws then can mean very little to one who travels. . . .

AT THE TWO ENDS OF THE BOSTON POST ROAD

ENGLAND is on the other side of the Atlantic, and almost a week away in time. But it takes only five hours to get from New York to Boston by express. Almost every book has become obscene in Boston in the last two years under the quiet little arrangement between the booksellers and the New England Watch and Ward Society whereby when the Boston Booksellers' Committee has notified its members that the Society objects to certain passages in a book which it believes to be a violation of the statutes, they refuse any longer to carry it in stock, and it is supposed to be heard of no more. The Massachusetts courts are very severe in their interpretation of the law, and although the statute says only books "manifestly tending to corrupt the morals of youth" are forbidden, they have held that it means not "obviously" but "conceivably" tending to corrupt the morals of youth. A bookseller naturally will not risk the vexation of a criminal prosecution for a profit of fifty cents. Upon the Boston Index Librorum Prohibitorum are over 100 books, which include such best sellers as *The World of William Clissold, Doomsday, The Sun Also Rises, Power, Young Men in Love, The Hard-Boiled Virgin, Nigger Heaven,* and *Manhattan Transfer.* The threat of the law in the background merely suffices as the pragmatic sanction for this list. But actual criminal prosecutions have been instituted in Boston against such books as Robert Keable's *Simon Called Peter,* Sinclair Lewis's *Elmer Gantry,* Upton Sinclair's *Oil* and Theodore Dreiser's *An American Tragedy.* Although under prosecution, the latter was assigned as required reading in one of the English courses in Harvard, across the county line! The condition will be rapidly achieved in Boston which is summed up in Shaw's epigram: "Censorship ends in logical completeness when nobody is allowed to read any books except the books nobody can read."

In New York the shocking-point is very much higher. Compared to Boston, it is a veritable sanctuary for literature. Since the death of Anthony Comstock, the New York Society for the Suppression of Vice has fallen upon evil days. It is still a potent cause for mischief but it has not the absolute sway of the good old days when it suppressed *Hagar Revelly* and *The "Genius,"* the latter without so much as having to bring a criminal action. Since then it has ventured upon many an egregious quest under the guidance of Comstock's successor, Mr. Sumner, but with

very little tangible success.   Since 1920, the Society has
attacked *The Story of a Lover, Jurgen, Madeleine, A Young
Girl's Diary, Casanova's Homecoming, Women in Love,
Replenishing Jessica,* Freud's *Leonardo da Vinci,* and two
such classics as the *Satyricon* and *Mademoiselle de Maupin.*
In the last case it was driven to cover by a suit for dam-
ages for malicious prosecution.   Although it sometimes gets
a verdict from the jury, it often loses by reversals in the
appellate courts.   The only case where the verdict was permitted to stand was in *Casanova's Homecoming.*   No wonder the courage of the Society has failed, and *Elmer Gantry,
An American Tragedy* and *Oil* are left strictly alone.   The
Boston and New York indexes agree only on *A Young
Girl's Diary* and the *Satyricon* as far as attempts at suppression go.   On the other hand, the New York Society has not
succeeded in so much as securing a warrant to halt *Simon
Called Peter,* against which the Watch and Ward Society
secured a verdict.

Obviously, the New York courts are slowly but surely
reflecting the greater cultural liberality of cosmopolitan New
York, where magistrates of Jewish, Protestant, and Catholic extraction sit upon the bench.   They have begun to undermine the rigor of Section 1141 of the Penal Law by
judicial construction.   While in theory a book may be convicted if it contains isolated obscene passages, in practice
they have begun to insist that the whole book which is introduced into evidence be taken into consideration.   Now
and then they talk almost like literary critics of the claims
of art.   Again they may exculpate a book if it teaches a
salutary moral, as happened when the conviction in the
Madeleine case was reversed.   The law is in flux, and all is
confusion, and cries go up to Albany annually for a Clean

Books Bill to restore the law to its pristine Comstockian vigor.

THE DEMORALIZATION OF DISSENT

BUT the New York situation is nevertheless so uncertain that both the temporal and spatial aspects of obscenity are illustrated within the limits of a single state and city. No one in his senses will any longer bet a nickel on the outcome of an obscene book trial in New York when a reputable publisher is involved. The lack of *esprit de corps* among the police magistrates and the disagreement of the lower and higher courts has brought it about that a book is obscene on a Monday when one magistrate has issued a summons, not obscene on a Wednesday when another magistrate refuses to hold the accused for trial, and obscene again on a Friday when, despite both magistrates, the grand jury decides to indict. This was the state of affairs when the publishers of *A Young Girl's Diary* and *Casanova's Homecoming* were indicted by a grand jury after the books were declared to be not obscene in the Magistrate's Court! A charge against *The Rise and Fall of Susan Lenox* was dismissed one year when it ran as a serial, and sustained the next year when it appeared in book form. *Madeleine* was an "obscene, lewd, lascivious, filthy, indecent, and disgusting" book in January, 1920, when the publisher was convicted, and a pure, moral, and uplifting book in July of the very same year when the Appellate Division reversed the conviction. *Jurgen* was an obscene book in January, 1920, when the indictment was issued, and a work of art in October, 1922, when the charge was dismissed; *Replenishing Jessica* was an obscene book in July, 1925, but ceased to be so before July, 1928, when a jury refused to convict. Judges of the New York higher courts who are men of the same profession, similar education, and the same social sphere have dissented from the majority of their colleagues in three of the leading cases, involving *The Gospel Worker,* an anti-Catholic paper, *Madeleine,* and *Mademoiselle de Maupin.* The figures are respectively 5–2, 5–2, and 3–1. The books were therefore obscene beyond a reasonable doubt 5–2, 5–2, and 3–1. The suit involving *Mademoiselle de Maupin* was one for malicious prosecution against the New York Vice Society after a jury had discharged the bookseller. In such a suit the question is not whether the book is obscene but whether the society had "probable cause," as the legal phrase is, for believing it to be so. The Court of Appeals could not even agree upon this more limited basis. No less than seven Supreme Court judges in the course of two previous trials had disagreed as to the obscenity of Gautier's masterpiece, and the second trial judge reversed himself when he allowed the case to go to the jury after he had determined the previous day that it was a matter of law for himself alone to decide.

A little guessing game is, perhaps, in order. Two New York judges are speaking. "I venture," says one, "that no one can read this book and truthfully say that it contains a single word or picture which tends to excite lustful or lecherous desire."

"This book," says the other, "is suggestive throughout. It offends decency and good morals."

Of what two books are the two learned judges (who happen to be of the Appellate Division) speaking?

The answer is that they are not speaking of two different books but of the same book—*Madeleine, the Autobiography of a Prostitute.*

An even more vivid illustration of dissent is to be found
in the fortunes of the issue of *The American Mercury*
which contained the "Hatrack" article.   H. L. Mencken
went to Boston and had himself arrested on the Commons
for the sale of a copy.   The next day he was acquitted in
the Boston Municipal Court by Judge Parmenter, who decided that the magazine did not contravene the obscenity
law, and added for good measure that Mr. Mencken, as
a free citizen, "had the constitutional right to raise hell."
A bookseller in Cambridge (which is just without the Boston city limits), previously arrested for selling a copy of
the same "Hatrack" issue, was, however, less favored.   He
was found guilty by a different judge and fined one hundred dollars for selling obscene literature.   To cap the climax Judge Mack, sitting in New York, issued an injunction restraining the post-office officials from interfering with
the magazine and ventured the opinion that "no one but a
moron would be affected by it."

All this is strongly reminiscent of the occasions when
the Supreme Court of the United States declares a statute
unconstitutional "by clear and undubitable demonstration"
although several of the eminent judges are dissenting.   The
ordinary mortal can understand when a higher court re-
verses a conviction in a case of robbery, murder, arson, or
larceny.   Certain evidence may have been wrongly admitted,
undue weight may have been given to certain factors (which
are quite tangible), new facts may have been discovered,
et cetera.   But the pages of a book are quite unchangeable;
the letters do not move and rearrange themselves; they remain the same on Monday, Wednesday and Friday, and in
January, July and October, and in fact will remain the same

for all time. All the changes that take place are confined entirely to the minds of the learned judges.

THE STATUTE OF LIMITATIONS ON OBSCENITY

FROM the fact that we have spoken of "the statics of obscenity," it may perhaps be supposed that the law is applicable only to modern literature. The literature of the past, however, proves also to be part of the same problem. In literature there can be said to be neither past nor present. We confront the now familiar dilemma of the Bible, Shakespeare, Rabelais, Boccaccio, the Restoration dramatists, Fielding, Smollett, and Sterne and the rest of the "obscene" classics. The Bible, moreover, is to be had in staggering quantities. It achieves circulation figures beyond any best seller; the numbers distributed (often gratis) by the American Bible Society, the English Bible Society, and the Gideon Society run into the millions. The classics are easily available in such popular libraries as the Bohn Classics, the Loeb Classical Library, the Everyman series, and the Oxford editions.

We have heard sardonic demands for the suppression of the Bible and the classics since obscenity laws have been enforced. The argument as to the Bible was most forcibly put by Annie Besant when convicted of criminal obscenity in England for publishing Robert Owen's *Family Limitation*. She compiled a pamphlet listing some 150 passages in the Bible which were "obscene" if obscenity had any meaning. When Vizetelly was in the toils of the British Pharisees, he increased the fury against him by sending the Home Secretary an eighty-page pamphlet (now the rarest among collectors' items) entitled *Extracts Principally from the English Classics: Showing that the Legal Suppression of M. Zola's Novels Would Logically Involve the Bowdlerization of Some of the Greatest Works in English Literature.* Incidentally, it is also a commentary upon the temporal aspects of obscenity: it includes passages from Swinburne and Rossetti which may now be freely quoted even in Boston.

When Upton Sinclair went to Boston to fight against the ban on *Oil,* he was told that everyone was sick of hearing of the Bible, Shakespeare and the Classics. Logic is always embarrassing. Yet the fact is that the *Decameron* is on the present Boston index. It was a New Englander, Noah Webster, who edited an expurgated edition of the Bible. "Many passages," he said, "are expressed in language which decency forbids to be repeated in families and the pulpit." In the early days of the obscenity laws the vice secretaries accepted the challenge of the classics more uncompromisingly. Rabelais, the *Decameron,* and the *Heptameron* have been hounded in London, Boston, and New York. In London the Vigilance Association is now content to leave them alone if they are not sold too brazenly. The New York courts have permitted an estate at a legal sale to dispose of Payne's *Arabian Nights, Tom Jones,* Rabelais, Ovid's *Art of Love,* the *Decameron,* the *Heptameron,* the *Confessions* of Rousseau, *Tales from the Arabic,* and *Aladdin,* and have enforced a contract for the sale of a set of Voltaire. We shall see, however, that such works are scrutinized much more closely under the Federal Postal Laws. The recent fiascos, too, in such a liberal state as New York over the *Satyricon* and *Mademoiselle de Maupin* should be a warning that perhaps they still lie in a shadowy legal realm.

Apparently, then, there is a statute of limitations on

obscenity. But when does a book become a classic? Is at least one prosecution necessary before the classicism of a book is recognized by the vice societies? Must a period of five, ten, twenty-five, fifty, or seventy-five years first elapse? A great man need be dead only ten years to be eligible for the Hall of Fame.

No wonder the New York Society was puzzled by *Mademoiselle de Maupin.* Only seventy-eight years had elapsed since its publication when the Society haled it into court. In 1835 it had shocked the immoral French and aroused the greatest indignation. In 1922, it was calmly accepted in America. Was the conclusion the uncomfortable and unreasonable one that the morality of France in 1835 was superior to the morality of such an idealistic nation as America in 1922? Had not a New York judge said in sustaining the conviction of *Casanova's Homecoming*: "We may assert with pride—though not boastfully—that we are essentially an idealistic and spiritual nation and exact a higher standard than some others."

Again, the paramount interest of society, this time in the preservation of the world's literature, bedevils the whole game. Is there any explanation possible? Does the Bible owe its immunity to the greater reverence with which it is supposed to be approached? Alas, this is not an age of reverence. The Bible has been secularized, and there is a whole movement which aims to teach it simply as literature. When interviewed as to the classics, the secretaries of vice societies excuse their leniency upon the ground that Shakespeare, Rabelais, and Boccaccio would not offend against the law today, but, living in a less refined time, they could not help but reflect the grossness of their age. (The implication is that this only shows the great advance in our own.) What age then did Theodore Dreiser, for instance, reflect? At any rate, is obscenity less lewd and lascivious *per se* if dated?

It is true that the whole background of a classic, especially if it is of foreign character, is often so strange and unrelated to the stresses of life upon the modern scene that its kinetic values are far less. Perhaps a youth who reads of prostitution in ancient Greece is not likely to go off to a brothel in London, Boston, or New York. However, one never can tell. A picture of Greek prostitution which was quite savory might make him mistake its present nature. When Charles Lamb attempted to excuse the Restoration dramatists upon the theory that their whole world was so unreal and fictitious that no immoral lessons could possibly be drawn from them, he was denounced as a sophist by Macaulay. After all, a youth is no philosopher, and he has no strongly developed historical sense. Perhaps, however, the secretaries of vice societies are cynics, and believe that the very definition of a classic is a book that is no longer read.

NOT INCLUDING THE SCANDINAVIAN

OBSCENITY is apparently also a lingual concept. When one investigates the activities of the vice societies, one discovers that their best energies are directed to books in the tongue of Shakespeare. Against books which are in a foreign language, they are not normally moved to action. With Rabelais in French or Boccaccio in Italian they refuse to concern themselves. The New York Vice Society secured a conviction against *Casanova's Homecoming,* but they let it circulate freely as *Casanova's Heimfahrt* in the original German. Schnitzler had become obscene in translation.

The English language was not to be sullied.   The same is
true of *A Young Girl's Diary,* which is also from the German.   It is true that there is the practical difficulty of prosecuting a book which is in a tongue that the jury may not
understand.   The spectacle of a jury of honest American
business men struggling through the intricacies of French
or German novels is one which we have been spared.   Yet
there are court interpreters who might be called in if real
earnestness were shown.   At least one foreign language is
a minimum requirement in our high schools, and our boys
and girls who are taught German and French and Spanish
may well go wrong if the obscenity laws are not enforced
against all languages.   Are we to follow the example of
the old English gentlewoman who consented to accept a
gift of a parrot with a rich vocabulary of profanity when
informed that although the bird swore horribly it did not
know one naughty English word but swore only in Portu-
gese?   Only two interpretations appear possible:

(1) If you are a foreigner, then obscenity cannot harm
you, but if you are an Anglo-Saxon you are susceptible,
and are to be protected—which is not very flattering to the
Anglo-Saxon; or

(2) If you are a foreigner, obscenity can harm you, too,
but our business is only to save Anglo-Saxons from ruin—
which is not very polite toward unnaturalized Americans,
however patriotic such a policy may be.

"If my name were Dreisershefsky," said Dreiser when
Sister Carrie was suppressed, "and I said I came from War-
saw, I'd have no trouble, but I come from Indiana, so good
night."

THE FOREIGN OFFICE VIEWPOINT ON LITERATURE

PERHAPS nationalism has made itself felt in obscenity, too. That is probably why we are slower to suppress a British book which we may think obscene although it is in our language. The fact that Joyce's *Ulysses* is openly published in Paris while it is always confiscated in England and America perhaps reveals in itself nothing as to the reputed immorality of the French. If *Ulysses* had been written in French there would be as little hindrance placed in its way to publication in London or New York. We are slow to attack a book in a foreign language by a foreign author when a slur upon the morals of another people might be involved. For all we know, international amity might be disturbed. However amusing such an hypothesis may seem, there is hardly any other explanation for the reception accorded Zola in 1893 when he visited the English Institute of Journalism in London as President of the French *Société des Gens de Lettres*. Hardly four years before, Vizetelly had been sent to jail for publishing English translations of Zola's works. Now the imp of Satan himself was the central figure in a triumphant procession to the Guildhall and a great dinner at the Crystal Palace, in which the Mayor and other dignitaries participated. But no sooner had Zola left England than the abuse of his works broke out again. At a later date, an English journalist said at a public dinner given to Anatole France in London that his countrymen were pleased to honor a master whom they undoubtedly would have put in jail if he had written in English.

DEMOCRACY AND SMUT

THE apathy of authority toward the classic and foreign books is less of a riddle if we realize that obscenity is apparently also a class concept. It is truly remarkable that no communist writer has yet composed a dissertation entitled: *Obscenity and the Class Struggle.* If obscenity is harmful, it is quite obvious that it will affect the physical and mental constitution of rich and poor alike. The educated are supposed to be able to absorb a quantity of obscenity that would wreck the lives of the uneducated. Yet it has always been supposed that education made one rather more susceptible to the influences of the passions. The upper classes lead a far more sensual life than the lower orders of society. We who live in a democracy cannot be particularly happy to recognize that there is no democracy of smut.

As it is, if one's education includes Latin, one is entitled to a much greater allotment, just as in the Middle Ages the knowledge of Latin privileged one in the commission of murder. When a Latin classic, for instance, is translated into English, it is the custom to permit the most obscene passages to remain in the original Latin. This ingenious device keeps the obscenity from the eyes of the vulgar. When, as Gibbon said, it is "veiled in the obscurity of a learned language," all is well. If the classics are tolerated, it is from the reassuring conviction that they are read only by the sophisticated and the serious students who even if young are protected by the atmosphere of college and the home. The knowledge of foreign languages, too, has always been the property of the educated—as the popularity of French among the European nobility illustrates. If foreign languages are now taught in public high schools, it is assumed with some justice that the pupils quickly forget the few phrases they have learned with such pains.

The acquittal of *Jurgen* is almost a perfect illustration of the rule of the aristocracy of smut. Its allusions and innuendoes make it more "obscene" than any book by Dreiser, Lawrence, or Floyd Dell. The amatory Jurgen proceeds from one seduction to another, and the phallic symbols are hardly to be misinterpreted. Nevertheless, *Jurgen* escaped, for the practical judge realized at once that it was the sort of book which could be read and understood by comparatively few readers. Its style and treatment made it caviare for the vulgar. Its world was as unreal as any Restoration dramatist's could well be, and it was in truth an imitation classic. It took a high degree of intelligence to perceive the trend of its allegory, and this fact in itself practically insulated it.

"PRIVATELY PRINTED"

THE same motive of policy results also in making cheapness of price an integral part of obscenity. A cheap reprint is held to be far worse than a *de luxe* edition. The practice of authority has always been to remain indifferent to the traffic in erotica while pursuing highly spiced popular novels. From this viewpoint, the formula may be laid down that the worse poison is *The "Genius"* or *Memoirs of My Dead Life* in a Tauchnitz edition, or *Mademoiselle de Maupin* in the Modern Library. Hence the greater immunity of the book which is marked "Privately Printed" and is issued for subscribers only. If you have ten, twenty, or thirty dollars you may have *The Divan: A Morality Story* by Crébillon *fils,* or *Venus in Furs* by Leopold von Sacher-Masoch, or *The Wild Party* by Joseph Moncure March, or *The Secret History of*

Procopius, or *The History of Prostitution* by Paul La Croix. The status of such books, too, is not sharply settled in law; but ordinarily the publisher, if he confines his advertising to "Physicians, Clergymen, and Lawyers," has not much to fear. For the wealthy, elderly satyr, the erotica are translated from all the languages of the world, including the Chinese. One wonders at the occult mathematical system whereby the publisher determines that in an edition of 1500 copies of a "Privately Printed" book, "one thousand copies are for America and five hundred for Great Britain," or vice versa. When we have the long end, are we supposed to be less decent or to have more money? The whole business recalls an old and favorite verse:

Lord Palmerston once with that off-hand felicity
    Which belongs to his Lordship in stating a case,
To a new definition of "dirt" gave publicity,
    As "nothing but matter left in the wrong place."

THE CIRCUMSTANTIAL ASPECTS OF OBSCENITY

This canalization of books with reference to age, language, origin, price, and format is again a sign of the circumstantial aspects of obscenity. Its nature must be mysterious if it often has to be determined not so much intrinsically as extrinsically. A great deal of intellectual exercise is to be had by posing various minor queries:

(1) Have vice secretaries a rule that a set of an "indecent" author's collected works is to be allowed freer passage than his single volumes? The finer the bindings, the more volumes in the set, the more expensive, and hence the safer? If Dreiser, Moore, or Lawrence go on writing till their de-

finitive" editions each reach a hundred volumes, will they eventually be left in peace?

(2) Is an "obscene" book by a distinguished author rendered less so by his distinction? Is reputation a criterion?

(3) Is a rather short "obscene" book to be more feared than a long book? Is the length of the book a guide? It was actually argued that as *The "Genius"* was in 736 pages no youth would have the curiosity to read it, especially also since it had no "plot." Does the presence of a "plot" make matters worse? How far from the beginning of the book must the first doubtful passage occur? Is a single obscene passage on Page 1 a justification for suppression when five such passages after Page 250 would not be? Thus, Upton Sinclair ingeniously pointed out to the Bostonians that the first possibly objectionable passage in *Oil* occurred on Page 193. What in particular must be the mathematical relationship of the entire number of "obscene" pages to the innocent pages? Is there a calculus for determining that? Is "obscene" verse to be more deplored than "obscene" prose? Are obscene suggestions "humorously" put less offensive than if "seriously" put? And are they more shocking in a dialogue than in an indirect description?

(4) What is to be presumed from the fact that a book is anonymously published, or has no publisher's imprint? Is the case worse when a book is surreptitiously sold? Then do we not encourage open and flagrant sale to avoid the imputation?

(5) Is the title a clue? Is a flaming title alone a sufficient condemnation? Does a sanctimonious title such as *Simon Called Peter* constitute a greater outrage when the text is carnal, possibly making it easier for the book to enter the home as a religious one?

(6) Does the fact that a book has appeared in many expurgated editions raise the presumption that another expurgated or unexpurgated edition is obscene? *Post hoc propter hoc*—is that the case with Rabelais and Boccaccio?

(7) Is a book safer if it has no index? No illustrations? No binding?

(8) Is the dedication of the book to be regarded? Is it to be considered *prima facie* innocent if the author has dedicated it to his mother?

With such bewilderments are men confronted.

A LAW WITHOUT PROVISOS

IN VIEW of all these circumstances, the fact that the obscenity laws are of a blanket character, containing absolutely no exceptions or qualifications, is truly remarkable. The greatest variety of policy has expressed itself under statutes that appear to be the very essence of simplicity. No sub-clauses, for instance, exempt the Bible, or the classics, or expensive erotica. But the law's sweeping inclusiveness, evidently intended to guard against pitfalls and embarrassments that might abet the forces of indecency in an emergency, is modified in practice by a great many tacit exemptions. This is, perhaps, the best indication of the enigmatic nature of obscenity. When the ultimate and central concept is elusive, every proviso is a challenge.

Moreover, nothing of real value actually could be accomplished if we did resort to legislation. The enigmas of indecency are insoluble. We shall see later that it is quite impossible to clarify the intrinsic nature of obscenity by definition, and, if we could, it would be futile. On the other hand, its classification under extrinsic factors would be, in-

deed, simpler but no less futile. As far as this goes, it is
forgotten that the Bible is often already privileged under
positive provisions of law. In England, it is the legally
established book of the Church of England. In thirteen
American states in recent years compulsory Bible reading
laws have appeared which require the Bible to be read to the
pupils in the public schools upon stated occasions. Such
positive provisions forestall the logical absurdity of applying the obscenity laws to the Bible. These Bible reading
laws, however, are carelessly drawn, for they permit the
old difficulty to remain. A sardonic schoolmaster might
choose to read such "obscene" passages to his classes as the
story of Lot and his daughters, or the Song of Solomon.
As we have already seen, to draw a law to exempt acknowledged classics would be difficult. But in any event both the
Bible and classics would remain available as sources of corruption. However much the logic derived from the law is
eliminated, the logic of life remains.

Finally a law might be enacted to permit specifically (*de
jure*) the "Privately Printed" erotica which are now merely
tolerated (*de facto*). The reasons for such a discrimination
would be the same supposedly as lie behind the movie censorship. But, assuming that the theory of democracy can
allow such an inconsistency, and democrats stomach such an
abomination, so positive a law would work to the greatest
disadvantage of literature. There would remain the insuperable difficulty of defining and determining in border-
line cases just when a book was an eroticon, making necessary a limited circulation, and when it was simply a sex novel
which might be generally circulated. The natural result
would be that a great many works which belong, perhaps,
to the latter class would be driven into the disreputable

former class.   Such a law should be welcomed, indeed, by
every shrewd vice secretary, who would bend all his efforts
to get every robust novel into a limited edition.   He would
always have ready the bland reply that he was not at all per-
secuting a book or its author but trying to confine him and
his work to the proper channels.   Under such a law *Jurgen*
and *Casanova's Homecoming* and all similar books would
undoubtedly have had to be published as erotica.   Great art
is, however, too democratic, aiming as it does at the widest
possible communication, to be hampered in this way.   The
assumption is that the reader of an ordinary sex novel has
not the intelligence to be safely trusted with one a little more
advanced in its eroticism.   That is drawing the line very
finely indeed.

IV

THE PERPLEXITIES OF FEDERALISM

An ideal State would be about the size of County Cork.—GEORGE RUSSELL (Æ).

THE enigmas of literary decency are embarrassing enough in any country which is governed as a political unity. The comedy of the sex censorship is, however, considerably heightened in the United States by virtue of the federal nature of the American government. When England makes a bad blunder in the suppression of a book, the combustions immediately resulting are internal. The inevitable comparisons are not so quickly instituted on each side of the waters except, perhaps, among very alert critics. In the United States, on the other hand, there are two immediate standards of reference in New York and Boston, and the Federal censorship of literature creates a third which makes the whole business still more inexplicable. If it is disconcerting to find that state officials do not agree among themselves, a greater confusion is to be expected when there are Federal officials to take still another view.

The Federal sex censorship is, moreover, a special problem in the administration of the obscenity laws. Considering that Federal laws override inconsistent State regulations, it is the greatest single element of importance in the game. Even if obscenity laws of an indeterminate nature are presumed to be entirely unobjectionable in the individual states

of a federalism, it is still in order to ask if the same is true
when a federal agency undertakes to intervene. Even those
who are for State obscenity laws, might still be against Federal obscenity laws. This was, indeed, the position of the
National Liberal League which in the early years following
upon the passage of the Comstock Acts led a forlorn hope to
secure their repeal. But it is not upon the barren con-
stitutionalism of states' rights that we wish to rest the
case. When Freeman, the prolific English historian, inspired by the comparative novelty of the United States of
America, launched his *History of Federal Government,* he
did not survey the Achæan League, the Italian States, the
Swiss Cantons, and the United Provinces of the Netherlands
from motives of political æstheticism but to discover their
essential limitations and advantages. If the size and diversity of the United States did not raise difficulties in
dealing with obscene literature, constitutional objections not
coincident with practical ones would not detain us.

THE LETTER CARRIER AS CENSOR

BUT we must recognize that constitutional limitations have
as a matter of history played a great part in creating the
peculiar vice of the Federal censorship. The Post Office
exercises censorship by indirection. A direct Federal statute against obscene literature would at least possess the virtue of common honesty. But as the Federal government is
not supposed to be concerned with private morals in the
States a devious course had to be taken. Before
Anthony Comstock secured the Postal Censorship Law in
1873, there had been vigorous objection to granting to the
Post Office the power of excluding matter from the mails.

When, in 1835, President Jackson urged Congress to pass a law barring anti-slavery literature from the mails in order to preserve quiet in the Southern States, no lesser persons than Clay, Calhoun, and Webster denounced the legislation as unconstitutional. When the first constitutional inroad was finally made by the exclusion of lotteries from the mails, such a conservative as Hannis Taylor declared tersely that the act had removed the First Amendment from the Constitution, no more, no less! It is simply for the purpose of irony that we recall that Washington believed a free and unhampered Post Office to be of such importance to the people that he declared himself in favor of no postage. It is even more ironic to recall that Hamilton expected so little danger from the grant of the postal power that he dismissed the whole subject with the remark that "the power of establishing post roads must in every view be a harmless power."

It was thus that Congress was driven to make the crime the indirect one of sending obscene literature through the Federal mails, and to convert the letter carrier into a *censor morum*. There are literal constitutionalists who insist that the only misuse of the mails which Congress may penalize must have a tangible and physical connection with the chance of injury to the postal service. Thus, the law against sending explosives through the mails is wholly reasonable. A delivery truck may go up in the air and postal employees may be killed. Many will argue that perhaps Hannis Taylor unduly excited himself when he objected to the exclusion of lotteries from the mails. The Federal Postal Laws also make it criminal to use the mails for the innumerable frauds and confidence games which may be practised upon the American public, from selling bogus oil stock to soliciting contributions to non-existent homes for dyspeptic cats. Some urge that it is too much to expect a government to permit the use of the mails to advance schemes which are quite generally regarded as criminal. But the chief vice of the Anti-Lottery Act was its value as a persuasive precedent. Although the Get-Rich-Quick Wallingford may consider a lottery entirely unobjectionable, and such a position is both human and understandable, its prohibition is both definite and objective, and the mails play a very important part in its management. But the delights of love cannot be enjoyed by mail. It is difficult to see how the seed catalogues and Congressmen's speeches can sustain injury from being in the same mail pouch with a volume of Rabelais.

In other countries, under the influence of the example of the Comstock law, if obscene matter is also excluded from the mails, the officials who adminster the law are part of the same set of officials which governs the country in all other respects. But a Federal postmaster is an appointee and consequently the chances are that he will be less responsive to the pressure of public opinion. He need not appeal to the verdict of a jury to support him in his private prejudices. It is in his discretion simply to exclude matter from the mails without prosecution, and this is, indeed, the usual procedure. In such cases it is extremely difficult to secure review of his action. In England and on the Continent the obscenity postal laws are rarely invoked because the same object can be effected in all parts of the state under the normal criminal law against obscenity. But in the United States it is no mere accident that the postal censorship has assumed such proportions. It has its darker aspects but its vitality arises from the very nature of the Federal structure.

Its indirection, above all, makes the postal censorship a subtle farce. Postmasters exclude and Federal judges convict for the crime of sending obscene literature through the mails. But, unlike a Boston or New York district attorney, neither postmaster nor judge can, if he has strict regard for the obligations of his oath, indulge in the luxury of such a remark as: "Are we to permit such vile trash into our homes to pollute our sons and daughters?" That they do must be set down to lamentable human weakness. Since the Federal government clearly has no control over individual morals in this sphere, it is not for them to say that they are barring a book from the mails for the protection of those immature or abnormal United States citizens whose minds it might corrupt by inspiring images of lewd and lecherous desire. Constitutionally, the purpose of the Federal law can only be to keep the United States mail pure. True, to determine if the book is obscene, its character must be ascertained by measuring its effects upon an immature or abnormal citizen as if the law was actually intended for his own individual protection. But this presumably is not the same thing. The citizen must be considered entirely hypothetical. The philosophy is entirely the philosophy of *Als Ob!*

THE AMORAL FEDERALISM

THE insuperable obstacle is the size and diversity of our Federalism. The no-less-than Seven United Provinces of the Netherlands might all be included with room to spare in many a single state of the almost seven times seven United States. Yet a single Federal law against obscene publications which is supposed to impose the same standards upon all the states controls the reading of New York and San Francisco, New Orleans and Boston. In a comparatively small country such as France a national law against the obscene is imposed upon a population which is on the whole homogeneous, so that uniformity of racial and environmental factors may be taken to supply some more or less constant and minimum criterion for judging the obscene. If savages or primitives possessed a literature, no divergencies as to the sense of the obscene would exist. The more civilization and territory the tribe acquires, the more marked the variations become. In other words, an obscenity law would work perfectly in that society where it cannot be conceived to exist.

But the United States is not only tremendous in size, stretching clear across a continent; it is also the most polyglot nation in the world, and has had indelibly impressed upon it the metaphor of the Melting Pot. There may, perhaps, arrive a time in the not distant future when the campaign for complete Americanization will have triumphed, and the Quota Immigration Act so insulated us against further inroads upon American civilization that no two Americans will differ in their moral sentiments. When such a degree of regimentation is reached, there might be little objection to a Federal law against obscenity—and perhaps no need. But at the present time the population of the states is still heterogeneous despite a superficial appearance of assimilation. The sense of modesty so deeply rooted in obscure racial taboos and antipathies can hardly be expected to operate in the same way in Wops, Heinies, Polaks and Yids. Moreover, the Sons and Daughters of the American Revolution themselves do not always react in the same way to the same samples of literature. A Methodist postmaster in the South may be expected to take a different view of the same law than a Catholic postmaster in Chicago, or a Jewish postmaster in New York. Neither our racial nor religious alignments augur well for a Federal control of the obscene.

Apart from such racial and religious differences in fact, there is no uniform sense of the obscene. The Federal post-masters have not even such slender moral clues for their guidance as state officials have in the enacted laws relating to the general protection of the public morals. State laws against adultery, fornication, and divorce may well be taken as some index of the public mores. The grounds for divorce show such variation in different states that it is generally admitted that a uniform law on marriage and divorce in this respect would be an imposition. Twenty-one states in the Union have no laws at all against fornication. Six states have no penal laws against either adultery or fornication. These are, curiously enough, Arkansas, Delaware, Louisiana, Nevada, New Mexico, and even Tennessee! The State of New Mexico has no law at all against obscene literature, and may well regard it as an impertinence for a Federal post-master to censor its reading.

AN INTRA-STATE MANN ACT

It sometimes happens in the states that Federal laws create moral crimes which did not exist there before. A singular one has resulted from the heroic effort to keep the mails pure. There is hardly a mature and sinful American who is not acquainted with the example known as the Mann Act. It is frequently denounced as an instrument of blackmail. Savage cynics and iconoclasts often point out the absurdity that while under the law of the wicked state of New York, for example, where fornication is not a crime, it is lawful for a man to take his mistress from Brooklyn to Manhattan, or from Albany to New York for illicit relations, neverthe-less under the Mann Act, which forbids the transportation of

women in interstate commerce for immoral purposes, it is
a crime for the very same New Yorker to take his mistress
for the same purpose from Manhattan to Jersey City.

The Mann Act was passed in 1913. Yet it is not at all
realized that as early as 1888 an even more curious mon-
strosity was evolved incidentally in the campaign against obscene literature. The passage of the original Comstock Act
in 1873 had left unchecked a ready means for at least securing information about obscene literature. The law as it then
stood did not penalize the sending of an obscene letter.
Thus, although a bookseller engaged in the immemorial business of selling the *Memoirs of Fanny Hill, The Thousand
and One Arabian Nights*, Rabelais, and the *Decameron* could
not send them through the mails, he might circularize prospects by letter to come to his shop to buy them. Where
bookseller and customer lived at considerable distance from
each other in the same or different states, the circular letter
alone would prove vain. But within the range of a single
city such as New York, Boston, Philadelphia, or Chicago, a
considerable traffic might still result despite the Federal
Postal Law. This was not to be endured, although it is to
be noted that in such cases the wretches might be prosecuted
equally well under the State obscenity laws which by now
had generally swept the State legislatures. That a Federal
law was therefore unnecessary proved, however, to be no
restraint. To protect the purity of the mails in 1888 the
amendment was passed including obscene letters. Now,
naturally, the law had to take a general form: the sending of
any obscene letter was made criminal. The Inter-State
Mann Act was thus rendered in comparison a benevolent act.
In its violation a state line at least had to be crossed and illicit sexual intercourse indulged in. But now an Intra-State

Mann Act had been quietly effected.   Under the law of 1888
if a man in Brooklyn writes a love note to his mistress in
Manhattan to come and spend Wednesday night with him
there, he is guilty of a felony which subjects him to both five
years imprisonment and five thousand dollars fine.   But, now
observe that if instead of sending the passionate love note,
he actually visits his mistress in Manhattan and has sexual
intercourse with her, he commits no crime at all since fornication is not criminal under the laws of the State of New
York.   Moreover, under this Intra-State Mann Act it has
been judicially decided that a man violates the law by sending
an obscene letter to his wife, and such convictions have
actually been obtained.   The logic is inescapable.   Constitutionally the object of the law is not the protection of the
recipient of the letter against lewdness.   It is simply to protect the purity of the Federal mails, and these are as much
defiled when a husband exceeds the bounds of familiarity
with his wife.   The theological doctrine that lust is the essence of sin has thus found magnificent substantiation in
Federal law.

THE ECCENTRICITIES OF BUREAUCRACY

ALL such factors make the Federal Postal Censorship fit the
habits of bureaucracy.   Much more so than State officials
Federal office-holders tend to become bureaucrats in the very
nature of things.   The incident of the dismissal of Whitman
from the Department of the Interior in the happy days before Civil Service Reform when its inhibited Secretary discovered him to be the author of *Leaves of Grass* may well
have its moral.   In Boston, the enraged William Douglas
O'Connor may have shocked his fellow citizens with the

intemperance of *The Good, Gray Poet*, but in Washington Secretary Harlan could afford to remain unperturbed. But if in all departments the decisions of Federal officials tend to be far more irrational and irreconcilable than those of local politicians who are more immediately responsive to local opinion, they are at least normally restrained by statutes which have some degree of definiteness and objectivity. In the exclusion of literature from the mails, however, they need act only upon their private prejudices.

This often explains the absolutely unpredictable nature of the postal censorship. A postmaster is, as an official, a free personality, and self-expression comes easy to him. One can make some rough guess as to the extremes to which a Boston district attorney will tend. One can expect that it will take a great deal to alarm New York appellate judges who have approved *Madeleine* and *Mademoiselle de Maupin*. But it is ever so much more difficult to anticipate the vagaries of the thousands of postmasters and United States attorneys. One finds at various times and in various places such very different magazines barred from the mails as *The Little Review, Life, The New Masses, The Birth Control Review, Physical Culture, Hearst's Magazine* and *The American Mercury*. It is significant that the most amazing cases in the history of censorship in the United States are Federal ones. There is, for instance, the attempt made to bar the official Field Museum importations of Chinese pictures and manuscripts in 1909 as obscene, and the even greater classic of the exclusion from the mails in 1911 of the Chicago Vice Report prepared by an official Vice Commission of the City of Chicago for circulation among clergymen, editors, and social workers.

A Federal postmaster is privileged to be as stupid as he

pleases. One of them once barred a copy of Ovid's *Metamorphoses* intended for an erudite professor of Johns Hopkins. Only recently a postmaster interrupted the passage of a reputable publisher's catalogue which listed an edition of the *Decameron*, and another has barred a catalogue listing *Elmer Gantry*. Sexual frankness is the not very satisfactory common denominator in such postal exclusions as (a) the *Kreutzer Sonata* by the New York Post Office in 1890, whose author, Tolstoi, the irate Theodore Roosevelt took the occasion to denounce as "a sexual and moral pervert"; (b) Swedenborg's *Amor Conjugalis* by the Philadelphia Post Office in 1909, although it had been published as early as 1768; (c) Ben Hecht's *Fantasius Mallaire* by the Chicago Post Office in 1922; and (d) in the same year an edition of the *Decameron* by the Cincinnati Post Office, for which the bookseller later incurred a fine of no less than one thousand dollars from the district judge.

But a bureaucrat is also privileged to be intelligent if he so inclines. There was, for instance, the United States Assistant Attorney General who refused to ban Upton Sinclair's *The Jungle* from the mails and whom the Boston authorities might now well emulate in handling *Oil*. If Whitman was dismissed from the Department of the Interior, it is equally true, although it is not frequently added, that another Federal office-holder gave him a post in the Department of Justice. But such liberality only encourages the logician to make capital of the resulting inconsistencies. He perversely declares that if it is *pro bono publico* for a Federal post office to bar Havelock Ellis's *The Psychology of Sex* when no State authorities have ever been disturbed by it in this country, then it is disgraceful for Federal postmasters to fail to concur on the ban on *Elmer Gantry* and *An American Tragedy* in Boston.

A LITERARY WEBB-KENYON ACT

BUT Federal officials often take strange and immoral pride in administering Federal law with little regard for State sensitiveness. The Federal Postal Censorship is a closed system. A theory may be advanced that exclusion of a book from the mails is even more serious than a State prosecution and hence that a greater skepticism among Federal officials is proper. But no such rationalization is possible. The result of the whole situation is that State laws are practically nullified. The banning of *Elmer Gantry* and *An American Tragedy* in Boston increases the demand, and then Boston booksellers take the increased orders, which are filled legally by mail. Under the sheltering ægis of the postage stamp which bears the face of one of the Fathers, the obscene books return in triumph.

There is Federal nullification for you! If both the State and Federal statutes against obscene literature are not to be brought into such derision and contempt that it will be impossible forever after to rescue them, perhaps a Twentieth Amendment to the Federal Constitution is imperative. Modeled upon the Eighteenth it might vest complete and exclusive jurisdiction over the traffic in obscene literature in the Federal Government, providing at most for a concurrent jurisdiction in the States. The technique of Prohibition enforcement might readily be adapted for the Obscene Literature Unit conducting raids and attaching padlocks to publishing houses and readeasy libraries. If this be fantastic a readier and likelier expedient suggests itself from an early period in the evolution of national prohibition. With its inauguration, the Wilson Act of 1890 and the Webb-Kenyon Act of 1913 became academic and it will not be long before only historians will remember their purpose. But the golden nineties regarded the Wilson Act as extremely vital. When the Supreme Court rendered the Wilson Act nugatory by interpreting it to allow the shipment of liquor into a State in the "original package," the Webb-Kenyon Act was passed by Congress to prohibit any shipment of liquor into a dry state. Few realized that a quite extensive form of Federal prohibition had thus quietly been established and the dry States in theory hermetically sealed against the wet. Similarly, to make the State statutes against obscene books truly effective, a literary Webb-Kenyon Act is indispensable. It would then be unlawful to send a book from one state into another where it had judicially been declared obscene. If this precaution is neglected, Boston will battle in vain for clean books.

THE BATTLE OF THE DEPARTMENTS

If it is lamentable to observe chaos in the Post Office Department among its own officials, and the disharmony in the relationship of the Post Office Department and the States, it is infinitely more so to find conflict among different departments of the Federal hierarchy itself. In the Federal Government it very often happens that one department works against the other. The bureau on the right knoweth not what the bureau on the left doeth. The story goes, for instance, that of late the Federal testing bureaus have incidentally been rendering invaluable service to the bootleg liquor trade. A sardonic friend of ours who has an acquaintance in a Government laboratory of the Federal Health

Service makes a particular point of sending him all his boot-leg whiskey to be tested there. So, too, the Post Office striving heroically to protect American youth from the suggestions of sex in American literature has first of all to contend with the depraved scientists of the United States Health Service who issue tons of official literature having to do with the disagreeable subject of sex. The Post Office at one time or another has suppressed Malchow's *The Sexual Life*, Clark's *Marriage Guide*, Butler's *Love and Its Affinities*, and Sanger's *History of Prostitution*; but the United States Public Health Service or the United States Bureau of Education has issued such obscene publications through the Government Printing Office as *Status of Sex Education in the High Schools, The Wonderful Story of Life*, and *High School and Sex Education*. Indeed the Division of Bibliography of the Library of Congress issues a List of References on the Sex Problem and Sex Instruction which includes a book by the troublesome Havelock Ellis. It also keeps on its open shelves for general circulation at least one book which has been suppressed in one of the states.

The Copyright Office is, perhaps, the most disgraceful unit in the game. Its dereliction of duty is all the more reprehensible since it stands at the very source of infection. The copyright law expressly commands the Copyright Office to refuse a copyright to books which are obscene. Yet it has issued copyrights to every one of the books which the Post Office has ever excluded from the mails or state authorities have ever suppressed or attempted to suppress, provided, of course, they are ones which have been published in this country. It has never examined for obscenity *Hagar Revelly* or *The "Genius"* or *Madeleine* or *A Young Girl's Diary* or *Jurgen* or any other of the American classics of the literature of suppression. If the copyright law were at all strictly enforced, then such a previous censorship as has always alarmed even the most moderate libertarians would come into existence. The very sinister nature of the copyright law against obscenity explains the state of desuetude into which it has been permitted to fall. Of course an author might still publish if a copyright were refused but then he would be deprived of all literary property. Probably even Blackstone would have condemned such a previous censorship. Apparently the members of the Congressional committee never envisaged such a possibility. A kind fate has allowed the copyright law to become the most moribund of all dead-letter laws in this respect. It is violated countless times by Federal officials if the present tests of obscenity have any meaning. If there are extremists who would welcome a rigid, national censorship of literature here is an instrument ready to hand.

THE BOOK IN QUARANTINE

THE Treasury Department through the Customs Bureau introduces the last but not least element of dissension. The Federal Customs had the dubious distinction of being the first Federal department to be entrusted with the fight against obscene literature. The Tariff Act of 1842, thirty-one years before Anthony Comstock secured his Postal Law, commanded the Customs to refuse admission of obscene books into the country. It may consequently well claim priority over the Post Office Department by virtue of seniority. The Customs censorship is, however, comparatively benevolent. A tariff act is not penal, and while the Customs may exclude and destroy objectionable books at its discretion, neither the importer nor exporter incurs any other penalties.

This may be the reason for the greater humanism it has shown in many instances when compared with the Post Office, which is at least armed with the power of imprisonment. Custom officials have shown perhaps a greater leniency because, stationed at the country's portals, they are subjected to corrupting and debasing foreign influences. The most important of the Customs is naturally at New York, and then come Chicago and San Francisco. The others have little occasion to deal with literature.

A little patience may perhaps make one understand the steadfast New York policy of the Customs in barring such contaminating works as Joyce's *Ulysses*, Pierre Louys' *Aphrodite*, the *Memoirs of Fanny Hill*, Forberg's *Manual of Classic Erotology*, the Machen *Casanova*, and the works of the profligate Earl of Rochester. But for a long time it has permitted entry of *The Love Books of Ovid*, unexpurgated *Decamerons* and Rabelais, and sets of the *Thousand and One Arabian Nights* which at one place or another in the country have been barred by postmasters. There is, however, a far more deadly division of opinion with respect to Dr. Marie Stopes's *Married Love*. The New York Customs has uniformly admitted it. All Federal postmasters have unanimously said No on undercover orders from Washington.

When a shipment comes into the country by express the Customs and Post Office do not come into direct conflict. But when books enter from abroad in the mails both the Customs and Post Office have jurisdiction. It is then that the real fun begins. Lately the Post Office Department at Washington awoke to the horrible fact that the Customs of New York were admitting Rabelais, Boccaccio, and the *Arabian Nights* into the country in unbowdlerized versions when they came through the foreign mails. The order went forth from Washington at once to hold the books till further notice. The Customs became so frightened that, as the story goes, they finally even barred a thoroughly expurgated *Decameron*. The expurgated editions were finally released when the publishers vigorously protested that the Customs had regularly admitted them hitherto, but they have been warned to make no future importations until further notice and rulings in the matter, which have been promised, but have not yet been forthcoming. The awakening of the higher officials at Washington has thus resulted in initiating a change for the worse in the New York Customs. It has of late, for example, barred the comparatively innocuous *What Happens*, by John Herrman, and *My First Thirty Years*, by Gertrude Beasley.

But the vigilance of both Post Office and Customs will in all probability prove futile. It is an old story, but it is not only in the United States that it has happened. The greatest federalism which the world perhaps has ever known is the Roman Catholic Church. When, as the great spiritual force in the Holy Roman Empire, it began to exercise a censorship over books in the sixteenth century, it, too, failed to avoid conflict and achieve uniformity. At first when different bishops independently undertook to publish prohibitory indexes for their separate sees, books which appeared on lists published at Rome as heretical did not appear on similar lists issued at about the same time in Louvain, Paris, or Valladolid. Moreover, when the Papal authorities later undertook to centralize the supervision of heretical literature at Rome, obstinate clerics in France and Spain, where national consciousness had taken hold, refused to accept a number of the Papal indexes at all. The Inquisition in Spain exhibited a similar recalcitrance. It condemned a number of books which do not figure in the Roman lists and conversely refused to include others which Rome had proscribed as subversive. In the Italian states, the intellectual freedom and liberality of Venice similarly served not only to undermine the Papal censorship but the repressive policy of the neighboring countries as well. In the North the enterprising cities of the Netherlands served as even worse centres of infection. Themselves remarkably free from censorship restriction, they poured a flood of godless literature past the customs of the Holy Roman Empire and the Papacy. In fact, they regularly imported the prohibitory indexes themselves to serve as guides to the interesting books to publish for a growing market.

THE FATHER OF THE POST OFFICE

TRUE history indeed is frequently disconcerting. When the biographers recently showed that Washington, the Father of that Country which nowadays has aimed at such high moral excellence, actually danced, drank and swore at times, all true patriots wept. Now, we have shown, we trust, that the very bulwark of the Federal censorship is the Post Office, and the object of the Post Office is pure literature in pure homes. But how far it has fallen from the ideals of the first Postmaster General! For the fact is that when in 1776 the First Continental Congress came to designate the first Postmaster General, it unanimously chose none other than Benjamin Franklin for the office. He is therefore rightly to be called the Father of the Post Office. Now this Father of the Post Office led a loose and immoral life, apologizing for his illegitimate children upon the specious ground that they helped to increase the population of a new and sparsely settled country; and not satisfied with this he published his famous *Letter of Advice to Young Men on the Proper Choosing of a Mistress*—so obscene a work that one hardly dares to send this production of the Father of the Post Office through the Post Office.

V

THE SUBTERRANEAN CENSORSHIP

*It seems to be taken for granted that the sub-
scriber is "powerless"—the word is frequently used
—and must sit, tied to her chair, while "doubtful and
objectionable" works are read aloud to her by an
emissary from the Circulating Library.*
—EDMUND GOSSE.

IF the Federal Post Office has been the institution of greatest single importance in the history of the censorship in the
United States, the explanation lies not only in the exigencies
of federalism but in the convenience of the instrumentality.
In England, the analogous form of control is to be discovered in the circulating library censorship, which until
quite recent years maintained its old power and influence and
is a factor with which the English reading public has still to
reckon at times. There is the immediate difference to be
perceived, of course, that the postal censorship has been one
exercised under the authority of the state, while, strictly
speaking, the English circulating library censorship has been
of a private nature. But such was the place of the circulating
libraries in England that their censorship can certainly be
considered as quasi-public in its operation. It had behind it
for decades all the prestige which came from its correspondence with the prevailing views of Victorian society.

In spite of their outward differences, no one will fail to
see the deeper morphological relationship of the postal and

the circulating libraries censorships. It is in the subterranean character of each that their similarity of function is revealed. The advantage of the postal censorship resides in the fact that a postmaster may exclude without resort to a public criminal prosecution; and this also was the effect when the circulating libraries refused to distribute a book to their subscribers. In any event the Anglo-Saxon hates to go to law when it can possibly be avoided. He will not budge from his stand but he hates to be disagreeable. It is such a nuisance. When the same result can be quietly effected without a clash or scandal or public notice, it is infinitely to be preferred. The fact that sex is involved (which of course is not to be dragged into the open) makes such tactics peculiarly desirable. In terms of tendency the sex censorship may be particularly described as straining towards the ideal of secrecy. This fits in well with the great variety of attitudes which sex sensitiveness always inspires.

Ultimately the method rests upon a threat of an appeal to law. But as we shall see when we come to trace the history of the English Common Law of obscene libel, the legal standards did not coincide with Victorian literary prudery until 1868, which is a comparatively late date. One reason was the remarkable degree of uniformity of attitude, amounting almost to a code as fixed as the law of the Medes and Persians, which came to express itself in the tyranny of the circulating libraries. Their strength, too, explains the fact that the actual number of prosecutions at law have been far fewer than in America. The attack on the novels of Zola did not materialize till the period of transition when the hold of the circulating libraries was beginning to be broken.

"GOING TO MUDIE'S"

IT so happened that all the circumstances of literary production and distribution among the Victorians conspired to give the circulating libraries censorship a perfection which has been equaled if at all only in a certain American city in recent years. It remains a satanic ideal to be approximated. A large reading middle class arose in England in the middle of the nineteenth century. A two-volume novel such as Wells's *The World of William Clissold* makes the modern reader sigh, but the leisurely mid-Victorian regarded a book "the longer the better." The English novel in the days of Fanny Burney, Richardson, Fielding, Smollett and Sterne appeared in from five to ten moderate volumes. The very birth of the English novel was closely related to the middle-class achievement of comfort and prosperity. But by the opening of the nineteenth century the English novel had settled down to three substantial volumes. The three-volume novel, or, as it came to be affectionately called by the Victorians, the old three-decker, became the standard and unalterable form.

The current price of the three-volume novel, however, was so high that until the early years of the nineteenth century only the most fortunate members of the very upper middle classes could afford the luxury of reading. The public library, the open-sesame to books, was still unknown, but the number of people who had the ability and opportunity for reading was growing. The law of supply and demand created the private circulating library. A three-volume novel cost no less than 31s 6d, or about eight dollars, a truly enormous sum when compared to the price of modern novels and popular reprints, which are much in demand, particularly in England. But for a guinea (or about five dollars) a year

the Victorian could obtain a continual supply of staple
fiction from the circulating libraries. The popularity of these
libraries in the later nineteenth century makes us forget the
great suspicion with which they were first regarded by respectable folk who looked upon reading as a secret and
shameful vice. Sir Anthony Absolute in *The Rivals*, for instance, observed: "Madam, a circulating library in a town
is an evergreen tree of diabolical knowledge. It blossoms
every year."

But no hint of indecorum attached to their patronage by
the time Dickens, Scott, Thackeray and George Eliot came
to write. The largest of the circulating libraries were
Mudie's, Smith's, Moses's, and Day's. But without doubt
the most popular was Mudie's, founded in 1842, which a
little over a decade ago celebrated its seventy-fifth anniversary amidst general rejoicing in church circles, and which
still enjoys its old favor. The Victorians had a phrase which
was on everyone's lips: "Going to Mudie's"—which expressed the fond place it held in their hearts. The package of
books from Mudie's was awaited with eager interest. The
fashionable congregated there: not only the wife of the prosperous merchant but the great lady and lord did not despise to
enter its portals. Of an afternoon the carriages of the gentry
drew up to Mudie's, and the powdered footman followed his
master or mistress carrying the precious burden of books
from the emporium on Oxford Street. Mudie's sent its
goods beyond the dominions. "I remember," we are told in
one of the Memoirs of the times, "when staying abroad at
his Excellency's, the Ambassador, the Government dispatch
boxes were awaited with eager interest because the Queen's
Messenger was the bearer of important novels from
Mudie's!"

The success of the three-volume novel and the existence
of the circulating library made the policing of Victorian literature comparatively simple. The publishers did not sell
directly to the reading public but only through the proprietors of the libraries as middlemen, who by virtue of the price
of books exercised a virtual monopoly. They usually had
agreements with the publishers under which they obliged
themselves to take a minimum number of copies of each
novel published irrespective of its quality—good, bad, or indifferent—just as jobbers agree to take specified lots from
factories. Mudie's once issued statistics showing that of a
million volumes which it took, 200,000 were history and
biography; 150,000 travel and adventure; 200,000 science,
religion and miscellaneous, and 450,000 fiction. While
novels constituted the staple wares, no less than 2000 copies
of Eliot's *Felix Holt* being bought by Mudie's, the largest
number of copies ever taken of a single book was 3250 of
Livingstone's *Travels,* with Macaulay's *England* and Mc-
Clintock's *Voyage in Search of Franklin* next in order. But
these figures are even more interesting in showing the extent
of the business of the circulating libraries. If they refused
to stock a book, the publisher might just as well sell it as so
much waste paper.

Now, the circulating libraries were representative middle-
class institutions which accurately reflected the tastes of the
times. Their proprietors were earnest Victorian Christians
who might be shocked by the very least suggestion of impro-
priety. It took only a very faint protest from a guinea subscriber to alarm them. As tradesmen, their whole prosperity
was bound up with keeping the three-volume novel pure for
their customers, and their relation to author, publisher, and
reading public made it easy for them to dictate terms. They

did not need to be bold, or venture into perilous experiments, when their income was assured under the existing arrangements.   When a book offended, it was entirely unnecessary to invoke the law, which was not on a firm foundation anyway.   The libraries simply agreed among themselves tacitly not to circulate a book, and that usually marked its relegation to limbo.

THE THREE-VOLUME NOVEL

THE Waverly Novels had given the first impulse to the three-volume novel.   The influence of the circulating libraries reduced it to a pathetic condition of feebleness.   The novelist had to write his stories to its fixed pattern, and if his inspiration did not warrant the whole three volumes, he stretched and padded until it did.   He was encouraged by his space to indulge in the moral tales, homilies, sermonizing, and reflection so dear to the Victorian heart, and virtue and style were thus inextricably intermingled and conditioned.   When one has nothing to say, one says the obvious, and platitude is the very foundation of decorum.   The second volume was always the great problem.   If Thackeray, Dickens and George Eliot, for instance, actually managed to produce literature in these trying times, the explanation is probably that genius can overcome any handicap.   But the three-volume novel in the hands of novelists of lesser endowments led to the absurdest inanity.   Forgotten are the hackneyed passions of the characters of such male novelists as Whyte Melville, Lawrence Lockhart, Guy Livingstone, or Frank Smedley, and such female practitioners as Ouida, Edna Lyall, Miss Braddon, Mrs. Oliphant, and Mrs. Craik. Only a few shades better were Charles Reade and Bulwer-Lytton.   The tales of the ladies, although provided with repentance and a proper moral, sometimes tended to a sulphurous passion; but this was exceptional. The taste of the times is illustrated by the story of the old lady who picked up a book in a circulating library, and asked: "You are certain there is no sex in this?" "Oh, yes, madam," the clerk assured her, "it is only a love story."

"Anybody," said the immoral and hopelessly lost Oscar Wilde, "can write a three-volume novel. It merely requires a complete ignorance of both life and literature." In *The New Grub Street* George Gissing has drawn a vivid portrait of the author of this period struggling with the incubus. The position of the proprietors of the circulating libraries, who, it is to be remembered, were only tradesmen, is hardly surprising when one recalls some of the notable examples of individual literary prudery at this time. It is hard for us to believe that *Jane Eyre* was attacked, that George Eliot's *Adam Bede* was characterized as "the vile outpourings of a lewd woman's mind," and that Elizabeth Barrett Browning's *Aurora Leigh* described as "the hysterical indecencies of an erotic mind." Even Charles Kingsley's *Hypatia* caused a considerable tempest, as a result of which he was actually forbidden to preach in London until after the investigation of the charges. "Your kind words about *Hypatia*," we find him writing to Bishop Wilberforce, "touched me more than those about *Westward Ho!*; for the former book was written with my heart's blood and was received as I expected with curses from many of the very churchmen I was trying to warn and save. Yet I think the book did good." Harriet Martineau, although a free-thinker, declared herself to be "unable to read *Vanity Fair* from the moral disgust it occasions."

MR. GEORGE MOORE AS DEUS EX MACHINA

AGAINST the interacting tyranny of the three-volume novel and the circulating library, men of letters had often protested, however mildly. In his rôle of satirist, for instance, Thackeray had delighted in mocking the institution. When the 1880's came along the dissolution of Victorianism was in sight, and the time was ripe for a direct assault. The Pre-Raphaelites had acted as the shock troops, but poets such as Swinburne and Rossetti were too occupied with their muses to be practical leaders against the censorship. But with the æsthetes of the 1890's on the horizon and the gospel of art for art's sake on the way, it was imperative to find one who should be both an artist and a fighter. Meredith and Hardy had given vent to their temper but usually suffered in comparative silence. The champion arose in the person of George Moore. He is to the history of Anglo-Saxon book censorship what Bernard Shaw is to the history of Anglo-Saxon play censorship. The respective champions, as all such do, needed specific figures to tilt against, and where Shaw had him in the Lord Chamberlain, Moore unerringly discovered him in Mr. Mudie.

In 1883, Moore had published *A Mummer's Wife*. One day he was informed that Mudie's Select Circulating Library (to give it its exact title) had refused to stock the novel because two ladies in the country had written in to say that they disapproved of it. Mr. George Moore was infuriated, and no wonder. Mudie's had taken only fifty copies and Smith's no more than half that. He at once determined to go and see Mr. Mudie personally, at the library. Moore waited below and soon the guardian of public morals descended the stairs from his sanctum. The man he beheld, to use his own words, was "an almost lifeless, thick-set, middle-aged man." Moore demanded to know the reason for the indignity which had been visited upon him as a man of letters. Mr. Mudie, however, refused to change his stand. Mr. Moore lost patience. "I will wreck this big house of yours, Mr. Mudie," he cried. "My next novel will be issued at a popular price. I will appeal to the public." The defiance delivered, he departed to compose *A Modern Lover*, which duly appeared under the imprint of Vizetelly & Co. in a one-volume format at the popular price of six shillings ($1.50), as he had promised. This may account to some extent for the selection of Vizetelly for martyrdom.

There are no reminiscences of George Moore which are more amusing than those in which he talks of his encounters with Anglo-Saxon prudery, and his favorite subject it remains to this day. Towards Mudie his personal vanity no doubt made him merciless. The suppression of *A Modern Lover* led him to join the ranks of the English pamphleteers with *Literature at Nurse or Circulating Morality*, in which he dubbed his victim the British Matron, and President and Founder of the English Academy. "The English novel is made," he observed, "so that it will fit in with the 'Maiden's Prayer.'" But his animus did not undermine his judgment and he perceived very clearly that the English censorship of his day was a censorship by virtue of thirty-one shillings and sixpence which would never be overthrown until the day of the three-volume novel was over. Otherwise Mr. Mudie's Select Circulating Library would remain as "select" as ever in a very morally discriminating sense of the term, indeed.

The success of *A Modern Lover* had not been such as to make all the London publishers agree to dethrone the old favorite. But the urge of the 1890's made the result inevit-

able and it was not many years before Mr. George Moore
was justified. The persuasion of the publishing world was
wrought ironically by that prince of best sellers, Hall Caine,
whose *The Manxman* was issued in a six-shilling edition by
Heinemann in 1890. When within a fortnight it sold 100,-
000 copies, the death knell of the three-volume novel was
sounded. It struggled a while but by the end of the
century was ready to give up the ghost. The figures in
Shaylor's *The Fascination of Books* tell the story of its decline. In 1890, there were 160 three-volume novels published; in 1891, 162; in 1892, 156; in 1893, 168; in 1894,
184; in 1895, 52; in 1896, 25; in 1897, 4. Its agony was
celebrated in a poem by Rudyard Kipling, entitled *The Three
Decker*:

Full thirty foot she towered from waterline to rail.
It cost a watch to steer her, and a week to shorten sail;
But, spite all modern notions, I've found her first and best,
The only certain packet for the Islands of the Blest.

Fair held the breeze behind us—'twas warm with lovers'
prayers.
We'd stolen wills for ballast and a crew of missing heirs.
They shipped as Able Bastards till the wicked nurse confessed,
And they worked the old three decker to the Islands of the
Blest.

By ways no gaze could follow, a course unspoiled of cook,
Per Fancy, fleetest in man, our titled berths we took
With maids of matchless beauty and parentage unguessed,
And a Church of England parson for the Islands of the Blest.

We asked no social questions—we pumped no hidden shame—
We never talked obstetrics when the Little Stranger came:
We left the Lord in heaven, we left the fiends in hell,
We weren't exactly Yussufs, but—Zuleika didn't tell.

No moral doubt assailed us, so when the port we neared,
The villain had his flogging at the gangway and we cheered.
'Twas fiddle in the foc's'le—'twas garlands on the mast,
For everyone got married and we went ashore at last.

I left 'em all in couples akissing on the decks,
I left the lovers loving and the parents signing cheques.
In endless English comfort, by country-folk caressed,
I left the old three decker at the Islands of the Blest.

With the passing of the three-volume novel, the absolute
monopoly of the circulating libraries was broken, and while
they were still to remain for many decades the most important distributors of books to the British public, the censorship which they now exercised was far less strangling. "One
day," Carlyle said, "the Mudie mountain, which seemed to
stand strong like the other rock mountains, gave suddenly,
as the icebergs do, a loud sounding crack; suddenly with
huge clangor, shivered itself into ice dust; and sank, carrying much along with it." The metaphor was entirely too
optimistic. The Mudie rock mountain cracked and shivered
but only into gravel and sand, which still reveal traces of the
rock. To undermine a traditional institution takes a very
long time. The circulating libraries attempt to supervise the
literature of their readers to a certain extent today, although
circumstances do not permit them to be as baneful as of old.
From force of habit they continue to feel a strong sense of
obligation towards their patrons.

THE LAST STAND OF THE CIRCULATING LIBRARIES

INDEED, a decade after the three-volume novel had finally
disappeared, the circulating libraries, still conscious of their

mission, attempted to restore through an artificial combination the censorial powers which they had enjoyed by virtue of an almost natural monopoly. The prosecution of *The Yoke* in 1908 seems to have prepared public opinion for the extreme measures which were now taken. According to Sir Edmund Gosse the immediate and moving cause of the uproar was the appearance of a volume of Recollections by an elderly lady of title like the one of the Vicomtesse de Chamilly published eighty years ago in Paris. "Their aunt Jemima, indeed," the noble authoress seemed to say. "Come a little nearer, and I will tell you all about Aunt Jemima. Oh, shocking!" During the time the moral wave lasted the circulating libraries took to banning all sorts of books. They refused to circulate Sudermann's *Song of Songs*, Neil Lyon's *Cottage Pie,* and finally to cap the climax Tyler's book on Shakespeare's sonnets! The Times Book Club refused to supply Henry James's *Italian Hours* to a subscriber, explaining that "it was not likely to promote the library's reputation as a circulator of wholesome literature," which raised the speculation that it had perhaps mistaken the title for the more voluptuous one of *Italian Houris.*

But apparently still unsatisfied in the last month of 1909 the circulating libraries (Mudie's, Smith's, Boots's, The Booklover's Library, The Times Book Club, Day's Library, and Cawthorn & Hutt, Ltd.) organized the Circulating Libraries Association. "We have determined," they announced, "that in future we will not place in circulation any book which by reason of the personally scandalous, libelous, immoral or otherwise disagreeable nature of its contents is in our opinion likely to prove offensive to any considerable section of our subscribers." Not content with this they further announced that they would require publishers to submit all books one week before publication, when they would divide them into three categories denominated "satisfactory," "doubtful," and "objectionable." The members of the Association agreed then that they would not circulate any book to which three of the members of the Association objected and pledged themselves to make the circulation of a "bad" book "as small as possible."

The impudence of this proposal was manifest. But in 1909 and the years following, the battle for pure literature reached such an intensity that to many of the good late Victorians (now unhappily converted into Edwardians) it appeared dictated by the very sternest necessity. They had been shocked almost into insensibility by George Moore's *Esther Waters* (which the circulating libraries had promptly banned on its first appearance in 1894), and almost floored by Hardy's *Jude the Obscure* (which the circulating libraries again had promptly banned in 1895). It was the publication of H. G. Wells's *Ann Veronica* in 1909, however, which made them feel that the world was coming to an end. It was denounced by a deputation of publishers and editors, headed by J. St. Loe Strachey, the famed editor of *The Spectator,* who made a personal appeal to the Home Secretary for the application of a rigorous censorship of literature. Hardly was this excitement over when Frank Harris wrote an article in the very radical *English Review* in which he compared the Japanese code of morals with the Ten Commandments to the disadvantage of the latter, causing J. St. Loe Strachey to announce that thereafter no advertisement of *The English Review* would be accepted for the chaste columns of *The Spectator.* Frank Harris, who like George Moore was a fighter, began a very discomforting campaign against English hypocrisy, and soon it was discovered and pointed out

that J. St. Loe Strachey was the publisher of the passionate
Byron, and of unexpurgated editions of the plays of Beaumont and Fletcher!

Now the proprietors of the circulating libraries could contend blandly that since the purchase of novels had been put
within the reach of the purse of the general public the outcry
of the authors against this "suppression" and "censorship"
was quite irrelevant! Certainly they were merely private
tradesmen who were trying to regulate their own business
and that was nobody's business but their own. The speciousness of this argument deceived nobody. The united libraries still were too important as book distributors for their
action to be regarded in this light. The authors revolted
and the publishers refused to submit their manuscripts to
this privately instituted Inquisition. To the indefatigable
George Moore there now rallied Sir Edmund Gosse, John
Balderston, Austin Harrison, Charles Tennyson, and Sir
Oliver Lodge, who filled the current magazines with indignant articles, and Hardy, Bennett, Wells, and Shaw joined
the protestants. The proposed agreement was never formally
executed but the circulating libraries continued independently in their old ways for the next few years to supervise
English literature. The following are a few samples of their
selective efforts, and form a little *"Index Librarium Circulatorium"* :

HALL CAINE: *The Woman Thou Gavest Me*
W. B. MAXWELL: *The Devil's Garden*
GILBERT CANNAN: *Round the Corner*
W. L. GEORGE: *A Bed of Roses*
COMPTON MACKENZIE: *Sinister Street*
J. W. SHORT: *Black Sheep*
M. GAUNT: *The Uncounted Cost*
GRANT ALLEN: *The Woman Who Did*

Nowadays, when an English author boasts that books in Great Britain are not dragged before the criminal bar as often as they are in America, he forgets the unobstrusive protection which the circulating libraries still afford in some measure. For the rest, no English publisher dares to risk a test of the very inclusive Common Law. Even now, Mudie's, Smith's and Boots's have an informal agreement among themselves under which when one of the libraries comes across a book that it considers immoral, it informs the others and then they all refuse to place it on their shelves. Often, however, the banning of a book has beneficial results so far as an author's royalties are concerned. "Many people," as W. L. George, himself a banned novelist, pointed out, "buy what they cannot borrow." It is to be doubted, however, if there is any real gain for the author when the loss of revenue from library copies is considered. A curious and characteristic distinction is made in Boots's which well illustrates the spirit of the modern British circulating library. A book which Boots's considers improper it will under no circumstances permit to be rented from the library. But on the counters where books may be purchased it freely sells the same improper book to such as can afford to buy it! It is an evolutionary vestige of the old censorship of price.

MONOPOLY AND CENSORSHIP

WHEN one muses on the circulating libraries censorship, one is naturally led to think of Boston. There is little that is new in the show it has made of itself. When the Boston Booksellers Committee hands out the little slips of paper which spell the blacklisting of a book, it is the subterranean censorship in action again. Thereafter one has to whisper.

The agreement of the Boston booksellers among themselves
that they would not circulate any book to which the secretary of the Watch and Ward Society took exception is so
reminiscent in all essential aspects of the English Circulating
Library Association that it is only another instance of the
repetition of history.   Moreover, it is fitting and proper that
it should be Boston rather than New York, or Chicago, or
Philadelphia that has adopted the English ideal, for it above
all other American centres of culture has striven to uphold
the claims of English literature in all its purity.

.With the increased interest in fiction in these prosperous,
easy years, private circulating libraries in America have been
growing in importance.   But no one has concentrated on
them in the interests of literary decency as there are so many
other active agencies at hand.   For one thing the American
public library system has always been far better than the
English—which accounts in some measure, perhaps, for the
greater vigilance of the circulating libraries there.   In recent
years, the American public libraries, with their budgets remaining relatively stationary while the price of books was
rising, have fallen behind the demands for the latest fiction,
and circulating commercial libraries have grown enormously.
Last year alone sixty-seven new ones appeared, outnumber-
ing new bookstores for the year by five to three and new
free libraries by seven to one, with subsidiary chains, moreover, in drug stores and news-stands according to the English system.   It is to be doubted, however, if they will ever
reach a degree of consolidation in America which will put
them in the position to dictate the tastes of their readers.
Yet no one can really predict what might happen if a Smith
or Mudie appeared upon the scene.   For the present, rumor
has it that when a few years ago a protest was made to Wom-

rath's, the largest chain of circulating libraries in New York, that it ought to be ashamed not to take steps to check the spread of indecent literature, there came the reply that if Womrath's customers wanted to read "bad" books they would be supplied with them as long as they were not outside the law.

The subterranean censorship may appear in the public library as well as in the private circulating library. Do public libraries attempt to supervise the tastes of their readers by making it a fixed policy not to buy "objectionable" books? It is a simple expedient, and has often been applied. The public librarian often has the plausible excuse that as the funds of a library are limited, he must pick and choose, and naturally the more "wholesome" books are to be preferred. He insists that he is exercising not censorship but the prerogative of free selection. Nevertheless, the character of this choice is often suspicious. The Kansas City Public Library has explicitly banned *Elmer Gantry*. Many others accomplish the result more quietly, and this has been true in both America and England. American public libraries have at times excluded not only Robert Chambers and Elinor Glyn but *Huckleberry Finn* and *Les Miserables,* and English ones in the provinces have not so many years ago outlawed Kingsley and Scott. One will look in vain in a great many modern public libraries for *Jurgen, The "Genius,"* and *The Rise and Fall of Susan Lenox*. Often "sex" books are not listed in the catalogue. An examination of the catalogue of the great British Museum Library once showed that neither Ellis's *The Psychology of Sex*, nor Carpenter's *Intermediate Sex* were listed, although the library had both. Many public libraries have "private cases" of books in which are included such old classics as *The Arabian Nights*, the *Decam-*

eron, Rabelais, and often Fielding, which are handed out only after close scrutiny of the prospective reader.

The vice societies, organizing the frequent indifference of the individual members of a community into its authentic voice, are naturally to be regarded as the most vicious constituent of the subterranean censorship. We have adverted already to some incidents of their activity. Is it too much to assume from the mere existence of the vice societies that there must be something wrong with a law which cannot be left for enforcement to the normal machinery of public prosecution? Is the involvement of sex too disagreeable for a private citizen ever to want to complain? Why not special societies for the enforcement of the laws against bigamy, arson, and murder?

The subterranean censorship exists and is exercised in innumerable ways. Always there is the basic assumption that the law is not adequate. A babel of voices is heard. Even the churches attempt to play the rôles of censors, and threaten the wrath of God to the members of their congregations who will read a certain lewd book—and Protestants and Jews, as well as Catholics, have their lists. In a sense, too, every editor acts, perhaps, as censor. There is this distinction, however. He says simply: "I will not print this book." He does not say: "This book shall not be printed." Booksellers may refuse to stock books of which they do not individually approve. Some years ago, for instance, there came the news that a retired Oxfordshire farmer had decided to establish a 100 per cent pure bookshop in London in which no work of fiction would be found that might bring a blush of shame to a maiden's cheek.

From the promptings of the individual censors in each of us to the concerted voice of the community is a long

stretch.   When are we to give ear?   It is to be recognized
that some forms of individual interference with books will
occur in any but the absolutely perfect society.   No scheme
can be contrived to abolish every form of extra-legal inquisition.   But no one can have any objection to an individual denouncing any book as immoral in his own opinion as
long as he does not also cry for the police.   The history of
the circulating library censorship clearly suggests the only
principle for distinguishing those forms of the subterranean censorship which are benign from those which are malignant.   It is the principle of public use, which says that
there shall be no combinations, restraints, or monopolies—
no concerted action, no collusion, no agreements—and a literary trust is no less conceivable than a beef trust.   If,
for instance, such organizations as the Literary Guild or The
Book-of-the-Month Club ever come to imitate Mudie's or
Smith's, they should not be permitted to plead that theirs are
private concerns.   The degree in which an agency of a public
or quasi-public nature is in a position of monopoly should
be the decisive consideration.   Otherwise the subterranean
censorship would reach intolerable limits.

VI

ORIGINS OF THE ANGLO-SAXON GAME

*English literature had been at least as free spoken
as any other from the time of Chaucer to the death
of Smollett. Then, in twenty years at most, English
literature became the most "pudibund," the most respectful of the young person's blush, that the world
has ever known.*—ANDREW LANG.

*Mastering the lawless science of our law—
That codeless myriad of precedent,
That wilderness of Single Instances.*
                    —TENNYSON : *Aylmer's Field.*

THE story of the English circulating libraries forms one
of the major phases of the history of literary decency. And
when we inquire into the origin of that history, its English
manifestations appear, in other respects as well, far more
important than its American. The crime of obscene libel
represents the resolution of the conflict of the law with literature; and both have followed English example, especially
in earlier times. The world has long believed that the
crusade against indecent literature is an Anglo-Saxon game.
Its conventions matured first in England some decades after
our own separation from the mother country, but when
this happened American criticism with the connivance of
American judges transferred them to American soil. Every
notorious example of Victorian squeamishness is to be

matched with one from American Puritanism. Emerson,
for instance, was rebuked in company for using the word
"spermatic," and when Charles Sumner said in the debate
on Louisiana that the new state was "a seven months' child
begotten by the bayonet in criminal conjunction with the
spirit of caste," he was reminded that there were ladies in
the gallery.

With the advent of Anthony Comstock, America took
matters more into its own hands and the subsequent episodes of the Anglo-Saxon game which it contributed are
both more vivid and significant. But with Anthony Comstock the history of literary purity in America became essentially the biography of this one man, and this biography
has been excellently written very recently.* At any rate the
main outlines of his career are familiar to the average American of middle years, so that it is unnecessary for us to
pursue the subject. Comstock no doubt had numerous
predecessors in volunteer clergymen who led sporadic campaigns from their pulpits against "debasing" literature, and
one needs only to recall the reverend gentlemen who, when
The Scarlet Letter was published, reviewed it as a fitting
addition to a Brothel Library, and classed it with the *Decameron*. It was Comstock's improvement to have secularized and organized literary prudery and made of it a
profession. Shaw's invention of the opprobrious epithet
"comstockery" has tended to create the false impression that
the methods and machinery of the unsurpassable vice hunter
were American and new; but he was actually little of an
innovator. He added little except American efficiency to
the discoveries of Victorianism. An English Society for

---

* *Anthony Comstock: Roundsman of the Lord,* by HEYWOOD BROUN and
MARGARET LEECH. New York: A. and C. Boni, 1927.

the Suppression of Vice, for instance, antedates the New York Society for the Suppression of Vice by no less than seven decades.

When the Comstock Acts came to be interpreted after their passage in 1868, it was to the English Common Law that American State and Federal courts turned, as was their habit, for aid to define the terms "lewd," "lascivious," "indecent," and "obscene." The layman can understand more readily that there should be no national literary boundaries but notions of sovereignty lead him to expect a greater independence in legal institutions. To this day American law courts often follow in the footsteps of English decisions, and the King's Bench is listened to as respectfully as the Supreme Court of the United States. When Comstock secured his State and Federal obscenity laws, there were already a few in existence; for instance, a Vermont law of 1821, a Connecticut law of 1834, and the present Massachusetts law which goes back to 1835, and elsewhere it was a crime under the American Common Law. Theodore Schroeder in his *Obscene Literature and Constitutional Law* has questioned if the sale of obscene literature was a crime at all at the American Common Law until after the American Revolution. If it was not, then the importation of the crime of obscene libel was more than ever unwarranted, since only the Common Law in force in England at the time of the Revolution was legally supposed to be adopted into American Law. Although the English Common Law of obscene libel, making the sale of obscene literature a crime, was not fixed until the end of the eighteenth century, it was then nevertheless received as the American Common Law and as the basis of the interpretation of the statutes. The limitation of existence prior to the Revolution was conveniently brushed aside.

The concept of obscenity is so vague that it is quite meaningless to speak of an obscenity law existing at a certain date, or of obscenity having become established at the Common Law at a certain date, without inquiring immediately into the standards of literary decency which are imposed. It is important, if their significance for modern civilization is to be grasped, to realize that they are of comparatively recent origin. It is generally assumed from the fact that the insistence on sterilized literature became the fashion after 1800 that the law and the public taste corresponded; but no reconciliation in fact took place till the year 1868 in England, when the crime of obscene libel was defined by Lord Chief Justice Cockburn in such a way as to give expression to the hypersensitiveness of Victorianism. The date is interestingly the same as that of the passage of the first Comstock Act in New York. Before then the type of "obscene" literature which was criminal under the law was the grosser type which we usually denominate "pornographic." The vendors of such books and pictures were pursued upon rare occasions in America, and frequently in England, but as far as works which pretended to be literature were concerned, the denunciation of literary indelicacy was frequent, but prosecution unknown. The cases of both Whitman and Zola in America and England respectively testify to this. The attacks called for a self-imposed discipline, and submission was simply voluntary. We know from the efforts of another noble Lord that the change came about from 1857 to 1868. The debate upon Lord Campbell's Act (for that was the name of the noble Lord) proves the contention.

THE EARLY LITERATURE

FROM the time of Chaucer to the death of Smollett English literature is as frank and robust as Continental literature. The castigations of Addison in *The Spectator* did not serve to deter either Fielding or Smollett. The American Colonies naturally affected the same attitude. Although the early Americans had in general little time for reading, many a library of a Colonial planter in Virginia or a Colonial intellectual in New England boasted copies of *Tom Jones, Tristram Shandy,* Shakespeare, Ovid's *Art of Love,* and Rabelais, in addition to *The Whole Duty of Man* and Leslie's *Against Deism.* Many a theatre was closed in America by the Puritans, but they appear to have paid no attention to lewd books. There was, for instance, an early Colonial law in Massachusetts against the sale of obscene books, songs, and pamphlets, but with the limitation that these had to be directed against religion or a clergyman. That the reading of the Fathers was not entirely unimpeachable may be judged from Benjamin Franklin alone. But even young John Quincy Adams, for example, confided to his Diary: "At home all afternoon reading *Tom Jones,* one of the best novels in the language." The first thirty years of American literature has, indeed, been described as "the seduction period." One of its best sellers was the shocking *Charlotte Temple.* Washington Irving felt called upon to declare: "No author who writes for popularity would ever be guilty of the preposterous folly of polluting the public ear with licentious ribaldry unless tolerably well satisfied it was attuned to such harmony."

In his famous essay, *The Evolution of Literary Decency,* Andrew Lang attempted to fix the time of the transition

from the earlier frankness to our present preoccupation with
book morality.   We are told that it was beginning to be established about 1800.   By 1800 a poem of Suckling's which
is a ballad of marriage appears in an expurgated form with
lines and half stanzas omitted.   A singular revolution of
taste was effected on both sides of the waters within the
span of a single lifetime.   "Take away your bonny Afra
Behn," said one old lady in the same year, although "Astrea"
had delighted her in her youth.   The fate of Richardson's
Pamela is even more in point.   It was a very catechism of
virtue from its publication to 1780.   Although Lady Mary
Wortley Montague considered it more mischievous than the
works of Rochester, and Sir Walter Scott feared that it
would rather "encourage a spirit of rash enterprise than
virtuous resistance," such was not the prevailing opinion
of contemporaries.   It was praised from the pulpit and
said to do more good than twenty sermons, and recom-
mended for growing daughters.   But in 1815 a young
lady looked over the shoulder of Charles Lamb as he
was reading this very same *Pamela*.   She retreated
very soon, indeed, and, says the gentle author of the *Essays
of Elia,* there was "a blush between them."   The Lamb anecdote is classic.   A novel now had to have a moral purpose
and prove that virtue was more than its own reward.   It
had to avoid being "improper," it had to be fit for "the
young person," it had to be capable of lying inoffensively
upon the drawing room table.   Inevitably upon the scene appeared Thomas Bowdler, whose name has become a by-
word.   He took it upon himself to expurgate none other
than the immortal Shakespeare!   His brother was a vigorous
leader in the Society for the Suppression of Vice, and
Thomas did the best he could with his pen.   *The Family*

Shakespeare in ten volumes entered finally into every Victorian home. "It certainly has been my wish," he wrote
in the Preface, "and it has been my study to exclude from
this publication whatever is unfit to be read aloud by a gentleman to a company of ladies." He was the first of the
expurgators. Yet later in Victorianism, there often were
sensitive souls who found even Bowdler's Shakespeare a
little too frank for their taste.

THE EARLY COMMON LAW

BUT the law, which is always several decades behind the
times, was very slow to accommodate its doctrines to the
ideals of literary purity. The proof from Fielding, Smollett,
Sterne, Swift, and Defoe—who, after all, despite all their
lubricities, created literature—is more than reinforced from
my Lords Burckhurst, Smedly, and Rochester, who freely
created what is usually called pornography. The Common
Law of England, which for the Anglo-Saxon mind is the
sum and perfection of all the virtues, treated neither "obscene" nor "pornographic" literature as a crime! The
Common Law was administered by the aristocracy, and men
brought up in the great English public schools upon the
classical tradition, which involved a constant study of the
masculine Greek and Latin classics, refused to yield for
a long time to the prejudices of middle-class virtue. In
the year 1708 Lord Holt, one of the great masters of the
Common Law of England, decided without shocking public opinion that a book (whose very name would otherwise
be quite forgotten) entitled *The Fifteen Plagues of a Maid-
enhead,* was not indictable at the Common Law. If it was
any offense at all, it was simply a "spiritual" one: it was

cognizable only in the ecclesiastical courts, which had a general jurisdiction over moral sins from adultery to swearing. The Common Law courts very wisely took notice only of such forms of immorality as tended to actual breaches of the peace such as keeping a bawdy house. The publication of an obscene book constituted only (in the quaint language of the time) "a general solicitation of chastity," and as such was not actionable. We find that as late as 1733 an indictment against the super-erotic poems of Rochester was quashed. Moreover, in 1768, when the stormy John Wilkes was indicted for the publication of such pornographic poems as *An Essay on Women* and *The Maid's Prayer,* it was rather their impiety than their obscenity which disturbed the judges. However, an increasing number of indictments testifies to the growing public opinion against lewd literature, which in the end overcame the apathy of the noble Lords who manned the King's Bench. While there is no high court Law Report to fix the exact date of transition, by the end of the eighteenth century it was generally understood by the English Bar that it was a crime at the Common Law to vend obscene literature.

THE ENGLISH SOCIETY FOR THE SUPPRESSION OF VICE

THAT interest in obscenity had awakened by the dawn of the nineteenth century is clear from the incorporation of the English Society for the Suppression of Vice in 1802. It had a Vice Secretary, a list of subscribers, annual reports of a lurid character which were headed by a quotation from Bishop Porteus's Lectures, in fact all of the appurtenances of a regular vice society. It is also clear from its reports that although it was now a crime to sell "obscene" literature, the term had a very narrow meaning. The pornography in which England was so rich was beginning to be exploited for the purposes of booklegging, and it was against its dissemination that the Society fought. It would never have dreamed of crusading against the type of books which Victorianism was later to find so abhorrent to its moral sense.

The centre of the traffic in early Victorian times was in Holywell Street. All sorts of wild tales, some no doubt true, and some no doubt very much exaggerated, were current. It was said that Holywell Street was lined with shops where pornographic literature was sold. It was even said that circulating libraries of pornography existed where the early Victorian might read for a fee! It was asserted also that regular traveling salesmen of pornography toured the provinces, visiting fairs, races, and markets where they peddled their stocks. One of these, about to die while under imprisonment on a conviction obtained by the English Society for the Suppression of Vice, confessed that he regularly visited the two university towns of Oxford and Cambridge at least twice a year with a line of highly finished French prints. It was stated by the Secretary of the Society (one Pritchard who, had he lived when the American art ballyhoo prevailed, would have become as immortal a figure as Comstock) that in 1834 there were no less than fifty-seven pornography shops in London, which had been reduced to about twenty in 1857 by the Society's efforts. The total number of prosecutions instituted by the Society from 1802 to 1857 was 159, or an average of three a year. There were only five acquittals. The terms of imprisonment, varying from two weeks to two years, averaged about eight months, to which must be added the pillory till this mode of punishment was abolished, and later the fines. To show the extent of the stocks of pornography which the dealers were able to collect, the Secretary stated that from one alone who was allowed to plead guilty in the Central Criminal Court there were taken no less than 12,346 prints, 393 books, 351 copper plates, 88 lithographic stones, and 33 cwt. of letter-press. From another in the same year were taken 15,300 prints, 162 books, 1 cwt. of letter-press, 96 copper plates, 21 lithographic stones, and 114 pounds of stereotype.

One almost hears old Anthony boasting of his sixty-one coaches of obscenity law violators, and his 160 of captured obscene literature! That the English Society for the Suppression of Vice was unable to secure such spectacular results was due to certain defects of the law. The only statutory enactment since the establishment of the crime at Common Law was contained in a provision of the Vagrancy Act of 1824 against exposing obscene books and prints in "any street, road or public highway, or in the view thereof, or in any place of public resort." This made it possible to catch only the most unwary. But for the rest, the law of evidence and of searches and seizures under the Common Law, which was very jealous of personal liberty, made it difficult to deal effectively with pornographers. It was, indeed, a misdemeanor at the Common Law to sell obscene literature, but the stock could not be seized and confiscated. Whoever was willing to pay the penalty of imprisonment might engage in the business without being completely ruined. The trade was said to be so lucrative that dealers could well afford to risk short terms of imprisonment during which their wives could continue the traffic. Of two habitual offenders, one had nine convictions to his discredit and the other seven. The law, as it stood, moreover, was hard to enforce. The traders were always on their guard, the indictment had to be set on foot by private information and there was a general suspicion of spies and informers. To make their evidence acceptable they had to be accompanied by a policeman to the suspected place, and searched immediately before and after the visit, in order to make sure they had not concealed the pornography upon their persons, which was a cumbersome procedure indeed.

The reform of the law was effected in 1857 by Lord Campbell. The change made by his Act was of great importance to the technique of suppression, but the debate which preceded its passage is crucial for the purpose of fixing the limits of criminal obscenity. The record is fortunately preserved in Hansard's *Parliamentary Debates*. What a contrast to the casualness with which the Comstock Acts a decade and a half later passed the Congress of the United States.

PORTRAIT OF A NOBLE LORD

IT is perhaps the greatest of the many ironies of the sex censorship that it should have been Lord Campbell who supplied the instrument which was to lead to the terrorization of literature. He was actuated truly by the best of motives, never intending half the mischief for which his famous act was in the end responsible, but it was none the less inevitable in the sequel. Lord Campbell was himself a great lover of literature who acknowledged her as a mistress hardly second to the law. Despite the burden of his duties as Lord Chief Justice of England, he found time to compose a learned work on the legal allusions of Shakespeare (whom his Act was to expose to danger). His *magnum opus* was the ten-volume work, *The Lives of the Lord Chancellors of England,* and he had to his credit also four volumes of *Lives of the Lord Chief Justices of England.* It took energy to accomplish these feats, and he was, indeed, a man of gigantic frame who all his life suffered from nothing worse than toothache. In his *Lives,* he often poked fun at a lack of literary appreciation on the part of his colleagues. Of Lord Eldon, who expressed great doubt as to the innocent character of Southey's *Wat Tyler,* Byron's *Cain,* and Milton's *Paradise Lost* as far as charges of blasphemy were concerned, he remarked: "It must have been a strange occupation for a judge who for many years had meddled with nothing more imaginative than an Act of Parliament to determine in what sense the speculations of Adam, Eve, Cain and Lucifer are to be understood."

Lord Campbell, however, was very imaginative. It so happened that in his judicial capacity, he sat in a case in which the prisoner was charged with peddling pornography of a very disgusting and offensive nature. The noble and learned Lord on the woolsack was outraged, and sentenced the wretch to the maximum term of two years. The very vigilant Secretary of the Society for the Suppression of Vice took the occasion to press upon Lord Campbell some startling revelations of the traffic in Holywell Street. It so happened also that at this time a bill against the indiscriminate sale of poisons was being considered in the House of Lords. Lord Campbell's imagination at once connected the two events analogically. An explosion occurred in his mind. We are, indeed, not left to speculate, for the noble Lord stated to the House of Lords in introducing his bill: "He was happy to say that he believed the administration of poison by design had received a check. But from a trial which had taken place before him on Saturday he had learned with horror and alarm that a sale of poison more deadly than prussic acid, strychnine or arsenic—the sale of obscene publications and indecent books—was openly going on."

LORD CAMPBELL'S ACT

THE Act which Lord Campbell offered appeared urgent and simple enough. It provided for a system of domiciliary searches and seizures under which the police might raid a readeasy and carry off the stocks of obscene publications to be destroyed. A magistrate or the Chief of Police was granted the power of issuing the search warrant upon the presentation of an affidavit that obscene publications were kept in a certain place. Lord Campbell's dismay had made him overlook the most obvious safeguards. There was no stipulation that the place to be searched had to be a public shop, or that obscene publications had to be sold or offered for sale there. Thus a private library in a private house could be invaded by the police. No wonder many a noble Lord shuddered and feared for the safety of his books! When the bill finally passed, all such objections had been met. The affiant had to swear not only that he believed the obscene publications to be kept in the suspected place but also the grounds of his belief. The warrant could only issue if the obscene publications were kept for "the Purpose of Sale or Distribution," which exempted any private library; and it had to be further stated upon oath that "one or more Articles of the like Character have been sold" (which protected booksellers who often acquired large libraries which might contain indecent books without their knowledge until they attempted to make an actual sale).

Finally a right of appeal from the magistrate who issued the warrant was given to the Quarter Sessions.

Middle-class Victorianism had then triumphed completely, and it marshaled its sentiment behind the Act. Lord Campbell himself received scores of letters from agitated clergymen, fathers, mothers and spinsters. The Society for the Suppression of Vice lobbied for the bill. The Archbishop of Canterbury expressed the very greatest anxiety for its success. It is therefore remarkable to find that the Act met great opposition from its very introduction. It takes a bold statesman nowadays to oppose a moral law, but the noble and learned Lords did not hesitate. They at once attacked the insoluble enigmas of literary decency which have puzzled the minds of judges, legislators, and critics ever since. The debate on Lord Campbell's Act is of the very highest consequence. It is the first time that an Anglo-Saxon legislative body argued the nature of the obscene, and the participants included the Lord Chief Justice of England, the Lord Chancellor of England, and the leading law Lords whose opinions made the law of England. Obscene literature was criminal at the Common Law at the beginning of the nineteenth century, but the debate proves that as late as 1857 the law had not yet met the standards of public opinion which regarded Aphra Behn, Richardson, and Lamb with suspicion. The degree of obscenity still had to be very gross to be actionable, and had to be that degree of grossness which is usually denominated pornography. The aristocracy still refused to cry with the middle class: "Oh, shocking!"

THE PURPOSE OF LORD CAMPBELL'S ACT

THE Lords agreed that the trade in pornography was abominable; but how did the noble and learned Lord on the woolsack propose to avoid the difficulty of defining "obscene"? The two Lords who were most vociferous were the great Lord Brougham and Lord Lyndhurst. Lord Brougham went so far as to write an article on the bill in the important *Law Magazine.* Lord Lyndhurst was particularly active on the floor of the Lords. It appears that Lord Campbell in his *Lives* had not done entire justice to the biography of this colleague, which naturally hurt his personal vanity very much. Moreover, Lord Campbell had added insult to injury in such a way that the hostility was not suppressed but emerged in the debate in the august House of Lords. Lord Lyndhurst went so far as to reflect on the noble Lord's ineptitude in the matter of *"le bon mot, le mot juste."* Lord Campbell wanted to seize "obscene" literature, he said, but he understood that word's significance as little as he did the expressions he had applied to his adversary in his biography. "My noble and learned Friend," observed Lord Lyndhurst, "in a publication which he recently gave to the world inserted two or three paragraphs of a nature by no means complimentary to myself, and having done so, he selects the particular volume containing those paragraphs from the whole set and sends it to me as a present with the author's compliments. I conclude therefore that my noble and learned Friend does not, upon all occasions, understand the force of the expressions which he uses." But Lord Lyndhurst's hurt pride must not be taken to invalidate his arguments in the debate; in fact it sharpened his wits.

The attack was, however, started by Lord Brougham.

"For example," he asked, "how did he (Lord Campbell) propose to define what was an 'obscene' publication?" and "He would remind his noble and learned Friend, that in the works of some of their most eminent poets there were some objectionable passages which, under this measure, might cause them to be considered obscene publications."

Every word in the reply of Lord Campbell is as important as the language of a law decision. He spoke as Lord Chief Justice of England, and he may be presumed to have known the law of England:

"Lord Campbell said, he had not the most distant contemplation of including in the Bill the class of works to which the noble and learned Lord referred. The measure was intended to apply *exclusively to works written for the single purpose of corrupting the morals of youth,* and of a nature calculated to shock the common feelings of decency *in any well-regulated mind.* Bales of publications of that description were manufactured in Paris, and imported into this country. He was ready to make what was indictable under the present law a test of obscenity."

Under the definition of Lord Campbell, then, a work of art had little to fear from the Common Law of obscene libel. If it had application only to works "written for the single purpose of corrupting the morals of youth," an author would be permitted to explain his object. He could not then possibly be convicted upon a few isolated passages. If a work had to shock "the common feelings of decency in any well-regulated mind," then only the grossest forms of "pornography" could be criminal. If the test was the effect of a publication upon a normal mind then Rabelais was certainly safe. Lord Campbell, moreover, did not generalize

entirely: his pointed illustration was the pornography of
Paris. He had in mind the dirty picture post card.

THE DILEMMA OF THE CLASSICS

THE Lord Chancellor repeated Brougham's objections. He
still had fears despite Lord Campbell's assurances. Modern judges might well emulate the law Lord's scruples for
art and literature. Then Lord Lyndhurst put the dilemma
of Shakespeare and the classics of which we hear so much
nowadays whenever the sex censorship is debated:

"My noble and learned Friend's aim," declared Lord Lyndhurst, "is to put down the sale of obscene books and prints; but
what is the interpretation which is to be put upon the word
'obscene'? I can easily conceive that two men will come to entirely different conclusions as to its meaning. I have looked
into 'Johnson' to see what definition he gives of the word, and
I find that he says it is something 'immodest; not agreeable to
chastity of mind; causing lewd ideas.' These are the definitions
which he gives of the word. Suppose now a man following the
trade of an informer, or a policeman, sees in a window something which he conceives to be a licentious print. He goes to
the magistrate, and describes, according to his ideas, what he
saw; the magistrate thereupon issues his warrant for the seizure
of the disgusting print. The officer then goes to the shop, and
says to the shopkeeper, 'Let me look at that picture of Jupiter
and Antiope.' 'Jupiter and what?' says the shopkeeper. 'Jupiter and Antiope,' says the man. 'Oh, Jupiter and Antiope, you
mean,' says the shopkeeper; and hands him down the print. He
sees the picture of a woman stark naked, lying down, and a
satyr standing by her with an expression on his face which
shows most distinctly what his feelings are and what is his
object. The informer tells the man he is going to seize the
print, and to take him before a magistrate. 'Under what authority?' he asks; and he is told—'Under the authority of Lord

Campbell's Act.' 'But,' says the man, 'don't you know that it is
a copy from a picture of one of the most celebrated masters in
Europe?' That does not matter; the informer seizes it as an
obscene print. He asks if the shopkeeper has got any more
prints like it. 'Oh, yes, I have got several others,' is the reply.
Whereupon he searches the shop, and in so doing perhaps he
stumbles upon a print of the story of Danaë. There he sees a
naked woman lifting her eyes to heaven, but standing in a very
strange attitude, the shower of gold descending upon her, a
little Cupid peeping over her shoulder pointing with his dart,
and other circumstances which I will not describe. Well, is this
print also to be brought before the magistrate? These prints
come within the description in this Bill as much as any work
you can conceive. And yet they are both celebrated pictures;
the first is a copy of a famous Correggio which hangs in the
large square room of the Louvre, right opposite an ottoman, on
which are seated daily ladies of the first rank from all countries
of Europe, who resort there for the purpose of studying the
works of art in that great gallery. But this is not all. Our
informant leaves the print shop and goes into the studio of a
sculptor or some statuary and sees there figures of nymphs,
fauns and satyrs, all perfectly naked, some of them in attitudes
which I do not choose to describe. According to this Bill they
may every one be seized,—

" '*Nympharumque leves cum satyris chori.*'

"Well, I will now go to a third class—the poets—for the informant next proceeds to the circulating libraries. I do not
know whether my noble and learned Friend's extensive reading
has made him familiar with the poems of Rochester, but I think
they would come under the description of this Bill. 'The freedom of ancient satirists,' says Hume, the historian, 'no more
resembles the licentiousness of Rochester than the nakedness of
an Indian does that of a common prostitute.' Suppose that book
is in a certain library lent out for hire; under my noble and
learned Friend's Bill it may be seized at once—in fact, under
the Bill a circulating library may be searched from one end to
the other. In the same way the dramatists of the Restoration,

Wycherley, Congreve, and the rest of them,—there is not a page in any one of them which might not be seized under this Bill. One of the principal characters in one of Congreve's plays is Lady Wishfor't. Dryden, too, is as bad as any of them. He has translated the worst parts of Ovid—his *Art of Love*—works for which Ovid was exiled, and died, I believe, on the shores of the Euxine. There is not a single volume of that great poet which would not come under the definition of my noble and learned Friend's Bill. I need scarcely recall to your Lordships' remembrance that poem—*Sigismonda and Guiscardo*—I think it is, beginning—'While Norman Tancred in Salerno reigned,' in which occurs the description of the secret wedding, the scenes that preceded it, and the scenes that were immediately consequent upon it. I will not repeat to your Lordships more of it than this passage:—

> " 'The holy man, amazed at what he saw,
>   Made haste to sanctify the bliss by law;
>   And muttered fast the matrimony o'er,
>   For fear committed sin should get before.'

But I think your Lordships will see from this specimen that Dryden's poems must be placed in my noble and learned Friend's *Index Expurgatorius*. Take, too, the whole flight of French novelists, from Crébillon *fils,* down to Paul de Kock; nothing can be more unchaste; nothing more immodest, than they are; and when my noble and learned Friend's Bill is passed, every copy of them may be committed to the bonfire with as little mercy as Don Quixote's chivalry books were."

The article of Lord Brougham in the *Law Magazine* was far more outspoken along the same line than he had ventured to be in the House. One of Lord Campbell's literary diversions was the keeping of a Diary, and to its discreet pages he confided: "Brougham had hardly ventured to oppose the Bill as it passed through the Lords but afterwards he wrote a violent article against it in the *Law Magazine.*" Therein Lord Brougham observed:

"The difficulty of defining what should be reckoned obscene; *the impossibility of putting down all works containing passages offensive to morality, indeed, to common decency*; the admitted fact that this class includes many of the classics, now in the hands of all scholars even of tender age; and the fact that several of the most celebrated works of French and English poets come within the same description, was immediately suggested and it was urged that if the seizure of such works were permitted, any bookseller might be stripped of such works as Voltaire's in nearly a hundred volumes, because neither the informer nor policeman could confine himself to a volume or two, and if he did the whole set became unsalable. To this Lord Campbell could only reply that he had no intention whatever to make Horace, Juvenal, Voltaire or Lord Byron, seizable."

THE LADY OF THE CAMELLIAS

In a debate upon indecency in literature, specific illustrations are always more valuable than general definitions. If the privileged category which the classics have always occupied makes it possible to minimize Lord Campbell's willingness to exempt them, it is impossible to dispose of a certain book which the noble Lord brought into the House one day as a text for his arguments. It so happened that London was all a flutter that very year over a performance of *La Traviata* at Exeter Hall. But Victorian prudery interdicted a translation of the libretto, and the program bore the note: "Notice: The Exeter Hall Committee have interdicted the publication of an English translation of the above program in the form of a book of words." The book which Lord Campbell had chosen to bring was none other than *The Lady of the Camellias,* upon which the opera was based, and he declared it to be innocent under the law.

"But he held in his hands," we are told, "a volume which

would give their Lordships a notion of what was going forward. It was a *translation* of one of the novels of Dumas, the Younger, on which the opera *La Traviata* was founded and it was called *The Lady of the Camellias*. It gave a description of the white camellias and the red camellias in a manner which trenched upon modesty, and which he could not state. *He did not wish to create a category of offenses in which this might be included although it was certainly of a polluting character. It was only from the force of public opinion and an improved taste that the circulation of such works could be put a stop to;* but he was glad to inform their Lordships that there was a Society for the Encouragement of Pure Literature of which his noble Friend the Duke of Argyll was President. He was shocked to think that there should be so much circulation for works like the one in his hand—*The Lady of the Camellias*. In this work, the Lady described her red camellias and her white camellias; but he would not shock their Lordships by going further."

One could hardly demand a better proof of the voluntary nature of the mid-Victorian sex censorship of literature than is furnished by this declaration of Lord Campbell's upon *The Lady of the Camellias*. Although regarded with a distaste which a few decades later would have led to legal suppression, the only antidote now employed was Lord Argyll's Society for the Encouragement of Pure Literature! Mid-Victorianism was still too secure to be threatened, and tolerance came lightly to such an age. However objectionable the symbols of the red and white camellias may have been, they did not constitute the gross abomination against which the mid-Victorian law of obscene libel was aimed.

An incident which occurred in connection with *The Lady of the Camellias* speaks eloquently for the jealousy of the circulating libraries for their reputations. They were far more vital to the voluntary Victorian censorship than Lord Argyll's Society for Pure Literature. Lord Campbell had intimated in the Lords that *The Lady of the Camellias* was freely to be secured at Smith & Sons. These Christian gentlemen bombarded him for a retraction which he had to make without delay. Indeed, the Earl of Shaftesbury came to their defense. "The moment his noble and learned Friend produced that book, he ventured to assert it had never been sold by the authority of the Messrs. Smith. He knew those gentlemen very well, and he did not suppose that there were more unlikely persons in the world to assist in the circulation of such a publication. They had devoted much time to the examination of the subject, and undoubtedly they had been the means of diffusing throughout the country an immense body of the purest literature." The Earl, indeed, was so anxious to vindicate the reputation of the Messrs. Smith, whom he characterized as truly Christian gentlemen, utterly incapable of an unworthy act, that he paid them the tribute of asserting that the books in their library were as pure as any to be found in the country.

THE REVELRY OF THE COMMONS

THE debate in the House of Commons was along substantially the same lines as in the Lords, but much bolder. Even the representatives of the Victorian middle class indulged in ribaldry and raillery at Lord Campbell's expense. The M.P.'s who led the opposition in the Commons were Messrs. Roebuck and White. Lord Campbell was so anxious for the fate of the bill that he appeared in the gallery of the House of Commons during the debate there. We

learn again from Lord Campbell's Diary that Denison, who
was the new Speaker of the House and a friend of the Lord
Chief Justice, sent a message to him by the Chancellor of
the Exchequer in which he humorously complained that
he "had appeared in the House to overawe their delibera-
tions like Cardinal Wolsey and Charles I and that it would
become his duty to protest against such an unconstitutional
proceeding." Roebuck went so far as to state that "a more
preposterous bill had never been sent down from the House
of Lords, and that was saying a good deal. It was an attempt to make people virtuous by an Act of Parliament,"
and then went on to challenge the noble Lord with Shakespeare and the other classics. White was able to be far more
delightfully scandalous than any of the peers. "It was
whispered out-of-doors," he said, "that in the event of the
present bill becoming law, it was the intention of certain
persons to publish selections from the literary works of the
noble and learned Lord who introduced the bill into the
other House and, moreover, cause them to be made subject
to the effects of this new statute. He was not sufficiently
acquainted with the writings of the Lord Chief Justice
nor could he say whether any of them would be amenable
under the proposed law."

A mischievous person, indeed, must have been the Hon.
James White, M.P., restrained by no sense of public deco-
rum. He had as little regard for the international amenities.
The first Federal provision against obscene literature in the
United States had appeared in the Tariff Act of 1842,
which barred such matter from entry into the country. The
alert Mr. James White had a little anecdote to relate to the
Commons of those absurd, impossible, and uncivilized

Americans! He had, moreover, done a little research in the library of the House of Commons.

"In the United States," he remarked, "there was a law which decreed the destruction of any obscene publications which might be imported thither. It happened curiously enough, not long ago, that an American traveler, returning home from Italy, brought with him a copy of that well-known work describing with figures, the principal statues, paintings, etc., of the Royal Museum of Naples. The name of this work is *Museo Borbonico Reale*; its value some thirty or forty pounds; and we have it in the Library attached to this House. Now, this very work was by the Collector of the Customs at New York deemed obscene; and was then and there ruthlessly destroyed. Since the introduction of the bill under discussion, he had again taken the pains to look over this work in their library, and he would put it to any of the honorable members conversant with its contents whether such a work (published under royal authority) could be called obscene."

THE TRIUMPH OF LORD CAMPBELL

WHEN in the end Lord Campbell triumphed, it was only after he had repeatedly assured both Lords and Commons of the harmlessness of his intentions. When the debate ended, he had made it abundantly clear that any work which so much as pretended to be literature or art, classic or modern, had little to fear from the law. Moreover, we also know from another entry in his Diary at the end of the year that his Act was only enforced against the abominations which had roused him to action. "Its success," he wrote of his Act, "has been most brilliant. Holywell Street, which had long set law and decency at defiance, has capitulated after several assaults. Half of the shops are shut up; and the remainder deal in nothing but moral and religious books! Under the bill similar abominations have been cleared away in Dublin. Even in Paris its influence has been felt, for the French police, roused by the accounts of what we are now doing, have been energetically employed in purifying the Palais Royal and the Rue Vivienne."

It was all very gratifying, indeed. No wife or son would be able to make a shameful living from pornography while the wretched husband languished in jail. But in the end the anxieties of the opposition proved more than justified. Lord Brougham had warned Lord Campbell that once his bill became an Act of Parliament, his intentions would be perverted. A new content, indeed, was given to the Act in little more than a decade. In three decades it was invoked against the very classics which all the noble Lords had wished to guard, and especially against current literature far less allusive than *The Lady of the Camellias*. We must refer for the last time to Lord Campbell's Diary for the crowning irony. During the time when the Act was passing through Parliament, the spare time of this lover of literature was taken up in reading no other book than Disraeli's *The Calamities of Authors,* which recounts in very vivid detail the almost endless odds against which men of letters have to contend. Quite unconsciously Lord Campbell was preparing the most formidable calamity of all.

ENTER LORD CHIEF JUSTICE COCKBURN

IT was Lord Chief Justice Cockburn, the immediate successor of Lord Campbell, who scrapped all of the latter's scruples, in 1868. An anti-papist by the name of Hecklin published and distributed a pamphlet entitled *The Confessional Unmasked, Showing the Depravity of the Romish Priesthood; the Iniquity of the Confessional, and the Questions Put to Females in Confession.* The copies of the pamphlet were seized under Lord Campbell's Act, and when an appeal was taken against the warrant the learned intermediate Appellate Court held that, while they were undoubtedly obscene in the ordinary meaning of the term, they did not come within the Act as they had been distributed for the honest purpose of exposing the practices of the Catholic confessional. In other words, they had not been published "for the single purpose of corrupting the morals of youth," which had to be the case before a publication came within the declared intention of Lord Campbell's Act.

This was the last time such doctrine was heard in an Anglo-Saxon court. If Lord Chief Justice Cockburn knew that his predecessor's Act was only intended to appy "exclusively to works written for the single purpose of corrupting the morals of youth and of a nature calculated to shock the common feelings of decency in any well-regulated mind," he chose conveniently to ignore the limitations. He explicitly admitted that to attempt to "destroy and extirpate Roman Catholicism" was, indeed, a laudatory purpose with which he sympathized, but there was no real danger to be apprehended from the papists and it was frivolous to consider such a question in view of the greater danger to growing sons and daughters which might follow if such matter came into their hands. Upon the other side of the waters Comstock had arisen, and an agitated spirit was stirring in the Anglo-Saxon world. The English-speaking peoples were listening and waiting for an oracle to give them a new concept of obscenity which would save them from any threat to the prudishness which was soon to be challenged by birth control reformers, infidels and æsthetes in England and America; and the oracle spoke the words which gave authority even to the State and Federal judges who were to interpret the Comstock Acts in America.

"I think," spoke Lord Chief Justice Cockburn, "the test of obscenity is this, whether the tendency of the matter charged as obscenity is to deprave and corrupt those whose minds are open to such immoral influences and into whose hands a publication of this sort may fall."

With this utterance sanity was swept away, and Victorian literary prudery and the law made to coincide. Or rather law was swept aside to make room for hysteria. Almost any book which might have some evil effect upon any Anglo-Saxon, young or old, male or female, was made criminal. Anon the classics were being attacked, and then modern literature. A literary reign of terror had been instituted, and no rational being might tell who would be the next victim. Was the abdication of reason complete, or was there a driving force behind the oracle which represented some urgency of the times?

VII

THE EVOLUTION OF THE SEX CENSORSHIP

The Middle Ages produced no literature because they were afraid of heresy, and the Twentieth Century will produce none because it is afraid of morality.—GEORGE MOORE.

A GREAT many persons have chosen to remain mystified by the vagaries of the sex censorship. They prefer, indeed, that its operations remain covert. The defensive mechanism usually adopted is to accuse all others of showing too great "sex-consciousness." The *status quo ante* is taken as its own ultimate justification. To be curious is to incur the danger of psychic dislocation.

We now turn from the practical aspect of the workings of the sex censorship to offer a theory for its existence. The modern problem of obscenity may profitably be considered in a great many different ways: psychologically, psychoanalytically, culturally, anthropologically, physiologically. It depends naturally upon a great many factors in a civilization. When we say that it varies with national character, we express a resultant of many forces. It is not so very fanciful to say that it has a relation to changing mechanism, represented by modern sanitation and plumbing facilities which have relegated the grosser functions of metabolism (the excremental, with which the sexual are intimately connected), so much more prominent in the sixteenth and seventeenth centuries, to the background in our daily lives. We may prefer to emphasize such a social condition as the prevalence of early marriage in a particular society, or the subjection of women. Climate is not without its influence if we are to believe Byron's lines:

> "What men call gallantry and the gods adultery,
> Is far more common where the climate's sultry."

On any such fundamentalist basis, it is as hard to understand obscenity as to explain the conventions which determine the relative respectability of such feminine professions as the actress's, the waitress's, the milliner's, and the manicurist's.

Since we are here concerned with obscene literature as a crime, it is only necessary to consider the sex censorship as a political function. To lovers of literature—the true, the good, and the beautiful—it always appears philistine so much as to suggest that the sex censorship is, indeed, not concerned with its welfare. When Anthony Comstock proclaimed that his object was "morals, not art or literature," he simply expressed the traditional point of view of the State. Our first clue out of the labyrinth is to realize that the State has no concern with the crime of obscenity as a literary problem. The State as a political agent is not primarily interested in literature, and literary purity is not in itself its first solicitude. If the State is democratic and enlightened, it may endow libraries where literature may be read, and colleges where it may be studied. But all this is incidental. Politically, the safety of the State is the first rule of its existence. We know that the State has always scrutinized literature for opinion wherever it has had the civilization to produce literature.   As long as there have been books, there have been books suppressed.   It is in order consequently to inquire if the sex censorship is not merely a changing form of the control of the State over opinion, a phase of its evolutionary development.

A few years ago in England, Clive Bell turned his critical attention from Goya and El Greco and the mysteries of significant form, to the nature of British freedom.   He began his speculations by observing a striking contrast in the different types of freedom which seemed to obtain in England and France.   An Englishman in London had a great deal of political freedom; he could get up in Hyde Park Corner and declaim at the top of his voice about the tyranny and stupidity of the British Government.   But when it came to satisfying his artistic tastes, and his joy in living, he discovered serious impediments.   The Vigilance Association stood guard over his literature to save him from indecency, and annoying regulations interfered with his drinking at such hours as pleased him.   Now, on the other hand, while a Frenchman in Paris had to be far more circumspect in his animadversions on the government, he had the privilege of reading such books as interested him, and imbibing his liquors at such hours as suited him.   Then the critic observed that he did not care a fig for speaking his mind at Hyde Park Corner but would gladly exchange the native for the French brand of freedom.   He added, moreover, that such foreign observers as Montesquieu and Voltaire, after visiting England, had created the myth of British freedom merely from observing that the British had such very handsome Houses of Parliament.   We imagine the average Englishman thought this preference for artistic rather than political freedom highly eccentric, and to be expected of an art critic.

Clive Bell observed the phenomenon but did not inquire beyond this. Yet in the fact that the sex censorship has reached its most aggravated form in Anglo-Saxon lands lies much of the explanation for the evolution of criminal obscenity. We need but take for the sake of contrast a larger bird's-eye view than is afforded by insular England to understand the success of the Vigilance Association, the New York Society for the Suppression of Vice, or the Watch and Ward Society. When we also take into account the comparatively modern origin of the sex censorship, which really did not grow to serious proportions either in England and America or anywhere on the Continent till the nineteenth century, we have the other most valuable clue.

"THE SENSE OF ANTIQUITY"

UNDER this title old Jeremy Collier in his diatribe against the immorality of the English stage considered the views of the ancients upon the supervision of the drama. In that immortal broadside, the *Areopagitica,* Milton similarly inquired as to the liberty which books enjoyed in Greece and Rome. We can applaud only one of these pamphleteers, but both are indispensable to our purpose. Collier, the divine who published his *Short View of the Immorality and Profaneness of the English Stage* in 1698 which excited comment in London for months and achieved the distinction of inspiring a reply from Congreve himself, certainly had not taken the earlier plea of the great poet to heart. The merest glance at antiquity shows that while the sex censorship is modern, an awareness of the obscene in art has obtained among all peoples which have achieved civilization, pagan or Christian. Plutarch himself has recorded for us his opinion that the comedies of Aristophanes are coarse and obscene. In his sixth elegy, the virtuous Propertius devoted to the infernal gods the man who first filled Roman homes with obscene paintings. "My verses," boasted Catullus, "are spicy and gay, they stir desire." The ancients had generally a distinct notion of the mischief which might be caused by books. One may well suspect that the plaint of Solomon that of making many books there is no end is to be explained by more than boredom. There is, for instance, a passage in the *Tagenistæ* of Aristophanes in which, speaking of a young man gone wrong, the dramatist ascribes his ruin to "a book, to Prodicus, or to bad company." That Plato regarded poetry unfavorably appears from the famous passage in the *Republic* in which he considered its demoralizing effects upon the minds of youth. Indeed, he went so far as to recommend the expurgation of Homer for Greek minors!

We detect a particularly modern and familar note in a story which Plutarch relates. After the defeat of the Roman army sent against the Parthians, books were discovered in the camp of the hardened Roman legionaries. These were copies of the popular *Milesian Tales* of Aristides, very much a best seller at Rome. Surena, the barbarian chieftain, called a conclave of the Parthians, and expressed a lofty scorn of the Roman soldiers that "even in the wars they could not refrain from doing evil, and the reading of such vile books." The justification which Plutarch makes for the Romans is no less amusing: it is not that the *Milesian Tales* were works of art but that the Parthian chieftain had no right to object when he was himself a bastard.

Now and then in antiquity the book of a poet, historian, or philosopher met suppression. In China it is recorded that in the second century before Christ the Emperor Che Hwang-Ti ordered the destruction of all the books in the empire except such eminently pragmatic ones as those dealing with medicine, divination, and husbandry, and not even excepting the works of Confucius. Merely to mention such particularly objectionable ones as the *Book of History* and the *Book of Odes* was made punishable with death. The trial and condemnation of Socrates is not the only instance of the suppression of a philosopher in the Athenian State. The writings of Protagoras were also condemned as pernicious and burnt in the Agora; and King Ptolemy forbade the philosopher Hegesias to demonstrate in his public teaching that life was an evil, because he did it so eloquently. In Rome there frequently took place the burning of books of magic and pseudo-Sibylline works, and occasionally the emperors issued decrees against subversive writings. Caligula, for instance, undertook (according to Suetonius) to suppress Homer, no doubt from patriotic motives as a 100-per-cent Roman, for Homer was a foreigner, and quoted too much in the cause of Greek liberty. The same author also relates that the Emperor Domitian had Hermogenes of Tarsus killed because of certain expressions in his history, and even had the booksellers who had circulated the work crucified. He also ordered the work of Junius Rusticus to be burned in the Forum under a *senatus consultum*.

The total of the suppression of books of all kinds in the Græco-Roman world was, however, inconsiderable. When a book or the teachings of a philosopher did fall under the ban, it was invariably a case of bringing the immortal gods into open contempt, or of undermining the peace of the State.

There is not a single well-authenticated example of the censorship of a book in antiquity solely upon the score of obscenity. "We do not read," as Milton tells us, "that either Epicurus or that libertine school of Cyrene or what the cynic impudence uttered was ever questioned by the laws." Only the fate of the poet Ovid, whose *Art of Love* these days frightens postmasters so much, may give rise to any suspicion. We know that Augustus banished him to the desolate shores of the Euxine, now called the Black Sea, but we do not know if the character of his masterpiece played any part. The usually accepted version is that Ovid had insulted the Emperor's daughter, perhaps by attempting to put the *Art of Love* into practice.

THE POPULARITY OF ART AS A CONDITION PRECEDENT

IF we have introduced all this ancient history, it is not for its own sake. We might have chosen a more modern period when criminal obscenity was quiescent to emphasize the first element for its comprehension as a political function. It is simply that the story of the censorship in the Græco-Roman world exhibits the moral most neatly. At no other time is it possible to remove so completely the differential factors which perplex the mind nowadays in the rationalization of the sex censorship. The comparative rarity of all kinds of literary censorship makes it idle to speculate upon the distinctive features in the make-up of Greek and Roman societies which might have failed to exempt them from a preoccupation with obscenity. The turbulent character of the Greek democracy, the love of art and philosophy in Greece, the old Roman Puritanism which has been exemplified for all time in the figure of Cato the Censor, the spirit of paganism, the vestiges of phallicism, the personal whims of Roman emperors or Greek tyrants of which Demos was the worst, all these are of little significance.

To be a problem to the State, an art must achieve that degree of popularity which may make its effects dangerous to peace, good order and safety. To do this it must reach the masses of the population. While an aristocracy may play with ideas with perfect immunity, the common herd is to be sheltered from their influence. Now the advantage of observing Greece, Rome, China, or for that matter any ancient commonwealth is that we are dealing with a period before the invention of printing. We could hardly conceive of the necessity for any kind of literary censorship in a civilization which wrote in cuneiform characters upon clay tablets. In the Graeco-Roman world, which had reached the manuscript period, we begin, indeed, to find instances of suppression, but, after all, when a book had to be produced painfully by hand, it could work little mischief. The slaves and the plebeians of the ancient world could hardly be disaffected by books when, first, they could not read, and, second, books cost too much to be within their reach. Plato, for instance, is reported to have paid over three thousand dollars in present money value for three books of Philolaus. Roman enterprise made books very much more accessible and cheaper, regular publishers arising who employed large numbers of educated slaves to write manuscripts down simultaneously from dictation, in this way producing editions of as many as one thousand copies of a best seller. Yet this distribution of books is not to be compared with the output made possible by the printing press. Precisely, however, because books were more numerous in Rome, we have more frequent exercise of the prerogative of censorship.

In considering the drama as a superior Vehicle of Infection in contrast with books, we have observed the greater degree of supervision which it has always inspired, so that today an English playwright requires the permission of the Lord Chamberlain for the production of his play while the novelist is under no such guardianship. It is recognized that Puritanism from the very beginning of its course has constantly attacked the theatre while only of late has it concentrated upon books, but the practical genius which went instinctively into this direction of attention has remained obscure. To the extent that the book and the play do not differ in force, the secret lies in the older place of the drama as a popular art. The popular art of the ancients was in the theatre, and, as we might expect, there is the corresponding difference in attitude which is shown in a quicker reaction against demoralizing plays. "The law," said Aristotle, "ought to forbid Young People the seeing of Comedies, such permissions not being safe till age and discipline had confirmed them in sobriety, fortified their virtue, and made them as it were proof against debauchery." When Jeremy Collier came to marshal the sense of antiquity upon his *Short View of the Immorality and Profaneness of the English Stage,* he was able to adduce Plato, Xenophon, Livy, Tully, Valerius Maximus, Tacitus, and even Ovid in support of his position. A form of censorship existed through the office of the choragus in the Greek drama, and in the Latin by virtue of the fact that the ædile who was charged with securing plays for public performance was an officer of the State. One thinks naturally of the comedies of Aristophanes; but it must be remembered that to be a free Athenian and Greek citizen no matter of how little pretension was already to be a member of an aristocracy in a sense. When

it is remembered, moreover, that women did not attend the
Greek theatre, the toleration of the coarseness of Aristophanes appears less exceptionable. Even Aristophanes, however, was suppressed at a later period, and Euripides was
punished for exceeding the bounds in his own life-time.
There was probably a formal censorship in the late Roman
Empire, if we may judge from expressions in Horace. By
the time of the Theodosian Code, no doubt under the influence of early Christianity, it was a cause for divorce for
a wife to go to the theatre without her husband's knowledge,
and to become an actor entailed the loss of Roman citizenship.

THE CHANGING INDEX OF CENSORSHIP

WITH the invention of printing in the middle of the fif-
teenth century, the first condition for the censorship of literature began to be fulfilled: literature was on its way to
popular distribution. The three forms of censorship which
we know today began to develop: (1) the religious (2) the
political (3) the sexual, which is the modern culmination.
The course of evolution may be stated to be from heresy to
treason to obscenity. The purpose of authority remains
always the same, but the index of censorship changes. Each
age produces those formulæ of suppression which coincide
with its dominant interest. It hits upon the test of virtue
and the good life which, when the individual meets it in the
conditions of the time in which he happens to live, constitutes the assurance of his regularity. It leads only to be-
wilderment to take the formulæ of censorship at their face
value. Witchcraft, for instance, appears to us now to have
been simply a demoniac possession of the Dark Ages of
Faith, and we do not perceive that the witch was often a

heretic, a member of organized cults which had survived from paganism, such as the Manichæan sects which numbered their tens of thousands, and that witchcraft supplied merely one of the naïve formulæ of the Age of Faith for dealing with them.

It did not take long after the printing presses began their work for both Church and State to take measures of censorship. The first *Index Librorum Prohibitorum* was instituted in 1559, and to this day the Church still issues its index to guide the reading of Catholics. The changing index of censorship is best observed in those troubled times when the State was struggling against the mediæval authority of the Church. The conflict which arose made the burnings of not only books but their authors all the more savage.

In this, which was the Age of Faith, the Church in its supervision of literature concerned itself almost entirely with its main interest, the extirpation of heresy. It naturally assumed that if one were a good son of the Church, the rest would be unimportant. A really good Catholic could commit no wrong which need alarm the Church. When the Catholic Church arose, it had combated the lusts of the flesh and the carnalities of paganism. In its confessionals it dealt daily with such sins. A papal censor, speaking of Sanchez's work on the confessional *De Matrimonis,* itself an eroticon of the first order, remarked: "I have read this work more than once with the greatest pleasure." The monastic ideal in itself implied an obsession with sex. We might expect the Church then to take a very severe attitude toward obscenity. But for a long time it showed itself most tolerant in this respect. It had preserved the obscene literature of heathendom without fear. It is perhaps no accident that it preserved the comedies of Aristophanes, which are very gross, and permitted to be lost the comedies of Menander, which we know were singularly pure. But at any rate for the Church the index of the good life was freedom from heresy and not from obscenity.

It is true that in the very first *Index Librorum Prohibitorum* we find in the general rules for the guidance of the inquisitors a prohibition of "books which include the treatment of obscene and immoral subjects," and Lucian is condemned in this category. But it is to be remembered that Lucian was an atheist, and mocked the gods of his day. But the rule remained one decidedly honored in the breach. With rare exceptions, the Church did not object to the obscene when it appeared only in connection with profane things. We need but take as an illustration the single case of the much-expurgated and suppressed Boccaccio. He, indeed, appears upon the *Index Expurgatorius*, but the expurgated passages are not those which would be called nowadays lewd, lascivious, indecent and obscene. All the obscenity which secretaries of vice societies insist shall be removed before Boccaccio may enter the home are in the papal Boccaccio. The portions which are censored are purely those which reflect upon religion and the Church. There are no alterations where only the laity appear in passages of amour. Where a churchman appears in such worldly diversions, the changes which are made relate merely to the removal of the reflections upon the dignity of the Church which arise from such conduct. According to an' ingenious rule, erring nuns are converted into noblewomen, erring monks into magicians. At one place, an abbess becomes a countess, a priest Gianni "a certain Gianni," and the Archangel Gabriel, the King of the Fairies.

But a long procession of martyrs testifies to the zeal with

which the Church pursued heretical books and their authors. One may read a great deal of the bitter story in such accounts as Anson's *Books Condemned to be Burnt,* and Farrar's *Books Fatal to Their Authors.* An obscene book might lead to indulgence of the flesh which was not necessarily a mortal sin; but an heretical book might lead to the loss of an immortal soul. We consider the suppression of the Bible nowadays as a *reductio ad absurdum* of the sex censorship, but the popularization of heresy appeared such a frightful danger to the Church that it did not hesitate to suppress translations of the Bible. The revealed word of God could not be entrusted to the masses of its communicants. One could prove anything from the Bible. Tyndale, Wycliffe, Bruccioli, Montanus, all the early translators of the Bible had to dare the wrath of the Church. To such extremes did the dread of heresy lead that when after the Reformation the State finally permitted translations, the severest punishments were visited upon careless printers who permitted such unhappy misprints to creep into the text as the omission of the "not" in the Seventh Commandment.

With the Reformation, which was itself hastened by the invention of printing, the index of censorship began to change and grow more complicated in Protestant as well as in Catholic countries. The weakening of the Church, which assured the ultimate unification and centralization of the states of Europe, had progressed to such an extent before the Reformation that the censorship of the Church of Rome had to rely largely upon the temporal power of the Catholic states to insure its prohibitions by adding the pains and penalties of this world to the dangers which excommunication incurred in the next. While the triumph of Protestantism did not mean the end of censorship, it made it the duty of the State, a burden which it only too readily assumed. Luther, Calvin, and Zwingli urged a censorship which was as savage as that of the Catholic Church. No amelioration was to be expected, for Protestantism had incurred the danger of stimulating individualism and emphasizing the importance of individual conscience. It was in itself a heresy which had to combat enemies both within and without.

Protestantism admitted the absolutism of the political state, and so no conflict for the direction of the censorship arose. But in such Catholic countries as Spain, France and Italy, the growing spirit of nationalism raised a conflict of purposes between these States and the Church. The success of the temporal powers resulted in a growing nationalization of the Catholic Church itself in the different countries. In the first place, the temporal princes began to insist that for an *index librorum prohibitorum* to be effective within their dominions it be left to them to declare its authority. Thus, a number of Papal indexes of the sixteenth century were never accepted in France, where the greatest degree of national consciousness existed. While the State permitted the ecclesiastics still to exercise the censorial function, it wanted it clearly understood that they acted only in the capacity of officials of the State, not of the Church. But a change in the focus of the censorship appeared which was much more fundamental. The States began to insist that the ecclesiastical inquisitor limit his examination of books to their theological and dogmatic aspects. The views of the Church and the Catholic States upon theological dogma had diverged, and censorship began to accommodate itself to the change of interest. What was sound doctrine to the Church was then no less than sedition to the State.

The transition may, perhaps, best be observed in Catholic

Venice, which in the sixteenth and seventeenth centuries was the leading publishing centre of Europe. The question, it is significant, was raised in Venice by Fra Paoli Sarpi, who, although a cleric himself, represented a modernist view upon the right of the civil authority to resist ecclesiastical interference in temporal matters. The good father submitted a report to the Venetian Republic in which he declared that the books of four classes of writers ought to be prohibited by the State: "(1) Those who attack the Constitution of the Republic and its laws by name; (2) those who attack the Constitution and the laws of the Republic without naming her; (3) those who within the limits even of fair controversy argue against the legislation of the State; (4) *those who attack no laws of the State but who broadly maintain the absolute and universal authority of the ecclesiastical over the temporal authority.*" After the usual interdicts and excommunications, the matter was finally settled by a concordat in 1596, but difficulties nevertheless continued to arise. Thus, for example, in 1602, the Church put upon the *Index* a commentary by Suarez on the *Tractate de Censuris* by Thomas Aquinas for the very reason that the commentary had received the imprimatur of the Venetian authorities after the expurgation of passages attacking the temporal power of princes! Other books which the Church approved but the Venetian Republic suppressed as inimical to its temporal power were Thomas Preston's *Apologia Cardinalis Bellarmini*, the Archbishop Spalato's *Recantation*, and Cardinal Palavicini's *History of the Council of Trent*.

The absolute political state was emerging. Both Catholic and Protestant monarchs ruled under the doctrine of the Divine Right of Kings. But their temporal power was their fundamental interest and security. While the support of

religion was still of the greatest import, it was secondary,
deriving its sanctions from the necessities of the State. The
integrity of religion was a greater concern to the Protestant
State, which had destroyed the absolute authoritarianism of
the Catholic faith. But all rulers remained Defenders of the
Faith. In Protestant states, there was merely a change of
terminology. It now called the heretic an atheist and the
crime of heresy became the crime of blasphemy. Sedition
was to become the most hideous of all crimes and thus also
the test of a meritorious book. As we approach modernity,
the secular censorship becomes more and more exclusively
political. If the State still insists that the subject shall not
be a heretic or blasphemer, it is from the conviction that
heresy and blasphemy are often antecedent steps to treason
and sedition.

ABSOLUTISM AND THE SEX CENSORSHIP

ABSOLUTISM quickly established itself in Europe, and with
varying degrees of success maintained itself on the Continent till well along in the nineteenth century. Even the ex-
plosive force of the French Revolution did not undermine
its hold entirely. The Holy Alliance did not work in vain.
In the Russian Empire it triumphed completely in reaction
and superstition, and elsewhere, despite currents of counter-
revolution and flurries of discontent, maintained some measure of the *status quo*. It took a long time, indeed, for Europe
to shake off the shackles of mediævalism. In such par-
lous times, little attention can be paid to books which are
merely sexually *"contre bonnes mœurs."* There are few
rulers in the history of the world who better understood the
political means than Napoleon, and in one of the most

troubled decades of the century, he thus declared the duty of the State with regard to censorship: *"Le, droit d'empêcher la manifestation d'idées qui troublent la paix de L'Etat, ses intérêts et le bon ordre."* Significantly, towards attacks upon religion he was indifferent, unlike most rulers; but, after all, he was a son of the French Revolution which had enthroned the Goddess of Reason. *"Qu'on laisse donc écrire librement sur la religion, pourvu qu'on n'abuse pas de cette liberté pour écrire contre l'Etat."*

A successful absolutism in the very nature of things is not concerned overmuch with the sex censorship. The good European submitted to State and Church, and led his personal life in his own way. The masses, ignorant, illiterate, and oppressed, had no interest or connection with art and literature in the vehicle of the book. When it is said that the invention of printing had popularized literature, it is true, after all, in an intermediate sense only. The book made its appeal directly only to the comparatively learned who then preached its message to the common people. The reformer may blaspheme and be heretical in a sermon, or be seditious in a political harangue, but he incites no one to be obscene. The absolute political State had no objection to the obscene in art upon such doctrinal grounds as influenced the Church. Noble lords and privy counsellors might read such erotica as they pleased so long as they raised no public scandal. The rule of good order was then disturbed. There was usually such a motive behind the confiscation of obscene books which has taken place occasionally in all centuries since the spread of printing. But as far as political danger from the licentiousness of an aristocracy is concerned, there is little to fear. Such laxity is, indeed, its privilege.

THE MECHANICS OF CONTROL

PREVENTIVE censorship remained the dominant European ideal and practice. Volumes have been filled with its history from the sixteenth to the nineteenth centuries as it fluctuated with the tides of revolution and unrest. There was the censorship of the rather liberal Frederick the Great, the patron of Voltaire, which he developed into a political system enduring in Prussia to the days of Kaiserism and the Kulturkampf. There was the censorship of Maria Theresa which, established under the influence of Jesuitism in Austria in 1753, remained in existence till 1848, when it succumbed to the temporary disturbances of revolution. In France, the censorship was maintained rigorously from 1521 till the French Revolution. Then followed the censorship of Napoleon in 1810, to be abolished at his overthrow and restored with the Empire. The State censorship in Spain dated from 1558, was dissolved in the French Revolution, only to be re-enforced after the restoration of Ferdinand VII. The more modern censorships are within the memory of the middle-aged: the political censorships of Russia, Kaiserism, Turkey, Japan, where absolutism remained unrestrained.

The absolute political state made possible the retention into the nineteenth century of the mechanism of censorship which had developed all over Europe in the sixteenth. This, too, had its effect in retarding the sex censorship. There is a remarkably close morphological similarity in the essential methods which developed. These could be maintained only under rigorous political control. Censorship on the Continent aimed to be preventive rather than punitive as it is mostly today. It was accomplished in three ways:

(1) The author, to protect his literary labors, had need of the power of the State against plagiarism. When he appealed to the State to grant him an exclusive privilege of selling his book, the State censors had the opportunity of examining the contents for objectionable passages. If none existed, he received the Imprimatur. It is thus interesting to observe that the copyright, which was originally intended as a protection to the author, was of even more benefit to the State as a guarantee against pernicious doctrines. Moreover, this censorship at copyright was alert and active, quite unlike that of the American Copyright Office in this respect.

(2) This preventive censorship was at first often lodged in the faculties of the mediæval universities, and in Europe often remained there for a long time. Thus, the censorship over some classes of books, exercised in England in the sixteenth and seventeenth centuries by the Universities of Oxford and Cambridge, was similarly the duty of the University of the Sorbonne in France, the Berlin Academy of Sciences in Prussia, the University of Padua in the Venetian Republic, the University of Munich in Bavaria.

(3) Later, more specialized bodies came into existence which would nowadays be called Boards of Censorship. The function was exercised in the sixteenth and seventeenth centuries in England by the Star Chamber. On the Continent, the preventive censorship was entrusted to variously denominated Colleges of Censors to which were often attached till quite recently Commissioners on Heresy.

(4) The mediæval trade guild system supplied another means of control. The English reader is familiar with the Stationers' Company which was founded in England in 1557. The members were given a monopoly of all printing so that a supervision over mischievous printers and authors might

be exercised through the responsible officials of the Company. Exactly the same object was effected in Venice through the Venetian Guild of Printers and Publishers, which was founded, several years before the Stationers' Company, and in Paris through the Syndics of the Guilds of Publishers. It is to be observed that membership in these printers' and publishers' guilds was made compulsory, and the officials were sometimes ordered to employ jobless printers in order to keep them from printing unlicensed books.

THE CONDITIONS OF THE SEX CENSORSHIP

To summarize: there are certain major elements which must be understood as conditions precedent to the development of the sex censorship. First of all, literature must achieve popular distribution. This was brought about by the invention of printing, the signal for innumerable mediæval book-burnings. The spread of knowledge was, however, still to be accomplished. Secondly, it is observed that the index of censorship changes in accordance with the prevalent interests of any age. The bitter conflict of Church and State clearly illustrates the tendency. Thirdly, and most important of all, the sex censorship bears the closest relation to the degree of political liberty which has been won in any state. This is only another way of saying that the printing press had done its deadly work with such good effect that absolutism both of dogma and personal fealty was ultimately doomed to extinction. A new orientation of society was imperative.

VIII

SEX CONTROL

When morality triumphs, nasty things happen.
—REMY DE GOURMONT.

THE triumph of Mrs. Grundy in the Anglo-Saxon world ceases to be inexplicable as soon as it is considered in terms of the three indexes of virtue. If the Age of Faith adopted the index of heresy, the Age of Divine Right, the index of treason, it was inevitable for the Age of Democracy to adopt the index of sex. The shift from the first index to the second has been made clear. It remains to show the transition to the Age of Sex Control.

It is customary to rail against the sex censorship. It is declared to be an insuperable obstacle to civilization. But we will be much nearer the truth if we say that it is one of the penalties of civilization. The paradox is that it came into existence as the first consequence of our enlightenment. Rightly regarded, the sex censorship is the measles of civilization. In evolving a politically free man, the life force made him a sexually inhibited one. In an ultimate sense, Galileo and Bacon are responsible for Lord Chief Justice Cockburn. The absurdities and inanities of the modern dread of the obscene have simply obscured the relationship.

Where the conditions of political liberty and intellectual emancipation have been first fulfilled, we may expect the sex censorship to appear. It is no mere accident that the symptoms first made themselves visible in England. For almost three centuries, the closest parallelism is to be observed in the evolution of Continental and English censorship. Substantially the same social, economic, and political conditions made the mechanism of censorship almost identical and kept its focus at the same points. Then, at the end of the seventeenth century, the divergence begins. The preventive censorship of the Star Chamber, the Licensing Acts, disappear in England at the same time that they are still the normal mechanism of control on the Continent.

Indeed, England emerged from the barbarism of the Middle Ages so much earlier than the rest of Europe that whenever the history of liberty and democracy is discussed, we naturally turn first to England. It is customary to say that England took the lead in the emancipation of the serfs, in the formation of Bills of Right, in the removal of religious disabilities, and in the establishment of representative government. The Anglo-Saxon speaks proudly of Magna Carta and the Petition of Rights. The early collapse of preventive censorship under the assaults of English libertarianism was an indication of this weakening of authority. The censorship was now administered under the criminal law in the punitive manner we know at present, and freedom of the press became the Englishman's ironic privilege of going to jail for his opinions. The right which an Englishman now had to a public trial and the verdict of his peers under a clear definition of the issues not only made it easier to escape a charge of sedition but made the crime itself increasingly unpopular.

THE BLIND OF PURITANISM

WHEN the evolution of criminal obscenity is discussed with reference to continental countries, it is much easier to avoid confusion and obscurantism. But when we turn to England we discover that it is the usual custom to ascribe the whole business to Puritanism. It is the particular habit of literary critics to set Puritanism up as a windmill, and then like so many gallant Don Quixotes to charge straight at the monster. We are told again and again of the Puritan's hostility to joy, his suspicion of art, his intolerance of infidelity. Puritanism is shouted as a dreadful accusation which is expected to bring to their knees the weaker, more easily intimidated Puritans. It is thus made to assume an objective reality which it is far from possessing. For Puritanism, which is offered as an explanation, is simply the label for a conclusion upon a very complex state of affairs. When it is used as a descriptive term for the sake of brevity, it serves a legitimate purpose. But unfortunately it has become perhaps the most frozen formula in the English language. It has resulted in our thinking that a peculiar kink exists in the English mind which separates it from all others.

When we say that the sex censorship is the creation of English Puritanism, all that we can properly mean is that the conditions which favored its existence appeared sooner in England than on the Continent. What is important to remember is that it was precisely the Puritans who had been largely instrumental in insuring English political freedom. Puritanism, which was bound up with the rise of modern capitalism, had need of such liberty to pursue its practical and worldly enterprises. But, again, it must not be forgotten that Magna Carta was the work in part of the barons and nobility who were in revolt against the excessive claims of prerogatives in the Crown. When we inject the economic necessities of Puritanism into the discussion we need only take into account the fact that the creation of a large middle class led to popular education, which first resulted in an increased reading class, and then ultimately made for such a spread of enlightenment that a new sanction had to be discovered.

It is no paradox to say that the Puritan had little conception of the modern sex censorship of literature. What attention he paid to obscenity in books arose merely from his inability as an earnest and practical-minded man to distinguish between lewdness in books and lewdness in life. He was against sexual immorality in life because he knew that a profligate life led to the undermining of the virtues of sobriety, frugality and industry which were indispensable to his labors for civilization. Thus he was always concerned about the bad example which a lewd book or play might set. He had no objection to the depiction of vice and sin provided it was bound up with the proper indignation. His attitude toward obscenities consequently differed little from the prohibitionist's objections to intoxicating liquor in its effects upon a man's efficiency. It had as yet no connection with the censorship of ideas and did not constitute part of the political function. Hogarth exactly caught the Puritan motive when in one of his prints he pictured the wicked mechanic reading *Moll Flanders* while the good mechanic read the story of the apprentice who became Lord Mayor of London. This conception of the art of life which early displayed itself in a host of sumptuary laws so far antedates the evolution of criminal obscenity that no other conclusion is possible than that more than the Puritan state of mind was involved.

THE INTERMEDIATE STAGE

THE critics who treat literary decency by a biometric formula in accordance with which it rises and wanes in relation to "Puritanism" have gone far astray as is proved conclusively by the length of time which elapsed between the emergence of English political liberty and the appearance of the crime of obscene libel. The crime of blasphemy still sufficed against the winds of doctrine. However much deism may have been popular in the upper reaches of English society, the masses were under the influence of religious orthodoxy, and blasphemy was still a serviceable test of the good life. The blasphemy prosecutions of the eighteenth and nineteenth centuries still had public opinion behind them. It is a rule that when one of the safeguards against subversive doctrine is rendered less effective there is a compensating shift of emphasis toward another. The jurisdiction over blasphemy had been lodged in the ecclesiastical courts, but the pressure of political freedom transferred it to the temporal courts. The prominence of blasphemy prosecutions in England is no doubt partly to be explained by the English dread of Popery, a dread which had been ushered in with the uxorious Henry; but this was no less one of the signs of emancipation. The time had not yet arrived for the sex censorship in England, where the fear of blasphemy was so great that even in the middle of the nineteenth century successful prosecutions could be conducted against such rationalists as Carlyle, Cooper, Watts, Bradlaugh, Holyoake, and Foote.

If there is any doubt of the meaning of the application of the intermediate index, it is removed by the fact of the prolonged American insistence that it, no less than England, was a Christian country. It is true that political liberty under rigid constitutional guarantees became better established here at an earlier date than in the motherland. But the myth of the absolutely free and untrammeled American has become more and more discredited. The adoption of the Alien and Sedition Acts so soon after the great struggle over the Constitution is only one of the many qualifications which were made. The significant fact is, however, that in supposedly free America the necessity for maintaining the index of religion was recognized. The fact is that a direct union of Church and State obtained in the New England states and Maryland till the middle of the nineteenth century, and that England had effected complete Catholic and Jewish emancipation before at least one American state, New Hampshire. It is interesting that the greatest strides toward religious freedom were made in Virginia, the first of the Southern states which had a feudal aristocracy of slaveholders which was quite sure of itself. The First Amendment to the Federal Constitution was interpreted to limit only the powers of Congress in interfering with free worship. Christianity was declared to be the law of the land in the sense that it was entitled to preference and protection. Until the late years of the nineteenth century atheists were generally incompetent to testify in America, and still are in Arkansas, Maryland and North Carolina. Blasphemy was a crime in all the American states no less than in England, and the American and English Puritan still refused to take alarm.

THE INDEX OF SEX

THE sex censorship was the result of the secularization of life. From 1800, when the conventions of literary decency began to mature, to the time of Lord Chief Justice Campbell was the period of gradual transition. If the growth of the circulating libraries in England constituted a menace, a free public library was an even worse "evergreen tree of diabolical knowledge." The modern public libraries date from the middle of the nineteenth century in both England and America, but it took another quarter century before their resources became adequate. When the first public library in England was opened at Manchester, Thackeray improved upon Hogarth by picturing the Lancashire mechanic reading Carlyle, Dickens and Bulwer-Lytton. Popular education was introduced by Forster's Act in England in 1780, and alarmed satirists began to picture houses burning down while their cooks read hydrostatics in sixpenny tracts. The Civil War marked the same turning point in America. It is more than an extraordinary coincidence that Lord Campbell's Act, the final establishment of obscene libel as a crime at Common Law, the Comstock Acts in America, and the publication of *The Origin of Species* all occurred approximately in a decade. The cluster of the dates 1857, 1859, 1868, 1872 indicates that the late Puritanism which flowered in what we call mid-Victorianism was beginning to struggle with the Frankenstein it had created.

The organization of special vice societies seemed imperative in such an acute situation. The New York Society for the Suppression of Vice was becoming a terror which made its influence felt in all parts of the Anglo-Saxon world. Over three-quarters of a century of battle had apparently worn out the old English Society for the Suppression of Vice, and removed it far from its original inspiration. A successor arose in 1885 in the National Vigilance Association. It is almost a law of their evolution that vice societies arise to deal with tangible evils and then soon turn to imaginary ones. The immediate cause for its organization was the existence of a considerable white slave traffic which disgraced London at the time.   The cause was taken up at the instigation of several ladies by the eccentric W. T. Stead, who, as the result of a number of investigations, published that never-to-be-forgotten series of articles in his *Pall Mall Gazette* entitled *The Maiden Tribute of Modern Babylon*.   The revelations were so graphic, startling, and specific that the starved Victorians devoured the editions almost before they came off the press, and "a wave of public indignation" swept London. To deal with them the Vigilance Society was organized at a great all-day meeting in St. James Hall followed by a monster demonstration in Hyde Park to which contingents from all ends of London went singing hallelujahs.   The first contribution was a five pound note from none other than His Eminence Cardinal Manning.   It was significant that now the Anglicans and the Catholics were lying down together like the lion and the lamb.   The Vice Secretary chosen was William Alexander Coote, whose exploits came to rival Comstock's.   Within three years he was leading the attack against the novels of Zola.

When Darwinism burst upon a frightened world, the fear that was most expressed was that its materialism would shake the ethical foundations of society.   Without belief in the Christian religion, men would relapse into savagery. Without a system of rewards and punishments, there could be no compelling reason for right conduct.   With the religious test of life undermined, the Victorian world set out upon a quest for a secular system of ethics, and discovered its basis naturally in sex.   With the powers of the state also limited, the family was of peculiar importance as a medium through which to bind the conscience of the individual, and the deep loyalties of the family became paramount. When a modern employer, for instance, asks an applicant for work if he is married, he is only using a test of dependability and regularity which elevates the Home as the fountain-head of the State. With the secularization of life, a special stress is placed upon the institution of marriage, and the whole sexual life becomes a matter of grave concern. The secularization of life means, too, the triumph of individualism, and sex is the centre of the individual's life forces. The evolution of the sex censorship occurred so long before the advent of Freudianism that it is a remarkable tribute to the practical genius for government which marks the Anglo-Saxon. The use of the law of criminal obscenity for the regimentation of life is an instinctive historical anticipation of the vast import of the libido. When we understand the multiple sublimations of which it is capable in all the avenues of life, we are no longer surprised that sex control has become the very crux of the political means. The sex censorship is Freudianism in action. It was accomplished by the gradual dissociation of the carnal and spiritual aspects of sex.

The old Puritan horror of lewdness and obscenities is also part of the modern sex censorship. To the extent that they are identical we are not mystified. It is often recognized as a characteristic of autocracies that they permit greater sexual laxity while they savagely curb political freedom: the brothel and vodka performed the same function in Tsarist Russia. But in a democracy, which simply means a state which is concerned with the welfare of the individual, it is natural that an attempt be made to guard against the deleterious effects of obscenity *per se*. The tendency is for an excessive pornography to be envisaged as a dangerous drug which interferes with the life of democratic citizenship.

When obscenity is so regarded, its relation to the political means is very slight. To regard it even as the very mildest excitant to unconformity, one has to imagine a citizen in the lower ranks of society who has been so debauched by obscenities that he begins to give ear to the voices of disaffection.

At first blush, the transformation of the law of criminal obscenity into a normal method for the censorship of ideas is less obvious. Its duplicity has often been observed. There is a comparative frankness and straightforwardness about a charge of sedition or blasphemy. It is true that there may be differences of opinion as to the nature of an actionable sedition or blasphemy but the political dangers of such opinions are palpable. All the absurdities of the political censor or ecclesiastical inquisitor do not leave us in the dark as to his central object. Indeed his greatest alarm arises naturally from the fact that the tendency of treasonable and irreligious doctrine is more immediately convulsive. Sex, however, is a far more subtle index of virtue. A political censor objecting to such an expression in a geography as a "union of two rivers" as treasonable in its implications appears less egregious than the secretary of a vice society who objects to a union of lips for three minutes.

Nevertheless, it is true that the sex censorship is also a new metamorphosis in the control of opinion. The very name of the crime in English law, "obscene libel," shows that it is a substitution for "seditious libel" and "blasphemous libel." It has become one of the peace-time limitations upon free speech. It happens, for instance, that in war periods the barriers of the index of sex are always relaxed, since the State grows omnipotent and the censor turns his attention to patriotism. This was as true during the Great War as during the American revolutionary period, when *Charlotte Temple* was the most popular American novel. If censorship of jazz is unknown, the reason is that music has no articulate relation to ideas. If neo-Puritanism has receded from its early antipathy for the nude in painting, it is from a gradual realization that the same is true of art. But such old Puritans as Jeremy Collier and Anthony Comstock, who appreciated obscenity *per se*, knew better. The former remarked: "Music is almost as dangerous as gunpowder," and the latter hunted *September Morns*.

THE LINE OF DEMARCATION

VERY gradually the obscenity laws have been adapted to the safeguarding of the most vital interest of modern civilization. We may speak freely upon any subject except the one in which our age is most absorbed. There is an implicit line of demarcation drawn between the type of obscenity which merely outrages the sense of shame arising from existing sexual morals, and the type which questions those sexual morals themselves. Where the injury is offered to the sense of shame, it has to be gross before action will be taken. When it is existing sexual morality that is attacked, the degree of offensiveness need often be very slight. A Shubert review may approach the limits with impunity when a *God of Vengeance* or a *Mrs. Warren's Profession* are at once suppressed. An E. M. Hull and a Marie Corelli who do not attack the established order but indeed base themselves upon its standards in their exhibitionism of sex passion are exempt, but such writers as Zola, Dreiser, and W. L. George, whose work reflects upon current morality, have been subjected to prosecution. For instance, the Secretary of the

New York Society for the Suppression of Vice publicly stated that the trouble with *The "Genius"* was that "there are very vivid descriptions of the activities of certain female delinquents who do not, apparently, suffer any ill consequence from their misconduct but, in the language of the day, 'get away with it.'" George Moore will probably never achieve a state of grace, for *Esther Waters* has actually led to the foundation of an Esther Waters Home for Girl Mothers. The works of Shelley have been haled into the Old Bailey but Byron has always lain upon drawing-room tables, even though the editor of *My Grandmother's Review* protested. A criticism of established sin tends to become criminal obscenity. That many more authors are not called to account is due to the limitations of human energy and the stupidity of authorities who do not always fully appreciate when morality is involved. A few sacrificial victims are simply chosen every now and then to remind the iconoclasts that virtue is not to be flouted with impunity. This periodic character of all censorship makes its rules merely the rules of a game, and leaves only the central reality significant.

The modern sex censorship concentrates more and more upon the creative artist. A theorist is often left unmolested where a novelist, especially if he is a realist, has to show cause. When sex is the index of virtue, it is natural for the novelist to attract the first attention. The love story is watched far more carefully than in ages when theological and political dispute was the main theme of authors. It is through the vehicle of persuasive fiction that corrupting ideas are popularized nowadays. Long ago Anthony Trollope declared: "I have always thought of myself as a preacher of sermons"; and Galsworthy has commented on one of his characters: "Like most novel readers of his generation, literature colored his view of life." Where once the great agitator moved the multitude, and the great preacher his congregation, it is the creative artist who has become the middleman through whom the revolutionary ideas of the thinkers are spread. It is he who represents philosophy in action. It is the creative artist who is the true reformer and revolutionist, however unconscious he may be of such a mission. Mill's *The Subjection of Women* had gathered dust for many a year, but no sooner had H. G. Wells published *Ann Veronica,* which sounded the keynote of English feminism, than the hue and cry was raised. Hegel was called "an obscene bird of the night," but he elicited hardly more than this epithet, while Dreiser, who swallowed Hegelianism in his youth, has been the pet of the vice societies for a generation.

THE UNDERGROUND RAILROAD

IT is easy to fall into too great a Machiavellian acuteness if the qualification is not understood that sex censorship has a direct and indirect operation. The secretaries of vice societies are not philosophers and they are quite unconscious usually of the forces which support them. But that does not gainsay their reality. Many prosecutions are inspired simply by the hysterical attitude toward sex which the standards of censorship have themselves created. When they are a manifestation only of the tendency of the times, they are comparatively benign. But more often an ulterior motive, a personal animus, a political hostility is to be found.

The adoption of the index of sex was bound to make censorship far more sinister and dishonest than under the older tests. There are certain reticences which accompany sex in savage as well as in civilized societies, however much these

may vary. An injury offered to the vital instincts of sex at
once invokes the sacred name of morality, under which all
sorts of crimes can be accomplished with convenience. The
tests of obscenity are so comfortably vague. And many a
man who will brave a charge of open atheism with impunity
will fly when the spectre of obscenity is raised. There can
hardly have been a worse infidel than Ingersoll; yet when it
was rumored that he was for the total repeal of the Comstock
laws, he resigned from the vice-presidency of the Liberal
League. A combination charge of blasphemy and obscenity
was too much for him to bear. The Anglo-Saxon who
regards an assault upon free speech with horror views with
equanimity its suppression as obscenity. Sir James Stephens
has remarked upon the difficulty of distinguishing between
simple obscenity and immorality in sexual ethics. Even
more often heterodoxy in sex matters is confused with radicalism in general. The wise radical instinctively realizes
that he must avoid the bugaboos of sex if he wishes to speak
against social and economic evils. But he discovers soon
that this is the most difficult thing in the world. The
Achilles heel of the sex censorship is so large that a hidden
motive is behind most prosecutions. It is usually radicals,
reformers, eccentrics and trouble makers of one kind or
another who are involved.

It is important to understand that sex radicalism in modern life is the best general index of radicalism in other
spheres. The man who publicly upholds birth control, the
single standard, free love, companionate marriage, easy divorce, and legitimization is a man prone to play with subversive ideas on private property, to be attracted by criminal
syndicalism, to be dubious about the House of Lords, or
about the fitness of the Republican Party to govern, and to

question the general efficacy of prayer. When such an individual is attacked under the sex censorship, it is assumed that no very great tenderness for his rights need be shown.

From the very earliest days, the sex censorship has exhibited its affinities in this way. Charles Bradlaugh, Charles Watts, Annie Besant, who were all notorious infidels or rationalists, had to stand trial for publishing Malthusian pamphlets and were the first victims of Lord Chief Justice Cockburn's revolution in the law. The fact that they all had been indicted for blasphemy not many years before this indicates neatly, moreover, the transition to the sexual index of virtue. The Comstock Laws found their first victims in such vigorous apostles of discontent as Bennett, the Woodhull sisters, Harmon and Ezra Heywood, who were the subjects of prosecution again and again. When criminal obscenity laws are invoked for dealing with intemperate denunciation of the Catholic Church, it is really religious controversy that is thus controlled. The same use has been made in America of the Postal Laws to keep anti-Catholic literature from the mails. When such action is taken a Catholic bishop or the Knights of Columbus are often discovered in the background.

The desire to dispose of a vexing radical publisher is as manifest in the repeated indictments against certain publishers now as in the repeated indictments of Vizetelly in the eighties. The social and economic radicalism of *The New Masses* and *The American Mercury* supplies the impetus behind the crusade against them as it did against *The Adult Review* in 1898, when its editor, who also kept a bookstore, sold a copy of Havelock Ellis's *The Psychology of Sex,* unmolested till then. The hardest motive to trace is the gratification of private malice, but it undoubtedly can

be seen in the *Madeleine* case. The demand for censorship
was raised by politicians who had been investigated by the
grand jury of which an officer of Harper's was a member.

The most constant ulterior use which has been made of
the obscenity laws is in the battle against birth control. This
has almost the dignity of a settled policy. It has lapsed from
its early virulence in England since the famous prosecutions
against Bradlaugh, Annie Besant, and Edward Truelove
because the law itself was amended, but it has not abated in
America, where this ulterior motive still constitutes the
greatest incubus of the Comstock Laws. The hazards of Dr.
Marie Stopes in England were mild compared to the perils
of Margaret Sanger in New York. It must be obvious that
there is nothing inherently obscene in the rational exposition
of an argument for the prevention of conception. But the
fact that sex is involved has been seized as a pretext to charge
birth control reformers with purveying obscene literature.
In one-half of the American states there are no laws against
giving contraceptive information but the same result is effected under the obscenity laws. Where there are such
combination laws a great deal could be accomplished by a
preliminary campaign to separate the provisions against obscene literature and birth control information which are
mingled in the same statute. To the Anglo-Saxon mind they
are, however, almost inseparable. The greatest obstacle is the
example of the Federal Postal Laws. The best known case
is that of Carlo Tresca, who, offending the Italian Government, found himself in the penitentiary ostensibly for publishing an "obscene" birth control advertisement of two lines!
Speaking generally the United States Federal sex censorship
is more frequently invoked against radicalism than is the

State or English censorship. Its remoteness and irresponsibility give it the greater elasticity necessary for this purpose.

THE TRANSVALUATIONS OF VIRTUE

THE index, after all, matters little. A book which is obscene is very often also seditious or irreligious. It was G. B. Shaw who once pointed out that *King Lear* constituted an obscene, seditious, and blasphemous libel all in one. Life is too complex for these elements ever to be completely isolated. Walt Whitman's democracy, for instance, is a political nuisance, his sanctification of the Life Force is irreligious, and his frankness in sex matters is obscenity. It is interesting that while the latter character has condemned him in England and America, he has recently been proscribed as an anarchist in reactionary Hungary. Conversely, not so long ago a shipment of Lenin's and Trotsky's work, *The State and the Revolution*, was seized as obscene in Boston. Birth control is blasphemy as well as obscenity; it is an attempt to undo God's command: "Increase and multiply." Hawthorne's *The Scarlet Letter* is sacrilegious in the slur which it casts upon the uprightness of the clergy, and obscene in the sexual immorality which is the clergyman's sin. If the State assumed to protect the reputation of ministers, such a book would also be treasonable. *Elmer Gantry,* its modern successor, has been condemned in Boston as obscene because of the seductions of its religious hero. A hundred years ago, it would have constituted a blasphemous and impious libel upon religion. Two hundred years ago *The President's Daughter* would have constituted a seditious libel upon the person of His Majesty if written of an English King. As it is, an attempt was made to suppress the book as obscene and the Vice Society states its regret that it could not prevent a libel on a dead statesman. Shelley's *Queen Mab* was the subject of a prosecution for blasphemy in 1842. By the end of the century, the printed copies of *The Cenci* would have been attacked.

Mutatis mutandis, the very same rules of the game of censorship have always prevailed. The Sergeant-at-Law who defended *Queen Mab* employed the *reductio ad absurdum* of the classics in the same manner as Vizetelly, except that he chose the examples of blasphemy. He pointed to the slurs upon infant Christianity which are contained in the polished sarcasms of Gibbon's *Decline and Fall of the Roman Empire,* and he asked if Milton had not let his imagination run away with him to the point where he invested the Satanic Adversary with too great nobility of soul and splendor. Now The Song of Solomon is adduced from the Bible just as the story of Job, who wished to curse God and die, was then. Always censorship has been aimed at the lower orders of society, and always directed particularly against "penny treason" and "penny blasphemy." Pitt refused to prosecute Godwin's *Political Justice* because it was published at three guineas a set, and, he said, "a three-guinea book could never do much harm among those who had not three shillings to spare." The gratification of private malice as a motive for censorship is one of the ulterior objects which has always been the same. Socrates was not attacked for corrupting the morals of youth until after he had done so for decades, and the real animus of the prosecution was political, to punish him for his resistance to Athenian politicians.

Only the fashions change. The old game of censorship continues, even at the cost of all the psychic derangements of sex which sex control imposes.

IX

THE ASTERISK AGE

In most modern countries, the only state-supported orthodoxy is a sexual orthodoxy. There is a powerful religion, or rather pseudo-religion, of sexual purity.—ALDOUS HUXLEY.

IN almost any Christian country, sporadic attacks upon eroticism have occurred, inspired by religious intolerance of sexual pleasure and sexual delight. Into the great bonfire of Savonarola were cast "many erotic books, both ancient and modern, impious books, those which tend to corrupt: Ovid, Propertius and Dante." Pope Pius V held the figures of Michelangelo's *Last Judgment* to be indecent, and proposed to cover them in the interest of modesty. In the German city of Strassburg in the year 1669 a series of erotic books was confiscated which included the *Histoire Amoureuse des Gaules,* the *Histoire du Palais Royal,* the *Parnasse Satirique,* and the *Cabinet Satirique.* In Holland at the end of the seventeenth century the rationalist Peter Bayle was cited before the Consistory of the Church at Rotterdam to explain the scandalous obscenities of his famous *Historical and Critical Dictionary.* In France in the last quarter of the eighteenth century, upon the insistence of Madame de Pompadour, the mistress of Louis XV, who had one of her periodic flirtations with virtue, Crébillon *fils* was banished from Paris for five years for writing *Le Sofa, conte moral,* but was rewarded with a government sinecure upon his return.

It was the nineteenth century that Stendhal aptly called "this moral century." It is our own which is truly the asterisk age. If its conventions have held strongest and matured earliest in Anglo-Saxon lands, they have also made their influence felt in the rest of Europe. The Anglo-Saxon can claim only priority. Although we are directly concerned only with the English and American phases, it would leave an incomplete and even distorted picture if we did not venture a little further. The inroads of the sex censorship upon the Continent are the best and most conclusive evidence of the irrelevancy of all talk of "Puritanism." It should be true as a matter of logic that, where conditions have not varied much from those in England, the sex censorship should appear upon the scene. Precisely to the extent that the secularization of life has been accomplished the reflex of literary decency should follow.

In no European country, however, has the sex censorship had quite the same quality as in England. The difference is often a subtle matter of feeling but none the less real. If the business has often been no less stupid, it has been discharged with far less hypocrisy, with greater frankness, in a spirit of obstinate realism. In Anglo-Saxon lands, the primary object of protecting sexual morals has often been disguised as horror at obscenity *per se,* but Europeans have shown less readiness to excite themselves over mere allusiveness and double meaning. A far greater grossness has to be displayed to offend delicacy. There has been a greater tendency to go into the necessities of art when an author's work has been examined at the bar of justice. The censorship is, on the whole, more adult, and there is less heard of "the young person."

It is naturally in Western Europe where autocracy fell soonest that we must look for the signs of literary decency. Of all the countries in Western Europe it was France which fought the first great battle for liberty, equality, fraternity. The French Revolution accomplished ruthlessly in a decade the reforms which in England had marked the slow progress of the years. The change was so violent and sudden that all the sanctions of orderly life seemed swept away. There followed reactions which restored the balance, but when all the turmoil was over a middle class had emerged. The anti-clericalism which was necessarily a part of the revolution called for the substitution of a secular morality, and literary decency became a guiding principle. In France it ran its course far more swiftly than in England, perhaps because of the lethargic English temperament. The immorality of French literature has now become proverbial. To an Anglo-Saxon the terms "French" and "obscene" are often almost synonymous.

THE READING OF THE ANTECHAMBER

YET the first concerted efforts against literary indecency in France were made under the Napoleonic censorship. Although it was a previous one, and largely political in complexion, the obscene was not neglected in the stresses of this post-revolutionary and godless period. The censor's office under the methodical Napoleon kept a very good record of its activities from 1810 to 1815. The first censor was Count Joseph Portalis, but he was later succeeded by M. de Pommereul, an old military man inclined to be more tolerant. The first question to be asked, said Portalis, was :*"L'ouvrage est-il obscène?"* The phrase that was constantly on his lips had to do with "the reading of the antechamber"—a phrase which is eloquent of the anxieties of all censors. One manuscript is reported shorn of *"quelques détails obscènes,"* while in another the author is commended to cast a modest veil *"sur des nudités trop révoltantes."* The veil which one ingenious writer attempted to supply consisted of writing only the first letter of each objectionable word, but this was not regarded by Count Portalis as sufficiently dense. Another romance was prohibited on the ground of immorality in that it showed the adventures of two rogues ended by a happy and prosperous marriage. *"Le roman,"* it was stated, *"n'est pas précisément obscène, mais il est au moins d'une très mauvaise moralité. C'est le vice menant à un état prospère."* M. de Pommereul confined himself more to politics. The Napoleonic censorship achieved the victory of ordering a book which bore the title *Histoire de Bonaparte* changed to *Mémoire pour servir à l'Histoire de Napoléon le Grand.*

THE CLASSICAL CASES

THE three illustrations of the consequences of French bourgeois morality which are most familiar are the cases of Gautier's *Mademoiselle de Maupin,* Flaubert's *Madame Bovary,* and Baudelaire's *Les Fleurs du Mal.* The extent of the conquests of middle-class virtue in France by 1835, when *Mademoiselle de Maupin* appeared, is described by Gautier himself in his Preface to the book, which must indeed have appeared its most offensive part, so susceptible were the times: "I remember the jokes launched before the Revolution (that of July, I mean) against the fortunate and vir-

ginal Viscount Sosthène de la Rochefoucauld, who length-
ened the skirts of the dancers of the opera, and with his own
partrician hands applied a modest plaster to the middle of
all the statues." This ridicule and baiting was not half so
bad as Gautier's direct assaults upon virtue as an ideal and
his elevation of art for art's sake. He even declared for the
establishment of a Prix Monyton not for distinction in virtue but for the person who should invent another cardinal
vice.

The censorship of *Mademoiselle de Maupin* was voluntary
and subterranean, entrusted to the conscience of every
Frenchman. By 1857, however, the æsthetic movement in
France made the authorities under the very virtuous Second
Empire lose patience, and in this one year occurred the
criminal prosecution first of *Madame Bovary* and then of
Les Fleurs du Mal. Flaubert was summoned to answer for
his *"outrage aux bonnes mœurs."* "Gentlemen," said the
public prosecutor loudly and indignantly, "did Madame
Bovary love her husband, or did she even try to love him?"
Hardly better evidence could be found that the confusion
of book morality with the morality of life is not peculiarly
"Puritan." However, the prosecution had raised a false
alarm. A more truly moral book could not be imagined, and
the fate of the adultress was so terrible that her example
could hardly have served as an encouragement. The language of the acquittal reveals the greater restraint and intelligence of the European judiciary when it has been
confronted with "indecent books":

"Whereas, the work of which Flaubert is the author is one
which has been long and carefully prepared, as a piece of literature and a study of character; the passages cited by the prosecu-

tion, though reprehensible, are few in number when compared with the extent of the whole work. . . .

"Whereas, the book does not appear, like some, to have been written for the sole purpose of satisfying sensual desires and the spirit of licence and debauch, or to bring into ridicule things deserving of general respect. . . .

"The court therefore acquits the prisoners of the charges brought against them."

Baudelaire was not quite so fortunate. *"Les Fleurs du Mal!"* The very title constituted an *"outrage aux bonnes mœurs."* Perhaps Swinburne later adopted the less committal *Poems and Ballads* in hope of escaping the fate of the master. There were some poems in *Les Fleurs du Mal* which belonged undoubtedly to an earlier Parisian Fleshly School of Poetry, for there were such lines as:

> And her belly and her breasts, these clusters of my
>   vine. . . .

and

> Thus I should like some night
> When the hour of the voluptuous strikes
> On the treasures of your body
> To crawl like a coward, noiselessly.

These lines were among those charged with being an *"outrage aux bonnes mœurs."* Baudelaire's unholy and satanic communion with Evil, his search for Beauty in the sties of sin and degradation, was too much for bourgeois morality. The arch and desperate criminal was arrested in the cemetery of Montparnasse while peaceably reading Boswell's *Johnson.* He protested that he did not "confuse ink with virtue," and declared: "Chaste as paper, sober as water, eager for devotion as a communicant, inoffensive as a martyr, I am not displeased to masquerade as a monster of debauchery, a drunkard, a blasphemer, and an assassin." In another mood, when a friend asked him if he expected an acquittal, he replied: "An acquittal! I expect reparation to my honor!" Nevertheless, he was convicted and fined three hundred francs. Later the six fragments of *Les Fleurs du Mal* to be suppressed were brought out in Brussels as *Les Épaves* ("The Left-Overs") and enjoyed a wide circulation in France.

THE NATURALISTS OF THE EIGHTIES

BRUSSELS, indeed, came to constitute a source of infection for French literature against which official prudery struggled in vain. The nearness of the Belgian border and the possession of a common language made the evasion of restriction easy. If the eighties were the period when the Vigilance Association fell upon Zola, and the whole campaign against indecent literature began in real earnest in England, the eighties also witnessed concerted efforts against the Naturalistic School in France. In this contest the celebrated Belgian publisher Kistemaeckers played the leading part. He issued the early works of Maupassant, Huysmans, Lucien Descaves, Camille Lemonnier, and George Ekhoud, which were promptly banned in France. In the end, however, Kistemaeckers was victorious. He was tried no less than eighteen times in the inferior French courts but acquitted by the juries each time. In addition he had to answer criminal charges in the Court of Cassation five times but was convicted only twice. Kistemaeckers was a man of high principle, and when Louis Desprez, author of *Autour d'un Clocher*, was charged with the customary *"outrage aux bonnes mœurs,"* the publisher refused to interpose his Belgian citizenship as a bar to the jurisdiction of the French court.   Despite a eulogistic memorandum, signed by six of the leading members of the Belgian bar, and the distribution of an *édition de luxe* to each of the judges and each member of the jury, Kistemaeckers was convicted and had to pay a heavy fine.   The fate of the author himself was as hard as that visited upon Vizetelly in England.   He was sentenced to jail for one month and fined a thousand francs. The appeal of Clemenceau, Zola, Daudet, and Goncourt for clemency proved useless.   The authorities not only refused to commute the sentence, but confined Desprez with common thieves, and shortly after his release he died of the hardships and privations he had suffered.

THE 1890's IN GERMANY

THE ravages of literary decency came latest perhaps in Germany.   That land had been too busy, for one thing, with war and unification to discharge its duty to morality.   Before Darwin, indeed, Johann Friedrich Strauss had disturbed not only Germany but all Europe, but the German people on the whole were better regimented.   The German strain was quite akin to the Anglo-Saxon, and the consort of Queen Victoria had found his royal wife most congenial.   The monarchy, although limited in many ways, was strong, and the indexes of political loyalty and religious regularity continued for a longer time to be more important than the index of sex.   But *Kultur* had so progressed by the 1890's that the importance of sexual morality became as great as *Majestätsbeleidigung* and *Gotteslästerung*.   Young Germany was inaugurating a new period of storm and stress in literature.   German Naturalism went far beyond the Eng-

lish or French. The prosecutions were, indeed, far more
numerous than those in England, but it must not be forgotten that the provocations were far greater. The German
penal law was a Section 188 of the *Staatsgesetzbuch für das
Deutsche Reich,* and it became far better known than Section 1141 has been in New York. It is interesting to note
that the German law contained the limitation that the obscenity had to be "gross" to be criminal. In view of the
fact that the literature attacked described prostitution and
sexual perversions of all sorts, the prosecutions may be said
to have been conducted with great restraint. What was
condemned was comparatively little, and the punishments
were quite mild. The learned German jurists appraised
challenged books as works of art, and vice societies played
no part. Often, however, the charge of obscenity was
mingled with that of blasphemy.

In 1890, Hermann Bahr's collection of stories, *Fin de
Siècle,* was seized by the Berlin police when it appeared in
its second edition. One part of the Berlin Landgericht dismissed the charge but it was sustained in another part in
1892 and the author was fined 150 marks. The critic Fritz
Hammer protested against "this *Fin-de-Siècle*-business and
farrago of international lust masquerading as art." In
1891, meantime, Bahr published his *Russische Reise,* which
was a series of Russian sketches, many of them almost pas-
toral, but containing among them a scene in a Russian
brothel. This was too much. The author was now in Austria and not amenable to the jurisdiction of the court, but
the learned jurists examined the book and ordered the expurgation of the brothel scene. They held the book to be
bad art, and proved it from the author's own comments.

"The *Russische Reise,*" said the court, "has no unity, no

artistic motif. The author himself declares that this did not concern him when he wrote. His object was, as he says at various points, to botanize for new sensations, to grasp them with sharpened senses, to enjoy them with practised nerves, and to record them with the first appropriate phrase which occurred to him. He did not wish in this book any more than in his previous one to spoil the pleasure of his sensations by the painful search for *'le bon mot, le mot juste'*. He simply wished to gather his sensations and to set them down with the first words of common usage which entered his mind."

In the same year, but this time in Leipzig, the police seized under Section 188 Konrad Alberti's *Die Alten und die Jungen,* Hermann Conradi's *Adam Mensch,* and Wilhelm Walloth's *Der Dämon des Neides.* All three books were published by Wilhelm Friedrich, who was courageously taking the lead in bringing out the work of Young Germany. The novels were savage social criticisms, and Conradi's *Adam Mensch* particularly raw to a nice taste, pausing at exhibiting nothing, sexual debauch, degeneration, and perversion. The latter's *Brutalitäten,* indeed, had to be published in Zurich in 1885, as no native German publisher would dare. The French formula is *"outrage aux bonnes mœurs,"* but the German is even more imposing: *"das Scham-und-Sittlichkeitsgefühl in geschlechtlicher Beziehung gröblich zu verletzen."* Conradi died before the trial, and Walloth was more than ready to leave the defense to the brilliant Alberti, who was a leader in the new realism. But the Leipzig court proved very provincial. Alberti conducted his own defense, and asked the public prosecutor Nagel if he had heard of the great dramatist Hebbel. "Hebbel, no," replied Nagel. "Have his writings appeared in Leipzig?" Alberti echoed the "No" but added: "They have erected a statue to him in

Vienna." For stating that the public prosecutor could not
be expected to understand Ovid, Alberti incurred a fine of
40 marks for contempt to begin with. In his summation,
he remarked, moreover: "Only a small number of readers
have such a finely organized sense of shame and propriety
as the Public Prosecutor; he shudders at every mention of
the word 'flesh'—but everyone cannot be expected to read
a novel from the point of view of a vegetarian." Alberti
was spared imprisonment but was sentenced to pay the maximum fine of 300 marks. It appeared from his admissions
that he had actually intended to make some money on his
book, and naturally only privy councillors in Leipzig were
allowed to make money.

If England has had its Swinburne and France its Baudelaire, Germany has had its Richard Dehmel. His is the
cause célèbre of literary decency in Germany. In the decade from 1890 to 1900 his work, the powerful cycle, *Die
Metamorphosen der Venus,* was prosecuted no less than
three times. Thus Germany treated the poet whom many
contemporaries have called the greatest since Goethe. Swinburne simply played with words of passion in intricate arrangements, Baudelaire betrayed the subconscious accents
of perversion, but in Dehmel burned a love and passion
which was deep, and vital, and terrible, and completely dis-
ingenuous. *Die Metamorphosen der Venus* realized love in
all its phases and transformations. In 1893, the first series,
Aber die Liebd, appeared in Munich under the imprint of
Eugene Albert after it had been somewhat expurgated by
the publisher by the reduction of the poem "Venus Domes-
tica" to an incomprehensible fragment. In 1894 the publisher and a bookseller were charged with attempting *"das
Scham-und-Sittlichkeitsgefühl in geschlechtlicher Bezieh-*

ung groblich zu verletzen." Against "Venus Madonna"
blasphemy was charged and against "Die Beiden Schwes-
tern" obscenity. The charges, however, were dismissed, and
the publication of Dehmel's works taken over by the Berlin
house of Schuster and Loefler. In 1896, the firm published
Weib und Welt. This time the attack was led by a Göttin-
gen student of jurisprudence who had himself poetic as-
pirations, having indeed published a book of poems the very
same year. He appeared actuated by a most unreasoning
hatred of Dehmel, but he represented, nevertheless, a strong
public sentiment. "Venus Consolatrix" and "Mit Heiligem
Geist" were the poems chosen as the basis of the prosecution which followed in Berlin. The latter poem was charged
with encouraging women to seek love without marriage, but
the court pointed out that æsthetically the poem was so obscure that it could not possibly endanger morality. "Venus
Consolatrix" was held to be both obscene and blasphemous.
The canons of art did not require such detailed description
of the nudity of women to fulfill the poet's purpose. Moreover, the Holy Virgin and Mary Magdalene were pictured as
merging with a nude woman. The poem was consequently
ordered to be expurgated. The next three years Munch-
hausen continued his agitation, this time with the help of
the magazine *Die Gegenwart,* which was hostile to Dehmel's
publisher for some other reason. In 1899 *Aber die Liebe*
was prosecuted again, this time for the poem "Venus Per-
versa," which suggested masturbation, but the complaint
was dismissed. Thus the only result of the furious six
years' campaign was the condemnation of one poem, "Venus
Consolatrix."

THE ANGLO-SAXON EMPIRE

HOWEVER influential the literature of France and Germany may be, neither country shows fully the great strides the sex censorship has made in all four corners of the globe. One has to reckon with the extent and prestige of the British Empire. It is a fundamental doctrine of British colonization and conquest that wherever an Englishman goes he takes his law with him. A zealous regard for literary decency has become such a part of the Anglo-Saxon character that it no longer seems incongruous in an Englishman. One can only stutter, however, when English prudery is imposed on Hindus and South Africans. Perhaps, after all, no importance is to be attached to climate. The English Common Law of obscene libel has crept along the Ganges stealthily and Lord Chief Justice Cockburn has been dinned into Hindu ears. The law has been applied in the furious religious controversies which have raged between Hindus and Mohammedans, under the pretext that most of the personal mythology of Vishnu and Brahma was too indecent! English judges have sat in Indian courts and forgotten that Anglo-Saxon standards are not universal, and that perhaps many a story in the King James version is no more innocent than are some found in the Hindu legends. Similarly the English obscenity laws have been invoked in South Africa against indiscreet critics who railed against miscegenation and black prostitution.

In Ireland, Australia, and Canada the obscenity laws are very severe, but as the autochthonous literature is less important than English and American and other foreign importations the customs censorship is the most vital. Ireland is even more pudibund than England, and it is even true that in certain parts of the Empire precautions are often taken against the literature of the mother country. There is frequent talk of laws either to exclude or to tax prohibitively English newspapers and magazines. An alert Irish clergyman has heard of Justice Ford's unmarried daughter, and cites the Clean Books League as an encouraging sign and portent. The pious hope is often expressed that Irish youth will be Gaelicized as soon as possible so that the language bar thus created may save them from English filth! In Australia, customs inspectors are instructed to guard against not only "indecent" but "immodest" literature, and to be guided by their experience "of what is usually considered objectionable in the household of the ordinary self-respecting citizen." There is a legal standard for you! The best organized is the Canadian customs: it has, unlike the United States customs, a permanent blacklist of prohibited books and magazines which is added to periodically. Once upon the list the book is automatically excluded. Such old favorites of the smut-hounds as *The Arabian Nights, The Yoke, Droll Stories, Three Weeks,* and *Ulysses* are excluded. Almost everything Maupassant has written is on the Canadian blacklist.

THE INTERNATIONAL GAME

In this the twentieth century the Anglo-Saxon game has, indeed, become an international game. The problem has become a world problem. All agencies of government combine to fight immoral literature. The Catholic Church everywhere now unites with the State to battle against its influence, and White Lists of books and plays go out to good Catholics as warnings against contagion. Protestant min-

isters and Jewish rabbis give vent to jeremiads from their
pulpits. The sex censorship has so entered into the subcon-
sciousness of Western civilization that it is beginning to be
almost instinctively respected. The Communist state no less
than the Capitalist state has no use for erotic literature—aiming as it does at the complete secularization of life—and it
is significant that among novelists who have been barred in
Soviet Russia are Hall Caine and Marie Corelli, whose
works are recognized at once to be at variance with the
ideology of the Revolution. Certainly communists cannot be accused of "Puritanism." The international atmosphere is thick with mutual accusation. The nations form
a virtuous circle in which each in turn points the finger at
the other. We aver patriotically that the pornography which
floods our country comes from France, and France accuses
Germany of slandering its fair name by putting Parisian
imprints upon its native smut, and Ireland accuses England
and the United States. Several years before the Great War
an International Conference for the Suppression of Obscene Publications was held in Paris under the leadership of
immoral France, speaking through the morally indefatigable Senator René Béranger, at which fourteen European
powers participated, but the amenities were unfortunately
interrupted by Armageddon. The signatories turned from
saving a few hundred of their nationalists from the deadly
blight of pornography to sacrificing them by the hundreds
of thousands to the ravages of war and the lechery of the
camp. A great deal of nonsense, indeed, has been written
of the "interest of the State in the welfare of the individual"
to protect himself against himself.

Since the War, the sex censorship has received a further
impulse. The object of the War may not have been exactly

to make the world safe for democracy but it did nevertheless contribute vastly to the destruction of old loyalties.   In
1922, the pre-War International Conference for the Suppression of Obscene Publications was revived at the instigation of Great Britain and held the next year in Geneva at
the special invitation of France but this time under the aus-
pices of the League of Nations.   Even Japan and China
were represented now, and the delegate of Uruguay expressed his gratification that the powers had succeeded in
"drawing up a convention, the very mention of which would,
a little while ago, have given rise to sarcasm and persiflage."
The only difficulty was that the participating powers could
no more agree upon what constitutes obscenity than upon
naval armaments.   It is true, for instance, that erotic literature enjoys a greater freedom in France than ever before,
and that the initiation of these international conferences may
be no more than beautiful gestures, but the country is not
entirely lost to shame.   A worthy successor to Senator Béranger has arisen in M. Deschamps.   The defection of France
is more apparent than real.   It must be remembered that
the integrity of family life is the ultimate aim of the sex censorship, and it so happens that in France the rigidity of
family control has been insisted upon even since the War.
The young person has less liberty than in other Western
countries, and it is considered the duty of the parents to
censor their children's reading.   The adult therefore does
not have to tolerate supervision of his tastes for the sake
of the minor.   At times, however, the law or public opinion
still intervenes, as, for example, a few years ago when Victor
Margueritte was expelled from the Legion of Honor for an
"outrage aux bonnes mœurs" in writing *La Garçonne,* which
was published soon after in New York as *The Bachelor*

Girl. Frank Harris's *My Life and Loves,* seized by the police in New York, was the subject of an unsuccessful prosecution a few years ago in France. The zeal shown by the French was truly remarkable, moreover, when it is considered that for them the book was in a foreign language. In France the Catholic *Index* is also very active under the administration of Abbé Bethléem. In Germany, especially, there has been since the War a revival of the campaigns of the 1890's. The limitation that a book had to be "grossly" obscene to be actionable has been specifically repealed by statute. The drawings of George Gross have furnished one of the *causes célèbres* under the new German Republic. The case shows that the ulterior use of the obscenity laws is being mastered. It was the artist's political affiliation with the Left which undoubtedly was the reason for his selection. Not long ago a wholesale raid of books as obscene was staged in Württemberg, which resulted in the seizure of many books on sex, crime and psychoanalysis. Among them were books by Stekel, a star pupil of Freud, by Havelock Ellis, and by Magnus Hirschfeld. One recalls sadly that in the old days it was in Germany that the first volume of Havelock Ellis's *Psychology of Sex* was published (and in German, too!) when Anglo-Saxon prudery made it impossible to do so in England. Only last year a "Literary-Trash-and-Mud Law" was passed in the Reichstag by a combination of Catholics, Nationalists, and Populists. This *Schund-und-Schmutzgesetz* sets up a Federal Board of Censorship which is given the power to ban the sale of any books or magazines in any store or news-stand to minors under eighteen when it finds them "muddy" or "trashy." A book requires only a majority vote for condemnation but a periodical a two-thirds vote. The Younger

Generation, under democracy, will thus be trained in purity. Even more recently bills have been proposed to bar youths and girls from art classes where painting is from models in the nude. Exception was taken officially against the reproduction of a naked Christ Child in the *Kölnische Volkszeitung*!

The Associated Press begins to bring items whose headlines tell stories familiar to Anglo-Saxon ears:

CZECHOSLOVAKIA PLANS CLEAN BOOK BILL

A bill which the government is drafting will be based upon the Geneva international agreement for the suppression of obscene works. A clause of the bill especially penalizes those who are responsible for such literature reaching boys and girls under eighteen. A commission appointed by the Minister of Education consisting of writers, publishers, booksellers and teachers will act as jury. If Commission and Minister of Education agree, the State Attorney will then have the right to suppress or censor the book.

ITALY PLANS CURB ON PRESS, STAGE, ART, MOVIES, RECORDS

Previous censorship of stage, movies and dancing to be established.

Central Pornographic Office to be included.

Publication of details of scandals to be forbidden in the newspapers.

Bringing charges under the law will be entrusted to the police aided by the National Organization for the Protection of Infancy and Motherhood.

NEW "PURITY SQUAD" OF BUDAPEST
RAIDS BOOKSTORE

Exhibition of photograph of the statue of the Venus de Milo prohibited to be displayed in shop window.

A Comstock Era begins for Europe. The old sanctuaries fail. Purity goes marching on—even against the obstacles of the Eastern and Latin temperaments.

X

TOWARD A TEST OF OBSCENITY

The precise meaning of "obscene" is, however, decidedly ambiguous.
    —The Encyclopædia Britannica.

"My Lord," said she, "are you frightened by the word 'rape'?"—Tom Jones.

"Make this dash—'tis an Aposeopesis; take the dash away and write Backside, 'tis bawdy; scratch Backside out and put Covered Way in, 'tis a metaphor."
    —Uncle Toby in Tristram Shandy.

A PRELIMINARY acquaintance with the function of the sex censorship was necessary before considering the present judicial tests of obscenity. Their vagueness will be seen to be admirably suited for dealing with every conceivable attack upon the modern social order. That they are tolerated is perhaps the best evidence that the secularization of life has been only partially accomplished. In delaying examination of the ultimate tests for determining when a book is obscene, we have only followed the normal course of events in any prosecution under the obscenity laws. The great readiness of the authorities to make a bargain of a suspended sentence for a plea of guilty, when a work of literature is haled before the bar, is one of the best indications of the looseness of the law. The circumstantial aspects of obscenity cease to be enigmas of literary decency when their value as indirect tests is understood. The fact that these tests permit the illegality of a book to be judged extrinsically by secondary factors when its intrinsic character is in doubt often avoids a great deal of embarrassment. There does come a time, however, when evasion is no longer possible, and direct tests of obscenity have to be applied. It is to these we turn our attention now.

The Victorian judges had few doubts. Their moral fervor did not permit them to make very fine distinctions. A book was obscene when it "tended to corrupt." To English and American judges the test of Lord Chief Justice Cockburn was plain enough. It was, as will be recalled, "whether the tendency of the matter charged as obscenity is to deprave and corrupt those whose minds are open to such immoral influences and into whose hands a publication of this sort may fall." Living in agitated times, it was natural for them to take alarm. A Federal judge of the Comstock era achieved the distinction of asserting that since the Fall of Man and his expulsion from the Garden of Eden all civilized men have had a universal sense of decency. He forgot that shame was the first penalty of man's disobedience. Other judges stated that any book not safe for girls in a boarding school was obscene. For the rest, the judges paraphrased one another and lost themselves in quagmires of verbiage. We have culled a few typical declarations as to the obscenity of books:

"A book is said to be *lewd* which is incited by *lust* or excites *lustful* thoughts, leading to irregular indulgence of animal desires, *lustful,* lecherous, libidinous."

"A book is *lascivious* which is *lustful,* which excites or promotes impure sexual desires."

"A book is obscene which is offensive to decency."

"A book is indecent which is unbecoming, immodest, unfit to be seen."

"A book is indecent if it tends to vitiate the public taste."

"A book is indecent if it shocks the ordinary and common sense of men as an indecency."

Such definitions remind one of the judge who was called upon to define "a reasonable doubt" to a jury in a labor injunction case. "Reasonable doubt," charged His Honor, "is a doubt that is reasonable."

THE MYSTERIES OF TAUTOLOGY

NORMALLY a judge will not resort to a dictionary for legal terms in a criminal statute. Webster is only the last resort. When the Comstock laws were adopted, however, they used the words "lewd," "lascivious," "indecent," and "obscene." The judges were at once driven into the mysteries of tautology. Did these words describe a single crime or four separate crimes? The question actually arose when one of the adjectives was inadvertently omitted from an indictment. Learned counsel argued that the words of the statute were not interchangeable, and that if a book was described as "lewd, lascivious, and obscene," omitting the "indecent," it was not criminal. There were decisions both ways.

This very year in the trial of *Replenishing Jessica,* Arthur Garfield Hays, author of *Let Freedom Ring,* made the same argument in the discharge of his professional duties. The indictment happened to omit one of the six denunciatory adjectives of the New York statute. "Do you mean to contend, Mr. Hays," asked Judge Nott, "that a book which is lewd, lascivious, filthy, indecent and obscene but not also described as disgusting is not a violation of the law?" The laity in the courtroom gaped.

The judges struggled to give each word in the statute a special signification. When one is at a loss as to the meaning of a word, the natural procedure is to take down the dictionary. The judges did so, explaining that the law used no words which an ordinary man could not look up for himself. The early obscenity decisions are especially filled with square blocks of dictionary definitions:

Lewd: Characterized by lust or *lasciviousness* or given to licentiousness; libidinous; unchaste; as lewd actions or lewd persons.

Lascivious: Having or denoting wanton desires; lustful; *lewd*; as a lascivious person; lascivious feelings or words. Tending to produce sensual pictures, as lascivious pictures or books.

Indecent: Offensive to common propriety or adjudged to be subversive to morality; offending against modesty or delicacy; unfit to be seen or heard; immodest; gross; *obscene*.

Obscene: Offensive to chasitity, delicacy or decency; expressing or presenting to the mind or view something that decency, delicacy and purity forbid to be exposed; offensive to morals; *indecent;* impure.

The multiplication of adjectives is often a sign of uneasiness.

THE HOME FOR THE FEEBLE-MINDED AS THE CLEARING HOUSE OF IDEAS

It is remarkable that the views of the Victorian judges have never been overruled. They are still accepted as the law, and are often quoted religiously, however much the practice may not accord with the preachments. The situation,

indeed, is the exact reverse of the early Victorian era. The
standards of literary decency, as we have seen, were then
tacit and voluntary and the law did not accommodate itself to the ideals of Victorianism until the beginning of that
era's dissolution. Nowadays the law still expresses Victorian standards but we strain for a larger freedom. Thus the
same discrepancy remains.

Couched as they were in the broadest possible terms, definitions of Victorian judges included every possible affront
to hysterical prudery. They were not so much definitions
as confessions of failure to provide them. A guess was
made in each case by the exercise of a sixth sense—the sense
of obscenity. The theory was that if one libidinous man
existed in an Anglo-Saxon community, then all its members
would have to submit themselves to the inhibitions of the
censorship. The very lowest common denominator was
chosen. It was not, moreover, the normally intelligent minor.
If there were one feeble-minded adult in the community,
he set the pace for all the rest. If a book contained the re-
motest allusion of an indelicate character, its pages were
forbidden to all men. Every man was his brother's keeper.

Since we still live under the Victorian judicial logic, the
basis for the selection of our boards of censorship might
well be altered. A book as soon as it is published might
be rushed to the nearest home for the feeble-minded and be
submitted to a committee of its inmates. If its contents
did not demoralize a single one of them, it might then be
released to the general public. All further complications
of theory would thereby be avoided. The test is the effect
of the subject matter upon the abnormal, and their needs
are clearer than those of the normal.

If the mere possibility that a book might fall into the

wrong hands is sufficient to condemn its circulation, then a law book or law report which contains the facts in rape and seduction cases is obscene, too. When Justice Ford looked at *Women in Love* on the library table in his home, he shuddered to think that it had fallen into the hands of his unmarried daughter. Yet, presumably, as he was a judge, he had many law books in his home, and he may well have worried over his daughter's also examining these. The same applies to medical books which contain discussions of the psychology of sex with accompanying illustrations. A clergyman's daughter who looked into his theological works might find doctrinal searchings of sin fit to make her blush. A volume of really forceful sermons might do much more.

Indeed, the fear that a book *might* fall into the wrong hands would seem to dictate that no prosecution ever be brought. As a result of the attempt to enforce the law, the book usually *does* fall into the wrong hands.

INDECENT EXPOSURE: LITERARY

In late years American judges here and there, while still rendering lip service to the blanket rule of Lord Chief Justice Cockburn, have begun to refine the test of obscenity in such a way as either to import qualifications into it, or at least to make clear the constituent elements of the crime. One of the first to sound a note of doubt was Judge Hand, who, in the *Hagar Revelly* case, felt compelled to uphold the law, but added: "I hope it is not improper for me to say that the rule as laid down, however consonant it may be with mid-Victorian morals, does not seem to me to answer to the understanding and morality of the present time as conveyed by the words 'obscene, lewd, or lascivious'."

The courts, especially in New York, have begun to apply the following tests of obscenity:

    (1)   Does the book excite or repel?
    (2)   Does the book have a moral purpose?
    (3)   Is the book true to life?
    (4)   Did the author have a praiseworthy intention?
    (5)   Is the language indecent?

The test of intent is familiar as the one upon which Lord Campbell staked his hopes. The tests of sexual excitement and moral purpose recall the definition of the modern German law: *"das Scham-und-Sittlichkeitgefühl in geschlechtlicher Beziehung zu verletzen,"* which may be translated "to offer an injury to the sense of shame and propriety in sexual morals." It will be seen, however, that the tests, which appear helpful upon first sight, upon a little analysis resolve themselves into the strangest paradoxes. When the complex of the obscenity laws can be broken up, and the isolated factors defined, matters are only made worse. If the subsequent discussion often appears not so much legal as theoretical and literary, it must be remembered that the obscenity laws operate to convert judges into literary critics. In effect men are sent to jail upon the canons of literary criticism. In the end one is driven to the disheartening conclusion that if the obscenity laws are to be maintained at all the basic theories must necessarily remain unintelligent and unintelligible.

Most of the confusion has arisen from the failure to recognize that there are two types of obscenity. As we have seen, they have always been instinctively sensed. There is:

(1) The type of obscenity which consists of the outrage of the sense of sexual shame through the exhibition of an excessive sexualism. This we have called obscenity *per se*: the induction of sexual excitement.

(2) The type of obscenity which reflects upon current sexual morality in an offensive way through the choice of theme and the treatment of character.

The first type we may call "pure" obscenity, if it is permissible to do so, and the second "thematic" obscenity. Again, the first is really a law of literary indecent exposure, the fallacy of which men of letters never tire of explaining, and the second is the crime of subverting sexual morals.

To take "pure" obscenity first, the occasion arises for the test: Does the book excite or repel? Several incongruous conceptions are to be noted. The object of the law is to prevent undue sexual excitement but it is also to prevent a shock to the sense of shame. A book may therefore contravene the law although it does not excite but repel. If, however, it repels, it is its own antidote. The same book may excite one person at one time, and another person at another time, or the same person may be both excited and repelled at different times. Again this sexual excitement may be accomplished negatively. For instance, eccentrics who have preached abstention from sexual intercourse have been held to violate the obscenity laws although they were quite in earnest and quoted Scripture for their purposes. To preach asceticism then becomes criminal. No doubt this may be done in a manner which may become sexually exciting, but this is the case where "pure" and "thematic" obscenity are one. The motive is the same as that which is operative toward birth-control agitators. The ascetic, no less than the birth controller, interferes with the interests of the State in the propagation of the species.

Liberality in the administration of the obscenity laws usually means that they have become restricted to obscenity *per se*. That this has begun to happen in New York explains in part the tribulations of the New York Society for the Suppression of Vice. On the other hand, in Boston, the inhabitants suffer from a stringent application of "thematic" obscenity. The New York judges have imported into the law, which is of the complete blanket variety, the significant qualification that a book to be obscene must tend to excite "lewd and lecherous desire"—obscenity *per se*. If a book does not excite to, but repels from, vice, it is innocent.

If the object is to prevent sexual excitement, then it is in order to ask two groups of questions:

Whom does the book excite?
(a) The child. (b) The neurotic. (c) The normal person.
To what does the book excite?
(a) To a sensual thought. (b) To onanism. (c) To sexual satisfaction.

As far as the problem is one of classes of persons, it is intolerable, of course, to think that society is to allow itself to be tyrannized by the weakest of its members. Such separate care as the child deserves we shall consider later. But as soon as the normal adult is suggested as the proper object of the law's solicitude, one comprehends at once the ju-

dicial preference for the reactions of the abnormal. To
set up the normal man as the standard is to give the whole
game away. It is well known that no censor is at all
injured by his work—even if he be a bachelor. In no prosecution for obscenity is it at all necessary to introduce evidence that man, woman, or child has been corrupted by the
challenged book. Now the precise usefulness of taking the
lowest common denominator is that it is easier to convince
the jury of the fiction that somebody might be injured when
the weak and susceptible are held before their eyes than
if the normal and self-reliant are invoked. The jurymen
might see that they themselves, the judge, the district attorney, the court stenographers, counsel and vice secretaries
were absolutely unharmed although they were wading in the
very sloughs of obscenity. The skeptical might go a step
further and inquire if there were any excuse for criminal
obscenity at all.

As far as the effect of "lewd and lecherous desire" goes,
it will hardly be pretended that we are saints who must at
all costs be saved from so much as sensual thoughts. It is
possible, of course, that the sensual impulse may lead to
onanism. Medical science, of late, has tended to the view
that its evil effects have been exaggerated. At any rate, it
is not yet a crime to fall into this indulgence. But the effect of the obscenity laws is to make it a crime to incite to
the act. There is thus presented the legal anomaly of making it a crime to incite to an act which is not itself criminal.
The same is true if the person subjected to the sensual
stimulus is driven to seek normal sexual satisfaction. In
most civilized states fornication is not a crime. Moreover,
it is not true, although it is generally assumed as an axiom,
that obscenity always leads to unlawful acts of sexual inter-

course. It is only our prurience which makes us assume that unlawful pleasures will be the consequence. An obscene book may very well lead a hesitant reader to the highly social act of marriage.

One suspects that obscenity may accomplish as much good as evil. Havelock Ellis has asserted that adults need "obscene" literature as much as children need fairy tales as relief from the oppressive force of convention.

Not long ago a great metropolitan newspaper, the New York *World,* embarking upon a campaign against inflammatory magazines, sent a reporter to interview clergymen, educators, lawyers, and doctors, who gratifyingly declared that such literature was most debauching in effect. One neurologist, however, had the temerity to wonder if, after all, the magazines did not perform a useful function of sublimation, and help to keep men faithful to their wives. His statement was quietly omitted.

There can certainly be no test for fixing the exact point at which the expression of desire becomes "lewd and lecherous." The most scientific measure we can imagine is to watch the subject's face carefully, and see if a blush or a giggle follows his reading. We are inclined to suppose a giggle is less healthy and cathartic than a blush, but perhaps neither constitutes irreparable injury. The state of our own neuroses, in which the greatest variation is to be found, determines where we would draw the line at obscenity *per se.* No two expurgators have ever been known to agree.

CONCERNING CRIMINAL SEXUALISM

WHEN it comes to the type of obscenity which endangers current sexual morality, the law in one sense proves to be certain enough. The author knows that the obscenity laws constitute a general injunction to respect virtue. In the manipulation of his characters, he is aware that he must not explicitly approve vice or denigrate virtue if he wants to remain eligible to lecture before Ladies' Clubs or to be buried in Westminster Abbey.

Beyond this there is first the difficulty that the author may not know when an act is immoral. The minor moralities as to permissible degrees of exposure of the human form depend on rapidly changing fashions. As to the major moralities, he might be more sure. What is illegal he actually knows, but often the law and morality are at variance. Adultery is clearly illegal but it may not be immoral, for example, if a man has an invalid wife. Many no doubt will say that there are moralities in life which are sanctioned in both law and morals, and these are so generally recognized that they are broken at peril. From this it would follow that there are certain situations in life which are immoral as themes, and that they are generally known.

But it is unnecessary to decide if morality is involved. The author contends that it does not necessarily follow from the fact that adultery is immoral in life that morality is violated when a fictional character commits the act. The great vice of the obscenity laws is not so much that they constitute sanctions of morality but that these sanctions of morality are indeterminable. All introductions of adultery are not considered criminal. Just when the line is passed depends in each case on indefinable circumstances. One author's adultery may be so handled as to be innocent while another's may be offensive. An affair of a President of a nation may be obscene but not so when the character is a mere banker. It is in this way that the obscenity laws operate advantageously to maintain morals as they are. A legislature would be outraged if a law were proposed to make it criminal to criticize current sexual morality "in any offensive manner." But this is precisely the effect of the obscenity laws.

If we are really in earnest, it will be far more honest for us to create the crime of "criminal sexualism." The statute might be modeled upon the analogy of the criminal syndicalism laws which appeared after the War in thirty-four American states, making it a felony to engage in the advocacy or teaching of "changes in governmental control." The convictions for mere violent speech under these laws brought innumerable protests from many lukewarm liberals who are yet quite indifferent to the obscenity laws. They might, however, change their minds if we drew a "criminal sexualism law" upon the model of any of the thirty-four criminal syndicalism laws. The crime would be to advocate or teach "changes in sexual ethics or control." Should not the ethics of sex be protected as explicitly as the ethics of property? . . . The criminal syndicalism laws are now dead letters.

The problem of "thematic" obscenity is not incapable of solution so far as legal science is concerned. If society thinks that there are certain themes which no author should touch under any provocation, it is comparatively easy to forbid any book or play which handles such themes. It may not be a good thing for either society or art, but an author will then know that he proceeds at his own risk. The treatment of *The Captive* shows that a few officials thought we were not yet ready for Lesbianism as a theme as some believed that we were not ready for homosexuality as a theme when Frank Harris published a life of Oscar Wilde. The depiction of Lesbianism and homosexuality can be forbidden till such time as we change our mind. Upon the subjects of prostitution and venereal disease there would be less agreement. Ibsen's *Ghosts* and Shaw's *Mrs. Warren's Profession* have as yet apparently established no precedents, as Gantillon's suppressed *Maya* will serve to remind us.

THE ABSENCE OF MORAL PURPOSE

THE balance of "pure" and "thematic" obscenity is supposed to be struck in terms of the test of moral purpose. Among men of letters, the test is, to put it mildly, considered Victorian. The dogma is now generally maintained as a canon of æsthetics that the writer cannot shackle himself to current morality in such a way as to make it impossible for him to create art. While his purpose may not be immoral, it may be amoral. It is agreed that we are no longer living in the days of the moral tales of Maria Edgeworth and Hannah More.

It is not our intent to venture into æsthetic disputation. The courts, however, still firmly rely upon the test of moral purpose. It is applied as a working rule in New York as well as in Massachusetts courts. In fact the late qualification of the New York courts that a book must tend to excite "lewd and lecherous desire" to be criminal is only a form of judicial neo-Puritanism. The chief difficulty of applying the test of moral purpose as a matter of law is that it squarely contradicts the test of sexual excitement. Take such a book as *Madeleine, the Autobiography of a Prostitute,* exculpated by the New York courts on the ground that it taught a moral lesson. It was said that nobody would want to lead the life the book describes. But in the course of the narrative there occur scenes of "lewd and lecherous desire" of the plainest sort. What guarantee is there that the reader will take the lesson but not be tempted to experiment? He may well read the book for the smut alone. If morality is to be inculcated, the teaching of positive precepts is to be preferred to the negative method of holding up bad examples. The test of moral purpose in effect creates two classes of writers. To the one, we say we will permit you a greater licence in treating the sexual life of your characters if you see to it that they never violate current morality, or that, if they do, a suitable retribution follows at once. To the other, we say we will not permit you the same laxity since you do not respect morality. The law can hardly be so inconsistent.

THE TEST OF TRUTH

IT is one of the disadvantages of the obscenity laws that they cannot allow the truth as an excuse. In an action for libel the defense may prove that the accusation was true. But truth is quite irrelevant as a test for obscenity. The only possible application of truth as a defense arises when it may be contended that some social object such as the exposure of vice excuses the obscenity which may be incidental to this purpose. The problem raised by *The Maiden Tribute of Modern Babylon* will be recalled. In such a case, the question would then be whether the vice did actually exist, and whether its exposure was for "good motives and justifiable ends," as is said when the truth is pleaded in libel. Such a distinction is one which ought immediately to be adopted into the obscenity laws.

If by the truth of the book truth to life is meant, then there can be no possible rule for determining this. The courts have wisely refused to deal with the problem. It is plainly silly to attempt to derive the permissible sexiness of a novel from a judgment as to the degree in which sex actually pervades life. W. L. George points out what a "true" novel would be under that dispensation: "There would be as many scenes in the bedroom as in the drawing-room, probably more, given that human beings spend more time in the former than the latter apartment." This would be akin to trying to prove that a character in fiction is "real" by offering to supply the critic with his address and telephone number. There may be in real life many persons who spend more time in the drawing-room than in the bedroom, provided that seven or eight hours' sleep a night is enough. The purposes of a work of art are too varied and life is too complicated for the truth to be anything but a very rough guide.

Moreover, a novel may be "false" to the verifiable facts of life, and yet be "true" according to a possible canon of æsthetics. "Art," as Alfred de Vigny has said, "is selected truth." The value of a work of art does not necessarily depend upon its verisimilitude. It may appeal to many precisely because it transcends the realities of life, which are to be discarded for the particular synthesis required in certain emotional states. The truth of a work of art is subjective and the greatest possible variation, to repeat, is to be discovered precisely in sexual reactions. Truth may be a law of life but it may frequently be tampered with in art. There is always the literature of escape. It may be important to consider the proper sexual ethics on the Albany Night Boat but all sorts of truth rules in the Forest of Arden.

A GILBERTIAN CRIME

SIMILARLY, the refusal of the courts to admit the author's intention has led to repeated criticism. It is a test that has a great deal of merit at first sight. Now there are only two possible methods for arriving at an author's intentions: the one is subjective, and the other objective. Proceeding subjectively means actually examining the author's motives, independently of his finished work. But is it permissible to attempt to discover these by putting him on the stand? We only can be interested in his intention, however, as it is manifested in his finished work, since it is this alone which is under attack. The criminal law (it is always to be remembered that obscenity is a crime) cannot be concerned with inner, subjective states of mind. It is the materialized, objectivized state of mind which is to be evaluated. We are not going to send a man to jail because he intended to be obscene when he did not succeed. The test of intent is not identical with spiritual sincerity. To insist upon earnestness is to be inconsistent. The law would then be admitting the truth of the frequent charge that the vice of the obscenity laws is that they are "subjective." The next step would be to call character witnesses to inquire into the author's personal life. We have it on the authority of the New York Court of Appeals that the immoral character of the author is quite immaterial. "Doctor Dodd was hanged for forgery, yet his sermons were not indecent. Oscar Wilde was convicted of personal wrongdoing and confined in Reading Gaol. It does not follow that all his plays are obscene."

Proceeding objectively, that is, to confine the inquiry to the author's works, it will soon be discovered that the test of intent for obscenity is little more than a matter of style. A book which appears to be crude, to contain sexual episodes badly delineated, to be untrue to life, may be written with the most honest intention. There are many misguided visionaries whose distortions, excesses, and inadequacies of language create the appearance of obscenity but who nevertheless have some altogether praiseworthy and ardent object of social criticism in view. It is only the acquittal of a bad book which is a triumph against the law, and which measures its efficacy. The masterpiece can always transcend the law. The master knows the tricks of style which transform the most unappetizing material into sheer delight. The most frankly amorous adventure may be so seasoned with wit and irony that however unmoral it charms and attracts. It is easy to imagine the much-maligned *Jurgen* in less competent hands. If, then, there is any good in the obscenity laws, it lies in this: they constitute a pressure for excellence of style. However, it is not comforting to reflect that we are threatening the poorer stylists with jail. The most that can be said for this is that it perhaps makes the punishment fit the crime.

ON EUPHEMISM

THE obscenity laws are only another illustration of mankind's habit of fighting its most intense battles over words. The relation of style to obscenity is fundamentally a verbal one. The man in the street, asked to define obscenity, would say that it is the use of "dirty" words. He would not stop to think further that, if such is the case, men are sent to jail for matters of taste. Does the use of bad language stamp a book as obscene?

The word is the medium of the book, and it is of the first importance to understand the limitations of language if it is desired to fix the possible harm which may result from a book. Words are merely symbols which convey meaning only to those who already have the experience which they represent. Consequently, only those who are already corrupted are subject to their influence. "The innocent," as Gilbert Cannan has aptly said, "are of all classes of persons the least in need of protection, for their innocence has no clue to the meaning of human expression. All books to them are fairy tales, as witness *Gulliver's Travels.*" A totally innocent person stumbling upon an "obscene" book needs no better protection than ignorance. A little girl, aged six, just learning to read, peered over the shoulder of her sophisticated uncle who was reading a Privately Printed Book. With great difficulty all she was able to spell out on the page was: "You——must——be——good!"

Are there words which are themselves obscene? Then the dictionary surely is. While that is not the view of the law, it is another matter where the words are transferred. There is a type of profanity which is often legally not obscenity, such as the mention of certain matters of personal hygiene described in detail in the thirteenth chapter of Rabelais. When a phrase has no sexual reference but is merely excrementitious, it is apparently privileged. Thus, a Federal court has held that the use of the expression: "Go wipe your dirty ass," is not obscenity but mere vulgarity. Even here, however, there is no hard and fast rule. Coarse language applied to the Mother of God will seem obvious obscenity to a religious judge, especially when, as is often the case, the epithets take a sexual turn. When the swearing involves unpatriotic allusions, most judges would be inclined to agree that obscenity is involved.

The safest course in any case is euphemism. The rule is to be obscene in a Nice Nelly fashion. The neuter gender is usually immune—though in German even the word for girl is neuter. There was a Federal postmaster not so long ago who objected to certain expressions in a radical magazine: "son of a bitch" and "bastard." He excluded the issue from the mails but lifted the ban next month when the editors substituted the expressions "son of a witch" and "bustard." But the best bred dowager, no more than the stable boy, cannot escape the ultimate idea. Its grossness remains even if it is put in the most delicate way. H. L. Mencken in *The American Language* has listed a great many of the euphemisms which we owe to Anglo-Saxon ingenuity. Whether we say "toilet" or "lavatory" or "water-closet," or "W. C.," we are reminded of our animal nature. Whether we say "whore," "strumpet," "courtesan," "prostitute," or "lady of joy" we recognize the woman's character. Whether we say "statutory offense" or "adultery" or refer to the Seventh Commandment, we know that the flesh has triumphed. No adult is at all deceived by the use of such phrases when they are substituted for the blunter ones. When the learned Peter Bayle was cited before the Consistory of the Church at Rotterdam for the manifold obscenities in his famous historical and critical dictionary, he published his *An Explanation Concerning Obscenities* in which he pointed out that the whole dispute was purely a grammatical one.

At best euphemism is a matter of taste and fashion. Morality is in no wise endangered or involved. Indeed, the insistence of the obscenity laws upon linguistic purity if it has any result is perhaps to put shameful conditions in a more pleasant light. There is prophylactic quality in calling a spade a spade. But a veiled obscenity stimulates the imagination of the reader to dwell upon and fix the outlines of the idea.

In the ultimate analysis, then, the obscenity laws act as literary profanity laws. The old Puritans had laws against "profane cursing and swearing." Most of these were carried over into American statute law after the Revolution, and a few are still on the books although rarely enforced. We have learned that no harm comes to us when "bitch," "bastard," and other heated expletives are *spoken*. We have still to learn that these words are no more to be dreaded when they are *written*. Apparently, we have not yet rid ourselves of the mediæval fear of the printing press as an agency of the Devil.

CONCERNING GOVERNMENT OF LAWS, NOT MEN

The impossibility of arriving at a satisfactory test of obscenity convicts the law of uncertainty. But the Devil's advocate rises to plead that there are many other laws which are uncertain, yet no reasonable man would contend that society could afford to dispense with them. The most carefully modeled statute leaves room for the personal idiosyncrasies of the judge, from indigestion to obtuseness, to intrude in the comedy of justice. After all, is not "the government of laws, not men," in Hamilton's famous phrase, only an ideal to be approximated? In the far from Utopian state in which we live there are many laws which expose the citizen to conviction for indeterminate crimes. There are, for instance, the laws against disorderly conduct, breach of the peace, reckless driving, driving in an intoxicated condition, or general drunkenness. There is also the whole problem of constitutional limitations and of bills of rights, which express only the most general principles.

Such contentions are not without force. There are many things in life which cannot be defined but which we easily recognize without much difficulty, and some of these things are the most important and profound in life. But in the first place, however uncertain are such laws as we have mentioned, there are always some objective factors which may be taken as guides. There is in a drunkenness arrest the prisoner's breath and the unsteadiness of his limbs, which may be observed from contact with him. When he is accused of reckless driving, it is possible to inquire into the turns of the road, the condition of the weather and the amount of traffic. Precisely in the degree to which subjective factors begin to enter, the uncertain law leaves much to be desired. The laws relating to breach of the peace and disorderly conduct have been made one of the bulwarks of the campaigns against troublesome radicals. The Supreme Court of the United States has held the use of the word "inclement" in a law which forbade the employment of railroad workers "in inclement weather" to be too uncertain to meet the constitutional requirements against *ex post facto* legislation. Yet it tolerates "obscene"!

We are no doctrinaires. We recognize freely that often the uncertainty of a law may be as much a charter of liberty as the opposite. A hard and fast rule often leads to the most fantastic dilemmas. The most notorious illustration is the Venetian law which, aiming at the outlawry of duelling, forbade the letting of blood in the streets of Venice, with the result that a surgeon who bled a man fallen in an apoplectic fit in the gutter exposed himself to the penalty

of the law, which was death.   There is no dogma to be maintained.   We might, for instance, be better off with prohibition laws which did not define intoxicating liquors as containing one-half of one per cent of alcohol, but only such
as were intoxicating in fact.   But even if we wanted to do
so, we could not very well define an obscenity law in terms
of one-half of one per cent of sexual kick.

A LAW WITH A CHANGING CONTENT?

No doubt an intelligent conservative could devise formulæ to give the obscenity laws a semblance of scientific
content.   It is always easy to play the sophist.   To begin
with he might say that not even their subjective uncertainty
necessarily condemns them.   Taking his cue from the con-
troversial dialectic of realism, idealism, and nominalism he
might observe that everything is "subjective" from a table
and a chair to a black cat, since they have no existence except for our own minds.   As well, then, insist upon the
subjective nature of the table, chair and black cat as upon the
subjective nature of an obscene book.   Obscenity may only
exist, as is often stated, "in the viewing mind," but that
does not gainsay the fact that a book may reawaken the
salacious images which might otherwise have slumbered in
the recesses of consciousness.   It is possible to talk myster-
iously of the "objectivization" of the subjective.   The
nexus of a civilization, holding for the members of a given
community the same emotional experiences, must condition
(within the limits of variability) the standards of literary
indecency, however perverted and indefensible these may
be.   While these are not to be defined, they are continually

operative, and impose themselves ineluctably on the average mind.

Thus, the differences of judges and juries as to the same book at the same time and as to different books at different times—the temporal and spatial aspects of obscenity in Anglo-Saxon microcosms—are converted by the mystical and magic power of words into, let us say, the relativity of obscenity. From the fact that a jury is the judge of this shifting and elusive sense (an Anglo-Saxon jury is supposed to be omnipotent and omniscient) may be derived a triumphant conclusion: a vision of a law fixed in form but with a changing content. If there is no such thing as fixed natural law (since obviously not all legal institutions agree), perhaps there is such a thing as a variable natural law which expresses a constant balance of given forces. Upon such an analogy an obscenity law appears a process of continuing legislation. This is carried on, however, not by a sovereign legislature but by a petty jury. To put it in the mildest way this is to shackle genius to the average prejudices of the times. When one speaks thus, there is a sweet reasonableness about the propositions which is almost reassuring. We are, nevertheless, in the realm of conceptual delusion. Obscenity remains still an *ex post facto* crime. The fine phrases merely conceal the ugliness, bitterness, stupidity, and confusion of judges, juries, district attorneys, moralists, and vice secretaries which go to make the myth of obscenity in action.

XI

THE CRITIC AS EXPERT

If it is deeply conceived, it cannot be immoral.
—George Meredith.

Among all the proposals made for the reform of the obscenity laws, the one urged most persistently has to do with the application of qualified literary opinion to the resolution of the dilemmas of literary decency. In other words, the still unsatisfied conservative is now pursuing yet another line of attack: Admitted that the judicial tests are poor; is it not true, however, that part of their inadequacy lies also in the very fact that they are judicial? Take the very same tests, and let them be interpreted not by judges but by literary critics and the results will always be happy. A judge and jury are not fit to pass upon an author's intention, but men of letters are equipped to make delicate distinctions. The trouble is not as much with the tests, then, as with the law, which entrusts standards of literary criticism to amateurs. Each test is not in itself satisfactory but perhaps all taken together are when left to competent hands. It is impossible to imagine the suppression of *Jurgen,* or *The "Genius"* by men of letters. A writer is not judged by a jury of his peers when he is judged by an ordinary petit jury. Thus the argument runs.

The literary critic as expert is urged upon all parties especially in times of stress. He appears the true deliverer when a book believed by most sane men to be an honest and sincere work of literature is suddenly assailed by a vice society. An appeal for a Book Jury was made, for instance, when *Jurgen* was suppressed. The services of the literary critic are usually invoked in one of three schemes: in a self-censorship in advance by a Committee of Authors and Publishers, in compulsory censorship in advance by a Committee of Authors and Publishers, and in the modification of the present rules so as to permit critics to testify as to the value of an author's work when it is at the criminal bar.

At first glance, the critic as literary expert appears to have a great deal to recommend him. It seems absurd that a work of literary art should be judged not by literary standards but by the rules of the criminal law which for the most part exclude him. Nevertheless the remedy is worse than the disease. The fact that vice societies at times have signified their entire willingness to have a board of literary men pass on manuscripts in advance should alone make us suspicious. A gift horse is to be looked very closely in the mouth even when he happens to be Pegasus.

THE ALTERNATIVE OF CENSORSHIP

INSOFAR as the admission of the literary critic as expert involves the alternative of censorship in advance, only the reactionary will welcome his entry. A voluntary Book Jury is not much better than a formal Board of Literary Censorship. It is true that previous censorship has one great virtue. We have spoken of the criminal obscenity laws as "subjective," "vague," "ambiguous," as imposing indeterminate sanctions of morality, as creating *ex post facto* crimes. The censor offers—certainty. This is, indeed, not a certainty of concepts but a certainty of immunity from prosecution—if his injunctions are obeyed. The author can no longer plead that he is not informed of the risks he takes. The hazards of punishment for subsequent crimes are removed. However much this certainty appealed to the mediæval mind it will hardly be accepted now after centuries of bitter conflict against the licensing of printing. With all their dangers and absurdities, the present criminal obscenity laws are to be preferred to such a retrogression of freedom. Liberty with danger is to be preferred to censorship with security. We have already sufficiently adverted to the neuroses of censors. No man of letters who valued the integrity of his mind would consent to act long in such a capacity. The problem of establishing boards of censorship has been called simply the problem of finding the perfect censor—he is as rare as the perfect fool. Training schools for neither as yet exist. The first censor appointed after a campaign for the creation of the office may be judicious, but his successors invariably prove to be of a progressively lower calibre. The stupidity of censors in all ages and climes has been proverbial. The examples are legion: a Russian censor once banned the Tsar's own speeches; a work by Pope Leo XIII is on the Catholic *Index Librorum Prohibitorum*; the Lord Chamberlain in England at first refused to permit the performance of Gilbert and Sullivan's *Mikado* for fear that it might offend the sensitive Japanese envoy.

THE PSEUDO-SCIENCE OF ÆSTHETICS

THE admission of the literary critic as a witness in a criminal obscenity trial involves the only proposition of the three that merits serious examination. The critic is not to act as censor but when called at the trial is to be accepted as an "expert" and asked his opinion of the challenged book as a work of literature. At present he is strictly excluded, and literary criticism can only be imported in indirect ways: if the book contains an introduction by a literary critic it will eventually reach the jury when the book is admitted in evidence. The contention is that if the judge and jury will permit themselves to be guided by the literary critic, the present miscarriages of justice will disappear. Such optimism is, however, based upon too many naïve assumptions. The inconsistencies of the position are too numerous and the compromise presented is an impossible one. The difficulties are both practical and theoretical. There are to be considered the limitations of æsthetics, the limitations of individual critics, the limitations of the legal system. It must now especially be kept in mind that we are dealing with the criminal law.

When the critic is called to the stand and declares that a book is "obscene," or "not obscene," he must be presumed to base his conclusion upon some standards. A doctor taking the stand as an expert can be examined as to the symptoms of a disease he has diagnosed in a patient. If the critic is to act as expert, he must be prepared to make similar explanations. Naturally he will rely upon the canons of æsthetics. He will ask: "Is the book 'art'?"

If æsthetics were a science, it should be able to limit the boundaries of the obscene. Its definition is of such vital moment to modern literature that one might have expected Anglo-Saxon critics especially to have devoted themselves to formulating a solution of the problem in terms of a system of æsthetics. When attempts have been made, however, they have been abject failures. It is only necessary to mention the theory of art for art's sake as the leading contribu-

tion. It is so unintelligible, that if it is interesting at all, it
is as a symptom of revolt against the rigid Victorian standards of literary decency. From the extremists who refuse
to admit any relationship between literature and life to the
more moderate critics who make some attempts to discover
the limits of the relationship is a long stretch filled with
every species of æsthetic theory.

In general, æsthetics rests upon no very secure foundation. Many a critical utterance as to the nature of "art" is
highly ingenious but not very illuminating. A judge may
have his shortcomings but generally speaking he is far less
generous in his dispensing of words than men of letters are.
To errors of critical dogma no penal servitude attaches but
upon errors of statutory interpretation may follow the loss
of life, liberty, and the pursuit of happiness. Except when
he is overcome by great moral fervor the judge as literary
critic realizes this. On the whole the canons of construction
have been kept more rigorous than the canons of æsthetics.
All æsthetic speculation leads simply into mysticism. A
great deal of it is charming and upon emotional levels affords satisfactions that may well be indispensable. Lest we
be at once accused of barbarism we hasten to say explicitly
that we are not concerned with the value of the critic, speaking as a critic, when he philosophizes on the nature of the
beaux arts. The question is simply his authority for juristic purposes.

At once the first sacrifice of consistency is perceived.
Most of the criticism of the obscenity laws has come from
rebellious men of letters. They are the ones who are constantly saying that the standards of the obscenity laws are
"subjective." They never tire of asserting that there is no
uniform sense of the "obscene," and are always asking (of

course, rhetorically) if it is so easy to recognize the "moral sense." Such cynicism is almost a standing obligation in radical literary circles. Having delivered themselves of very scathing remarks concerning "the Comstocks" and "the Sumners" and the enemies of literature at their respective corner speakeasies or tea-rooms, the critics depart for their studies, and begin to explain to their publics the nature of "art," the conditions of "significant form," and the way to recognize immediately "the æsthetic sense."

It must be obvious that art, too, is highly "subjective." For any number of judges who have defined "lewd" as "lustful," there are any number of critics who have defined "art" as the possession of "the æsthetic sense." But the "æsthetic sense" is no clearer than the "moral sense," and the test for "art" is as useless a working principle as the test for "morals."

The test of art is simply a highly organized complex composed of the tests of sincerity, truth, and intention. Of these, as criteria of crime, we have already disposed, and it is unnecessary to repeat the objections again. The appeal is simply from one mystery to another. Consider the remark of George Meredith that if a novel "is deeply conceived, it cannot be immoral." This is as helpful as W. L. George's dictum of the comparative importance in literature of the bedroom and the drawing-room which we have already quoted. Indeed, one has only to read some modern essays on the æsthetics of the obscene such as W. L. George's *The Publisher and the Policeman,* George Moore's *The Freedom of the Pen,* Grant Showerman's *Art and Decency,* Stuart P. Sherman's *Unprintable,* H. L. Mencken's *Puritanism as a Literary Force,* or John Erskine's *The Literary Discipline* to discover that the greatest variety of attitude exists among critics as well as judges.

A great deal naturally depends on the critic's position in the respective camps of "realism," "naturalism," or "romanticism." When romanticism struggled against eighteenth-century classicism, the Italian poet Monti declared that "the romantic was the cold grave of the beautiful," and similar laments are now raised over realism and naturalism. Art is eternal but artists are eternally quarreling. Æsthetics, it is true, once offered some semblance of finality, in the days when few dared dispute Aristotle's doctrine of katharsis, when the drama labored under the inflexible rule of the three unities, when the aristocratic tradition dominated art. But literary dictatorship is a thing of the past, and impressionism is the prevailing mood of modern criticism. When it comes to explaining the "obscene" and "the æsthetic sense," a modern critic has nothing more than his intuitions to go upon. The formula offered most frequently nowadays is that it is all a matter of "taste." Again we are told that the novelist may treat love and passion as "general forces in life" but the canons of æsthetics are violated when he ventures too far into their intimacies. A kiss presumably is art according to this theory but a seduction may be another matter.

Nevertheless, any number of critics may be found who are positive that they can infallibly recognize the obscene:

JOHN RUSKIN: "For the moral tendency of books, no such practical sagacity is needed to determine that. The sense to a healthy mind of being strengthened or enervated by reading is just as definite and unmistakable as the sense to a healthy body of being in fresh or foul air."

JOHN ERSKINE: "Well, if it is obscenity we war against by all

means root it out for it can be recognized at a glance, and
the reformer need not brood long upon it."

HORACE B. LIVERIGHT: "Every publisher knows the exact difference between frankness and obscenity, and functions
according to his understanding of this."

MERTON S. YEWDALE: "First of all the purpose of pure fiction is to stimulate the æsthetic sense. . . . Only people
of *innate* culture possess the æsthetic sense, for it is merely
the understanding and appreciation of the fine arts. Great
works of *art* stimulate the *æsthetic* feeling."

Each of these instances of critical dogmatism has its special irony. We have allowed Ruskin to speak for the Victorians. Whistler's suit for libel against him for calling a
nocturne of his "a pot of paint flung in the public face" may
well stand as a general warning of the difficulties of debating
"art" in the law courts. Sometime after Erskine declared
that obscenity could be "recognized at a glance," he published *The Private Life of Helen of Troy,* and one fine day
he awoke to find the front pages of the morning newspapers
filled with the story of the denunciation of the novel by
Rabbi Stephen S. Wise in a public sermon as "moral filth"
and "corruption." Liveright, who as a publisher may be
considered a practical critic, apparently knew the "exact difference between frankness and obscenity," although more
books under his imprint have been in the criminal courts in
recent years than any other publisher's. The remarks of
Yewdale are taken from a special introduction to Dreiser's
The "Genius" when it was issued in 1923, seven years after
its first suppression, and are offered thus as an explanation
to the reader to help him distinguish the innocence of an indicted book.

NOTES ON OLYMPIANS

WITH these examples we begin to pass from æsthetics in the abstract to æsthetics in the concrete. It is impossible to dwell long upon the contradictions of critical theory without entering into the contradictions of critical practice. The history of literary criticism is full of them. The changes of critical view come rapidly and unpredictably. Thackeray, who at one time declared: "Since the author of *Tom Jones* was buried, no writer of fiction among us has been permitted to depict to his utmost power a MAN," nevertheless excluded Elizabeth Barrett Browning's poem, "Lord Walter's Wife," from *The Cornhill Magazine* because of the immoral situation presented. Robert Buchanan, who thought Alfred de Vigny's *Chatterton* immoral (although the hero shows his love for Kitty Bell by giving her a present of a Bible) and caused a storm by attacking Rossetti in the famous *The Fleshly School of Poetry,* was one of the warmest defenders of Walt Whitman in England, speaking of his "ineffable goodness" and "beneficence." Swinburne, whose *Poems and Ballads* shocked England in his time, was himself shocked by Shakespeare's *Venus and Adonis* and the wasp dialogue of *The Taming of the Shrew.* On the other hand, he defended the language of Aristophanes. We need but take critical expressions upon the decency of Shakespeare to make us hesitate to grant critics ultramontane authority.

Charles Lamb thought Shakespeare would fill young hearts with "a withdrawing from all selfish and mercenary thoughts."

Emerson said: "What maiden has not found him finer than her delicacy?"

Coleridge observed: "Decency is a gift of reason and

morals, as indecency is rooted in nature and passion. Shakespeare's words are too indecent to be translated. His characters call things by their dirty names and force one to think upon particular images of physical love. His gentlefolks' talk is full of coarse allusions such as nowadays you could hear only in the meanest taverns."

The enthusiasm for the literary critic is based upon the erroneous assumption that all critics are "good" critics. From this point of view a "good" critic presumably is one who is less sensitive to morality than to art. The idea that writers as a class are immoral is one that is dear to the heart of the moral middle-class citizen. It is comforting to him to think that his virtue is exemplary. When he thinks of the boisterous Christopher Marlowe, the thieving François Villon, and the perverted Oscar Wilde, he experiences an inner glow of satisfaction. The truth is, of course, that writers as a class are no more immoral than other men. If a few immortals have been miscreant, the average man of letters has only failed to do his full duty as a taxpayer because of the slenderness of his income. It is wrong to expect him to be free of the moral taint of his times, to be entirely aloof and dispassionate.

Again literary history is overwhelming. In the sixteenth century Roger Ascham denounced the *Morte d'Arthur* as no more than "bold adultery and wilful murder," and in the next century Daniel Defoe is said to have declared in a vindication of the press: "The only objection I do not take upon me to defend is that against lewd, and obscene poetry in general (for sometimes the very great wit may make it excusable) which in my opinion will admit of but a slender apology in its defence." And this at a time when literary decency had not yet become the fashion.

Among the Victorians the greatest quantity of critical nausea was exhibited over what one of the critics called "the Ptolemaic system of sex." Some instances we have already mentioned in connection with the English circulating library censorship, but there are many others. Charles Lamb criticized the obscenity of Fletcher's *The Faithful Shepherdess* as "unfit for boys and virgins." When Shelley translated the *Cyclopes* of Euripides, which is the only extant satyr play, he softened the coarseness of the jests. Robert Hall found the moral tales of Maria Edgeworth debasing. Henry James said of Maupassant's *Bel-Ami* that it pictured "a world where every man is a cad, and every woman a harlot," and Baudelaire's *Fleurs du Mal* made him exclaim: "We are at a loss to know whether the subject pretends to appeal to our conscience or—we are going to say to our olfactories. 'Le Mal,' we exclaim, 'you do yourself too much honor. This is not evil; it is not the wrong; it is simply the nasty." Whittier threw his copy of the first edition of *Leaves of Grass* into the fire, and the same poems led Wendell Phillips to remark: "Here be all sorts of leaves except fig leaves." The whole period in this country was perhaps best summed up in the matter of fact remark of William Dean Howells: "Generally speaking people now call a spade an agricultural implement."

The objections against the literary critic as expert which are derived from the character of individual critics will, perhaps, raise some doubts. It is true, it will be said, that critics as well as the rest of men have opposed the new. One has only to recall the receptions accorded to Ibsen, to Nietzsche, to Wagner. One bright critic coined the word "Ibscenity" to express his moral disgust. Max Nordau's *Degeneration* challenged the sanity of all art. On the other hand, there have also always been more enlightened critics who did recognize originality. Most of the instances of literary prudery cited have been Victorian. On the whole are not modern men of letters freer from the preoccupations of decency?

The answer is partly in contradiction. There have been pudibund literary men since Victorianism passed away. Members of the old guard still live to uphold Victorian standards. There is a group of writers which is almost regularly quoted in the literature of the New York Society for the Suppression of Vice and of the Clean Books League: such erstwhile rebels as Hamlin Garland, Irving Bacheller, and Edwin Markham, whose respective comments upon the vileness of the modern novel have been carefully collected for this purpose. There are some unfortunate animadversions of Hendrik Willem van Loon's upon the smut of the sex magazines, concluding with the exhortation: "Smite these corrupters of our children's morals," which have been seized upon for the same purpose. The late Stuart P. Sherman is also featured, and it will be remembered that he concluded his review of The "Genius" with the observation: "And so one turns with relief from Mr. Dreiser's novel to the morning paper." Indeed, many writers refused to sign a protest against the suppression of The "Genius" even as in 1923 others refused to join in the protest against the suppression of Jurgen. Owen Wister, for instance, stated that he believed in a Book Jury. Professors Brander Matthews and Paul Elmer More thought too highly of the services of the New York Society for the Suppression of Vice to be able to sign, and Professor Linn of the University of Chicago went so far as to call Cabell "a prosperous and affected pseudo-litterateur." His self-righteousness was equaled only recently when Professor Bliss Perry, speaking at a dinner of the Watch and Ward Society, referred to George Moore as "a satyr in his seventieth year."

THE LIMITATIONS OF THE LEGAL SYSTEM

THERE still remains the intelligent and liberal critic who can perhaps be trusted. When he understands, however, the only manner in which he can function as an "expert," he will not be very eager for a call. The limitations of the legal system interpose. As at present constituted it is not adapted in any way to the adjudication of problems of literary art. When rules are applied its functional limits are made clear. At present a form of suit in which critics are often admitted as experts is found in actions for plagiarism. The dismay of the judge and jury, not to mention the members of the bar, is no less instructive than the perplexity of the critic. Given a problem of similar plots—say a Jew marries a Gentile. The critic takes out his æsthetic principles and solemnly measures the incriminated book or play to prove its source of inspiration. But all the while he must be wondering if *Abie's Irish Rose* was not much indebted to *The Merchant of Venice*.

In a criminal obscenity trial, a great many ludicrous matters may come to the fore when the critic is called to take the stand as "expert." A light-minded public prosecutor might make a great deal of the preliminary examination of the critic's qualifications for "expertness." A doctor's, an engineer's expertness is easily established. They have licences to practise which are granted after a prescribed course of training. But the State does not yet license poets, novelists, dramatists, or literary critics. If critics are to be called upon to advise the courts a great many more kinds of licences than the Poetic Licence of the wits may become necessary.

What will constitute an "expert" in literary criticism? Will it be inclusion in *Who's Who* as an "author"? Will it be the holding of an editorial or professorial position? Will the critic have had to publish a book or will a certain number of magazine articles suffice? Will the mere scribe who does reviewing for a small town daily newspaper be admitted? Will the proffered critic have to be a member of the Authors' Club or the Authors' League?

We may yet hear a public prosecutor thunder in Part I, or II, or XIV of the criminal courts as jurors and bailiffs listen agape:

"Do you believe in art for art's sake?"

"Do you mean to say you do not believe, sir, that a novel should have a moral purpose?"

"What do you mean by 'art'?"

"Have you read Aristotle's *Poetics*?"

"Have you read Schlegel's *Dramatic Criticism*?" (These last two questions might make many a modern critic nervous.)

"Do you believe in significant form, so help you Shakespeare, Goethe, and Michelangelo?"

"Are you a member of the Algonquin circle?"

"Have you ever had lunch with the prisoner?"

"Have you ever reviewed a book of his either favorably or unfavorably?"

"Have you any prejudices against his style?"

Perhaps it would be possible to establish a Literary Division of the Supreme Court which would eliminate such unseemliness—provided the very idea of the existence of such a court did not constantly provoke us to mirth. If established, however, it would very soon have sinister consequences. A Literary Division sitting in theory only to adminster the present criminal obscenity laws, which permit prosecutions only after a book is published, would set up in effect an active and self-perpetuating censorship in precisely the same fashion as the mere existence of vice societies does. The simple pressure for judicial literary business would tend in this direction. Consequently the critic will have to act as expert in the present criminal courts, and then he will inevitably do more harm than good. In the second place, he will be bound by the rules of evidence and procedure in the criminal courts.

The rules of evidence fairly require that, if the indicted author and publisher are permitted to call literary critics to testify, the public prosecutor also may have the privilege. At once the literary critic as expert proves to be such a boomerang that one wonders why all the forces of morality have not hitherto united to welcome him with open arms. The opposition must be ascribed to the moralist's deep abhorrence of the artist, and the mutual suspicion of both sides. When the secretary of a vice society is put upon the stand, a decent-minded jury can be made to feel somewhat that he is a literary spy and informer who is trying to make trouble for a reputable publisher. The cross-examination can reveal the underhand methods which vice agents use to secure a copy of the indicted book and all the other unpleasant tactics of vice hunting. But now the defense would be put in a much more difficult position. After it had called its liberal critics, the prosecution would begin to call its conservative critics, and there might appear upon the scene Professor Bliss Perry, or Professor William Lyon Phelps, or Professor Linn

who might say that the challenged book was very bad art
and detrimental to morals! Any other number of persons
of eminent academic standing might be called to testify similarly. The effect upon the jury can well be imagined. If
persons who are professors of literature in our higher institutions of learning denounce a book, it must obviously be
criminally obscene. The members of the jury, naturally impressed, would not hesitate long to bring in a verdict of
guilty.

It will be objected that the conservative critic might not
necessarily think that the book should be suppressed. But
again under the rules of evidence the critic would not be permitted to say so. In other words, he would not be able to
state his whole position. He would be permitted to explain
his conception of the book as a work of art but not to make
any recommendations as to the way it should be treated. To
state the point in legal language, that would be a conclusion
of law for the court to decide with the assistance of the jury.
When a psychiatrist is on the stand upon an issue of insanity
in a murder trial he is allowed to say that he thinks the
prisoner sane or insane but it is beyond his province for him
to add that he should or should not be hanged. Similarly the
critic would be reminded politely by the judge that he had
not been called to instruct the court as to its duty. The embarrassment which would result to the critics may be easily
illustrated. When Heywood Broun reviewed *Jurgen,* he
said the book tried to attain a "Rabelaisian flavor," and
added: "In the hands of Cabell, the joke becomes a bar-room
story refurbished for the boudoir. In such a refining process, it becomes a little nasty." What would happen if he
said the same thing upon the stand may well be imagined.
Yet surely he would not believe that the book should be sup-

pressed. The same dilemma would be experienced by H. L. Mencken if in a modern trial of Zola's work he spoke (as he does in the essay on Dreiser) of "the empty, meticulous nastiness of Zola" in *Pot-Bouille,* referring at the same time to Nietzsche's phrase "the delight to stink." The critic who thought a book bad art would be in a deplorable situation indeed. If he valued literature above the obligations of his oath, he would simply have to lie. The dishonesty of obscenity trials would thus become a burden shifted from the prosecution to the defense.

TRIAL BY EXPERT

It is unnecessary to repeat all the general objections to "trial by expert" in the law courts—the modern equivalent of wager of law and wager of battle. It is significant that the testimony of literary critics is also excluded in obscenity trials in France and Germany, where juristic standards are particularly rigorous. The judge as a literary critic certainly leaves a great deal to be desired. Shakespeare may be justified in his strictures upon the dullness of judges and Dean Swift in his animadversions on the folly of judicial determination. We do not, however, admit experts to tell a court what murder is and it is better to leave it also to struggle with obscenity. It is better that we maintain even the illusory semblance of objectivity which obtains under the present obscenity laws when the tests of sincerity, truth, and intention are excluded. The confusion would only be increased when men of letters trooped before the criminal bar to save one of their number from the fell clutches of the law. It is undoubtedly desirable that judges and juries should proceed in as civilized a manner as possible, but it is better that they get their æsthetic appreciations elsewhere than in court. Upon an argument of an appeal from the judgment of a jury, there is less to be said against counsel urging æsthetic considerations upon the members of the appellate court, for then the critic puts in no personal appearance, and his opinions are taken only as such. They are then to be regarded entirely as so much persuasive eloquence on the part of the counsel.

The fundamental incompatibility of the artist's and moralist's positions makes it idle to attempt any reconciliation. The assumption of the obscenity laws is that it is morality that is endangered, and if this is true, then it is obviously no answer to say that the ends of art are being served. It is better that art and morals continue upon two parallel lines. The point is not that a book be judged by this standard or that but that it be not judged at all. It is only when the need for censorship is admitted that there can be any question of referring to the literary critic as expert. His admission may spell an enlightened Puritanism but it is Puritanism none the less. The issue must be squarely fought until the case of either the moralist or the artist is invalidated. In the last analysis it is as irrelevant to take expert testimony upon obscenity as upon witchcraft. The adoption of any middle course will only delay the outcome of the contest.

MOBILIZING THE AUTHOR AND PUBLISHER

IN the conflict over the sex censorship of late, men of letters have with few exceptions been very indifferent champions. When the New York Society for the Suppression of Vice hailed *Jurgen* before the bar, James Branch Cabell sat quite calmly in Virginia indulging at the most in a few cynicisms.

Even Theodore Dreiser refused to be perturbed any longer when the Watch and Ward Society swore a warrant against *An American Tragedy,* and departed for a vacation in Europe. Authors apparently no longer thunder *Areopagiticas.* When they are wanted in connection with an "obscene" book trial, they are no longer within the jurisdiction. If authors are to presume to act as experts, the least that can be expected of them is a constant readiness to face the law.

Mediævalism with much greater logic imposed prime responsibility upon the author, and, as we have seen, burnt not only his books but his person. The modern author has been left so much alone that he has come to believe that ridicule is the best weapon against censorship. In this he has been encouraged both by the law and by the practices of vice secretaries and public prosecutors. When a decision is made to attack a book, the first problem is the selection of the victim. Under the law a great many persons are liable for participating in the preparation of the volume if the book is proved obscene: there are the printer, the author, the publisher, the jobber, the bookseller.

Every course possesses advantages and disadvantages. The technical legal condition must be met that the "obscene" book was distributed or held for distribution. Upon this score the printer is attacked less often than any others of the partners in crime: the seizure of Frank Harris's *My Life and Loves* at the printer's represents one of the exceptions. The author was in France, the book was not publicly sold, and such action was consequently the only one feasible. There is in addition the fact that usually the book is no longer in the printer's hands when it comes to the attention of the vice society. Thus the printer has put behind him the terrors of the days of unlicensed printing. The necessity for guilty participation also makes it possible for an officer of a publishing firm to escape when he did not personally pass upon the book and approve its publication although the firm itself is, of course, liable. Thus the president of Harper's was able to plead successfully in the *Madeleine* case that he had been in Europe when the book was accepted. As for the author, the mere writing of the "obscene" book is not a violation of the law and there has to follow some further act of participation in its production or distribution. The acceptance of royalties from the publisher is probably enough; but if the author has sold the rights of the book outright he may not be responsible at all; on this ground Maxwell Bodenheim was discharged as a defendant in the trial of *Replenishing Jessica*. Upon a balance of all the conveniences, it is the bookseller who has usually been chosen for arrest, and thus he becomes, in a sense, the critical expert in the case. The unfairness of such a course must be obvious. He has thousands of books on his shelves. Trade notices and book reviews can make him only slightly acquainted with their character. The ancient rule of the common law *"caveat emptor"* is but little protection to him. He knows not of what to beware. Under the present unknown rules of literary decency, he cannot insure himself against the penalties of the law even by reading all the volumes on his shelves. This risk, moreover, he takes for an average profit of perhaps fifty cents a volume. The jobber and the newsstand dealer are in the same position. The latter indeed has an even greater deluge of print showered upon him, his profit is only a few cents and his wares must be sold before he has time to read them. The fact that the average bookseller has very little capital makes him an easy mark. He has not the means to fight effectively.

If we are to have any obscenity laws, most reasonable men will at least agree that the bookseller should be exempted, unless his acquaintance with the contents of the book can be proved. A parallel practice has been in existence for many decades in connection with the sale of jewelry. A retailer who sells gold which is below the marked karat is criminally liable until he shows the court that he did not order the jewelry to be deceptively marked and until he can bring the manufacturer before the bar of justice. His responsibility ceases as soon as he has done so. If there is such a thing as obscenity, the bookseller should certainly be allowed similarly to transfer the guilt where it belongs.

The publisher and the author are at least fully acquainted with the nature and contents of the books they sponsor, and if it is possible for the critic to act as expert, the publisher's readers, who are critics, are in a position to do so. The publisher and author are partners in crime, if crime there is, and should bear the brunt of any attack. In contrast to the bookseller, the publisher usually represents a large aggregation of capital and has an influential place in the community. Even in the absence of a provision of law making the publisher specially liable, the practice of late has tended more in this direction. Some years ago a bookseller's clerk secured a substantial verdict against the New York Society for the Suppression of Vice in a suit for malicious prosecution following his arrest for the sale of a copy of *Mademoiselle de Maupin*. Thereafter the vice hunters changed their policy. It is easy to make a jury see the unfairness of an attack upon a bookseller's clerk, and he can bring his action for malicious prosecution without fear of reprisal. A publisher, however, cannot counterattack in this way. As soon as he brings such an action, the vice society is likely to at-

tack another book of his, and the continuous vexation and
expense prove too great a burden. It is little wonder then
that, striking a balance of all the conveniences, the vice societies tend to concentrate on the publisher.

This has been true especially in New York, where the
suit for malicious prosecution occasioned by *Mademoiselle
de Maupin* was brought. It is significant that precisely
where publishers have been most often brought into court, as
in New York, the greatest progress against the obscenity
laws has been made. The author, who is harder to reach
(he may be in London, Paris, or Peking), even though he
has not the wealth of the publisher, has the same potentiali-
ties for leadership. Where available, he should be enlisted
in the cause by indictment. Even if he may not act as expert before the bar of justice, his claims will be readily admitted at the bar of public opinion. If we increased the
burden of the author, we might have more *Areopagiticas,*
and a quicker end to censorship.

XII

AN APPEAL TO SCIENCE

All mere quarrels about the acquired meaning of what is "moral" is mere piffle. The whole issue is essentially one of genetic and abnormal psychology. Only in the field of psychology, and especially of abnormal psychology, will we ever get an adequate understanding of the sources and damnation of our sex censorship.—THEODORE SCHROEDER.

There is no need to be over-anxious about the effect a book or a play may have even upon a child.
—GOETHE.

ALTHOUGH the debate on literary decency has proceeded for centuries, it has remained strikingly inconclusive from any rigorously scientific standpoint. The chief weapons have been those of logic. Where logic has proved unavailing, resort has been had to intuitions. The disappointing truth is that, although we live in an age of science, it has furnished scant help thus far. Is it possible to measure the quantity, quality, and effects of literary influence? Can science collect the data for judging the consequences of the printed word? Can analytic methods answer the basic questions: In what ways do books stimulate you sexually? If so, what books? What is their relation to other exciters?

Until very recently these have been literary problems exclusively, and the critic has been the sole expert. We have noted the inconsistencies and dangers of his position. At

234

the start we may agree that books undoubtedly have potent influences. But to credit books with too much power is to discredit the factors of heredity and environment. It would no doubt be very flattering to any author to believe that the printed word in itself could be responsible for human acts. To accept such a hypothesis is to impose upon him too awful a responsibility. On the other hand, the mere urge to write refutes the contention that the pen is totally without might. Literature has vitality because man's picture of himself comes in part from books. It is difficult to determine precisely the respective shares of "guilt" between the two sources. There is involved the fascinating enigma of causes —remote and proximate.

Upon a few of the collateral issues science has contributed some insight. It may be that ultimately we shall come to rely upon the trained psychiatrist who is not interested in definitions at all but only in pathological mental states. When he has made sufficient progress in his investigations we may be able to appeal to him rather than to the literary critic as an expert. When we come to consider the child, behaviorism may do a great deal to rid future generations of its fears of the obscene. Meantime, psychoanalysis has at least served to illuminate the fear and compulsion neuroses of the censors. On the other side of the equation, however, is to be reckoned the fact that psychoanalysis has given much encouragement to the censors' apprehensions: it has emphasized the importance of the sex instinct to such an exaggerated extent that it would seem more imperative than ever to direct it in healthy channels, and to spare no precautions.

In every statement made in favor of suppression of books there is the assumption that no sexual excitement arises without stimulation. Medical science, however, has known for many years that the activity of the sexual organs is not dependent necessarily upon external influences. Studies have been made of the auto-activity of the sexual organs—denominated the gonadic urge. It has been shown that the periodicity of sex desire in women bears a high correlation with the menstrual periods. That natural form of birth control known as the "safe" period for women forms part of the gonadic cycle.

"This statement," to quote from the *Journal of Abnormal Psychology,* speaking of a contrary assertion, "is based upon the fallacy, exposed by recent biological studies, that the fundamental sexual stimulus comes from without the organism. The innate drive of sex is not aroused by sight of sexual objects, not even fundamentally by the contact with the external genitalia, but by the action of sexual hormones and changes (more or less rhythmically recurring) in the smooth muscle of the internal sexual apparatus. There is, therefore, a true biological need for sex activity in no way dependent upon the social environment, though often enough harmfully repressed by the latter."

GETTING DOWN TO BOOKS

SCIENCE, however, can offer no very definite conclusions upon the central problem of the effects of books when the gonadic urge is discounted. The case and questionnaire methods which are usually employed in sexual psychology have just begun to be appreciated. Some day possibly schools and colleges will apply them widely to the mysteries of literary decency. It is obviously the only way in which they can be objectivized. Even the advocates of sex censorship often realize the importance of supporting their mere conjectures with more tangible and convincing proof. But they find that they have no facts which directly connect the reading of books with "libidinous thoughts" or "sexual desires." The sole exhibit of the vice societies, the entire extent of their case proof is an affidavit by an official that a boy was once seen masturbating while reading a French joke paper. When a juvenile delinquent commits a crime, society is inclined to breathe a sigh of relief if he confesses to having read penny dreadfuls. This represents an immemorial tendency. In the mediæval trial of Gille de Rais, his ecclesiastical judges tried to get him to admit that pagan literature had inspired him to his crimes. Man has always grasped too eagerly at the comfort of any suggested cause for any unexplained effect.

The secretaries of vice societies will doubtless refer all students of this particular subject to that entertaining volume written by a presiding judge of the Court of Appeals of Rion, France—the Hon. Louis Proal: *Passion and Criminality in France—a Legal and Literary Study,* originally published in 1901 and circulated surreptitiously in the United States for more than two decades. This is a case book derived from the experiences of an active jurist. He gives examples of suicides determined by passion, and from the diaries of the dead traces the motives to literature. He delves into the records of the defendants who came before him in cases of seduction, desertion, jealousy, and adultery. Judge Proal's creed is that each writer moulds his readers in his own image. Does it follow that Pierre Loti created sailors, and Jules Verne travelers? It would be all just as simple as that if we could be sure that the famous roués of history ever read a book. But after giving the salacious details of these crimes of passion, the jurist who believed that books, more than life, are inimical to morals, listed the authors of meretricious influence—Byron, Musset, Ovid, Voltaire, Rousseau, Goethe, Plato, Molière, Paul Bourget, Petronius, Dostoievsky and even St. Augustine! It would be hard to assemble a more motley group.

But this is not the only treatise on the subject of book influence. We find innumerable reports of •opinion-evidence. The National Committee for Mental Hygiene, Inc., in 1920 published *A Consensus of Medical Opinion Upon Questions Relating to Sex Education and Venereal Disease Campaigns.* Here we find the untamed guesses of about seventy members of the Psychopathological, Genito-Urinary, and Gynecological Societies. But this report, prepared under the direction of Dr. John B. Watson and Dr. K. S. Lashley, lists no facts, only opinions. Naturally, their expert testimony on the subject of the educative effect upon the public of motion picture films was of little value to the vice crusaders because the replies were partly from doctors who favored absolute sexual continence for the unmarried of both sexes, and partly from others who indicated that continence is "rarely harmless."

Of course, we cannot overlook the serious study of book influence on patients in tuberculosis hospitals made by the Federal Government. Acting Medical Director Winthrop Adams, in October, 1927, canceled as unsuitable reading for such patients, Wells's *The Sixth Commandment*; Kemp's *Tramping on Life*; Wiggin's *The Next Age of Man*; Stephens's *Etched in Moonlight, The Yale Review,* and *Motor Age.* But the entire list, prepared by the high authority of the United States Veterans Bureau, Medical Division, offers little aid in the quest for sources of book influence.

THE WORK OF A ROCKEFELLER ENDOWMENT

FORTUNATELY at this stage of our research we began to study the work of the Bureau of Social Hygiene of New York City.

This scientific organization sent out ten thousand questionnaires to unmarried women, college graduates. The interrogatories covered twelve pages and contained two hundred and eighty-three questions. The accompanying statement adequately expressed the purpose of the study:

"For most cultured women the emotional and idealistic aspects of sex experiences are probably more prominent in consciousness than the sensory and physiological phases of it. For unmarried women this is particularly true because the whole trend of education for women stresses the suppression of physiological sex experience of any type and tends to bring about a sublimation of sex impulses so that they become expressed in forms not immediately or consciously related to sex. Nevertheless, no educated woman questions the reality of actual sex impulses, physiologically conditioned, nor their importance as the starting point and substratum for one of the most vital and fundamental realms of experience."

This study was frankly intended to apply not to the merely emotional and idealistic aspects of sex experience, but to the physiological sources of sex as they find expression in the conscious acts of unmarried women. The entire problem of what should be taught young girls on this most vital subject ought to rest upon a much more adequate knowledge than we now possess of the actual experience of normal women. The hope of the Committee was that educated women would be willing, in spite of the social taboos with which the entire topic is hedged about, to state frankly and fully just how much of a foundation of knowledge and experience with regard to the physiological aspects of sex had formed the background of their own attitudes and emotions.

The questionnaire was safeguarded so that the identity of the girls would be unknown. It included inquiries as to sources of sex information, sex instruction, sex feeling, sex experience, sex reveries, and sex problems. Masturbation, other erotic practices, and promiscuity of relationship were confessed in the answers. Several invaluable pamphlets have been published. The Journal of Social Hygiene has printed partial reports. This work, under the direction of Dr. Katherine Bement Davis, has been a painstaking quest for knowledge in a field where romance and emotion cloud the paths and where only the abnormal has been the concern of the medical profession.

The questionnaire contained two inquiries directly in line with the problem of books and obscenity:

1. "What things are most stimulating to you? Please answer as specifically as you can, e.g. certain types of men (what types); dancing, sex dramas, pictures, etc." and
2. "How and from whom did you receive the earliest information about sex matters which you can recall?"

Before analyzing the answers, it is important to understand the types of women to whom the questions were directed.

Ten thousand college and normal school graduates geographically distributed over the United States were selected at random. The ages ran from twenty to seventy. Some had attended co-educational institutions. A card was sent out asking if the recipient would co-operate. Two thousand five hundred and fifteen agreed. Of this number, a considerable group finally failed to reply for lack of time or other known or unknown reasons. Twelve hundred sets of answers were finally tabulated.

The material which we are presenting has not been indexed by the Bureau of Social Hygiene but through its courtesy and interest in the subject of this book it has permitted us to retain Miss E. M. Hubley, a former employee of the Bureau, to do this work.

The results are extremely interesting to anyone who has ever puzzled over the banning of books or the bringing up of children.

The question relating to the origins of earliest sex information shows the following results:

Source	Number in Group
Parents or Guardians	351
Children	570
Information in high school or college	27
Miscellaneous	155
No information received in childhood	7
Do not recall	35
Unanswered	55
	Total, 1200

It may be that the parents and schools are doing a better job today than during the childhood of the girls approached by the Bureau. Probably the ninety who did not recall or failed to answer were the most truthful—for it is difficult to remember the source of first information as to the actual sex act. Often it comes little by little—observation of animals, adult words overheard. To many children the information has such terrifying connotations that the facts sneak far back under deep-folded brain layers to come out later in life in curious ways.

Our main concern is with the one hundred and fifty-five who answered under the caption of miscellaneous. This subdivides as follows:

Source	Number in Group
Reading (books, pamphlets)	72
Conversation	14
Teachers, governesses, nurses	6
Servants	16
Observation (animals, boys, babies)	26
Relatives	8
Older people	13
	Total, 155

No broad general deductions can be made from such a small group, but the conclusion here is evident that reading represents only six per cent of the total sources of sex information. The gossip of other children is eight times as great an influence. Possibly the vice societies will see the humor of attacking a non-usurious six per cent. When finally we examine the seventy-two who correlate books with earliest sex information, we find listed to our interest not the banned books of Boston nor the privately printed erotica, but for the most part old friends and respectable in the publishing world:

The Bible—Old Testament, *Genesis*
The Dictionary
The Encyclopædia
Novels from Dickens to Henry James
Shakespeare
Circulars for venereal diseases

Medical books
Folder around a bottle of medicine
Eve's Daughters
Spenser's *Faerie Queene*
Mother's Magazine
Thackeray
George Eliot
Scott
What a Young Girl Should Know
Toxology
Household doctor's book
Lydia E. Pinkham advertisement
Woman
Missionary pamphlet
Motley's *Rise of the Dutch Republic*

Where is shocking Boccaccio, and *The Perfumed Garden?*
Surely these women who wrote so fully about actual sexual
practices did not modestly and dishonestly substitute the
standards of missionaries and the classics of the home for
the reputed schoolgirl smut.   Their honesty must be assumed.   Of these seventy-two girls who claimed books as
sources of sex information, nineteen mentioned the Bible
and eight the dictionary.   The Bible naturally is in the lead.
It is accessible and full of sex.   The chapters on birth, masturbation, birth control, rape, and perversions are approached
in later life with a reverential but uninquiring mind.   To a
child the intellectual curiosity as to sex dominates the mood
of religious awe.   The "begats" chase the reader to the dictionary, second on this list.   This volume, open in the schools
and the home, is usually thumb-marked at the definitions of
"prostitute," "harlot," "sodomy," "masturbate," "courtesan," and "whore"—unless the child has searched in vain
for the latter word under the letter H.

But for our purposes sources of sex information are not as important as causes of sex stimulation. Even though the above answers may create new ideas as to the basis of sex knowledge and minimize books as part of the problem, let us draw no conclusions until we examine the titles of the books which these twelve hundred women listed as creators of "sex desire."

The other question taken from the questionnaire related directly to the prevalent definition of obscenity: "What things are most stimulating sexually?" Of the twelve hundred women replying, two hundred and eighteen had no doubts—the answer was Man. To be sure, a similar problem propounded to men would probably be still more complimentary to the opposite sex. The conclusion is obvious: if we could only do away with men and women, the problem of what is obscene would disappear. This may be the only solution.

In combination with men, many women include dancing, drama, pictures, and music as the highest stimulants. Dancing alone is, for twenty-nine, the great sex stimulant, and forty designate drama. Eighteen thrill before pictures and nine find themselves most stirred by music. A great number are unable to separate any single emotional stimulus from among combinations of music, dancing, pictures, and drama. Everyone recognizes the integrity of such answers. Time, mood, state of health, light or darkness, even the biological periodicity of sex desire are inseparable ingredients of sex urge.

And where in this list of erotic stems do books come in? They are disgraced; only ninety-five out of the total twelve hundred declare for books and books alone. True, three hundred and two give books a place, but it is not an exclusive one.

We cannot close this summary without mentioning those queried thirteen who "don't know," confused no doubt by the flood of stimuli; the sad sixty-four maidens who admit to having felt no stimuli at all; and the two hundred and eighteen who fail to answer. In brief, only ten per cent credit or accuse books as being the main stimuli. In a land of no books we still cherish the hope that these ninety-five would not have gone to loveless graves. Glands functioned before printing was invented, and sex-life antedates literature.

The legal authorities, judges, juries, prosecutors, and officers of vice societies might try in vain to guess the titles of the books cited by the ninety-five as sex stimuli. To our chagrin as members of the bar we note that the law has been aiming at the wrong criminals. Schools and colleges, it seems from this research, are the main propagandists of vice. Spenser, Shakespeare, Conrad and Hardy, required reading in our institutions of learning, are among the authors cited as sexually thrilling. On the same showing the dictionary and the encyclopædia must be banned from now on. *The New York Times, The Churchman,* in fact the entire press must be censored for advertising or reviewing books by Hutchinson, McFee, Swinnerton or Galsworthy.

THE DIRECTORY OF SMUT

THE list is as follows:

Poetry	Literature of *Madame Bo-*
Leaves of Grass	*vary* type.
Simon Called Peter	*Decameron*

If Winter Comes
Mexican novel
Kreutzer Sonata
Elizabethan drama
Books—modern decadent
   type
The Sheik
Modern drama and novels
Literature from Aristophanes
   to Dante
Sons and Lovers
Together
World's Illusion
Joanna Godden

Cytherea
The "Genius"
Venus and Adonis
Old English drama
Jane Eyre
Restoration play
Many Marriages
Poetry of Middle Ages
French literature
Mademoiselle de Maupin
Song of Songs
England, My England
Introduction to *Getting Married*

Authors on the roll were:

Ellis
Walt Whitman
Boccaccio
Dreiser
Sudermann
D. H. Lawrence
Herrick
Marguerite de Navarre
Anatole France
Sherwood Anderson
E. M. Dell
Rose Macauley
Ben Hecht
McFee
Hardy
Walpole
Swinnerton
Freud

Robert Keable
Hergesheimer
W. L. George
Galsworthy
Fielding for College English
   Courses
Rabelais
Pierre Loti
Paul Bourget
Shaw
Wassermann
Floyd Dell
Hutchinson
Conrad
May Sinclair
Sheila Kaye-Smith
Mary Ware Dennett

The answers also included:

Newspaper reporting
Books about control of prostitutes
Stories of happily married people
Reports of Courts about delinquent girls
Mediæval literature
Descriptions of well-built men
Playing cards
Sex stories
Scandals in newspapers
Artistically done literature
Reading when tired
The lovers' kiss in stories

These questions and answers are not numerically large enough to lead to final conclusions. But like direction posts they stand, silent, pointing the way. It is at this place that the vice societies should begin their research. "How far was this group a cross section of American life? Was this class of girls more sophisticated than the average? Was the influence of schools and parents more pronounced? Would less wealthy girls be more vulnerable to obscenity? How can a girl give the answers without delving into the subconscious? What sexual disturbance, if any, did these books create? Did they bring joy and happiness?" There is no end to this type of musing. We might, for instance, ask whether blondes or brunettes vibrated to Conrad or Hardy. Professor William M. Marston, of the Department of Psychology of Columbia University, very recently noted a variation in emotional reaction between these two types. Perhaps Galsworthy is poison to the one, calories to the other. Hardy may excite a Swedish maiden who is unaffected by May Sinclair, the possible stimulator of an Italian.

But after ending the inquiries at any point short of exhaustion the residuum is sure and clear. In this compartment of life books are not the mainspring of early sex information nor of sex stimulation. In the second place, look at the books cited. Not a single book on the lists is now suppressed in New York State. Not even the most passionate vice crusader would dare ask to have one of them suppressed—except in Boston. Surely most of these books and authors have been read and enjoyed by the directors of the vice societies. And yet here is guilt self-confessed, if it is guilt to react normally. No prosecutor ever brought forth such candid evidence against *What Happens* or *Jurgen,* as these women do against the Bible, the dictionary and the encyclopædia.

Perhaps, however, vice societies will point to the revelations with triumph. Actually, books of sixteen out of the thirty-four authors who are listed in our Directory of Smut have been scrutinized under the obscenity laws in either New York, Boston, or England. These are Ellis, Whitman, Boccaccio, Dreiser, Sudermann, Lawrence, Marguerite de Navarre, Anderson, Hecht, Hardy, Freud, Keable, George, Rabelais, Shaw and Floyd Dell. But there is no book on whose guilt all jurisdictions have agreed. Moreover these college graduates must have read some of these volumes while under the ban. The vice secretaries must be indeed chagrined when they look at the books which have never been suppressed. Many of those formerly incriminated now have clean bills of health, and the most passionate vice crusader would not dream of touching them. The questionnaires do not permit of conclusions as to the effect of these books on these girls. We may well be thankful that they do not testify that they had been injured by the Bible, or duty would re-

quire proceedings against God's work.   The answers to the
questionnaire do, however, establish this one incontrovertible
truth upon which we have insisted all along: the whole business of suppression is futile and absurd; no one can know
which books to suppress.

The scientific work of the Bureau of Social Hygiene ought
to call a halt to the prevailing ignorant attacks on literature.
In the face of this preliminary scientific data, the vice societies should divert their energies to further search in order
to isolate those books which sexually excite.   The Bureau
has assaulted the old gossipy methods.   In the previous
utter darkness an unquestioning course was sinful but possible.   The light of science on this subject, once lit, may soon
outshine the old fires employed by vice hunters to burn up
books of science.   At any rate, it is along these lines that
vice secretaries should divert their energies.   *In any society
based on the scientific principle any law restraining knowledge should have to prove its way onto the statute books.
We must start with a presumption in favor of liberty of
thought.*   When a book is haled before the bar of justice, its
author should not be condemned upon unverified hypotheses.
His guilt should not be presumed.   It will be time enough
to invoke the majesty of the law when actual witnesses whom
the book has debauched come weeping into court, and cry
for punishment on their seducers.

XIII

CHANGING FASHIONS IN OBSCENITY

*There is scarce a principle of morality to be named
or a rule of virtue to be thought of which is not
somewhere or other slighted and condemned.*
                                                —LOCKE.

SEXUAL immorality and obscenity, as we have seen, do not
always coincide. Often, not morals but only literary im-
modesty is involved. However, the fashions in obscenity
are always predicated on prevailing sex customs. The attitude of a community toward the sex act, the subjection of
women, and the conventions of mating determine the obscene.

The present pace of change in customs is swift and fierce.
It is difficult to keep up with it, and each person has his own
standards of sin and wickedness. During periods of great
transition the moral customs alter so often that they are difficult to follow. The proof of this rapidity of variation
should create a modesty, a confession of objective uncertainty sufficient to shorten the long arm of any censor.

The controlling sex mores are laid down by the elders
just as wars are ordered by those who have long passed the
conscription age. Standards of sexual morals are imposed
by those who are beyond the age of temptation. But the
vitality of the young combats the experience of the old. The
existing mores are always under attack. The next generation shouts aloud the thoughts which the outgoing genera-

tion has only whispered or used in dreams. The relations between boys and girls change so quickly that few parents are able to remain en rapport with their own children. Dad remembers his excitement when he returned a scented handkerchief or when his fingers involuntarily touched a voluminous overflowing sleeve, or the time when he laced the uppermost part of a girl's high boot. His son has not imagination enough to translate such events into the slightest thrill. The corresponding modern memory is the feel of the corsetless waist or the glimpse of the bare knee.

Nevertheless the quantity of sex stimuli does not vary and the effects are similar though the causes may change. Sexual excitement is one of the factors of what we term moralities; and moralities are supposed to be more fixed than stars, because it simplifies life to cherish a faith in a clear and constant distinction between morality and immorality. The resulting false idea that morality never changes leads to the disastrous concept that obscenity is inflexible.

However, the world is beginning to be educated to the fact that there is no natural law of morality, particularly not in the field of sex. Whether the standards set up by society in different ages are for the better or for the worse cannot be judged by any of the species affected. The inhabitants of Mars or any other planet may be viewing with amusement our advances or retrogressions just as we, from our watch towers of civilization, can objectively see the pathetic inability of the buffalo to survive as a species or the bright prospects of development for the musk-ox. For the purpose of this discussion we can disregard the enticing problem of direction or kind of change in moralities and customs, but not the changes themselves, particularly in those mores which are the mainsprings of obscenity.

OBSCENE STYLES IN MATRIMONY

THE oft changing attitudes toward marriage, fornication, and adultery should make us proceed with caution. Hymen in our civilization arose from conflicting sources—the Jewish and the Greek. The Jews were a small race with great ambitions. The economics of their very existence dictated the command of Jehovah—"Multiply." Therefore celibacy was a disgrace, and onanism and homosexuality offenses. Fornication and adultery put limits upon licit pregnancy and were considered anti-social while polygamy was the fashion of the day. No literature consonant with these standards was considered obscene.

The Greek civilization, on the other hand, arose in small states and restricted areas, where the scarcity of food supply called for the limitation of population. Hence the sex code invited fornication and adultery and in some communities where the divine Greek culture thrived, it was a disgrace for a young man to be without a male lover. Infanticide was an established custom. The bounds of Grecian obscenity were prescribed by these practices.

Christian society, only a third of the world's population, has adopted segments of these antagonistic philosophies. Although the Christian marriage code rests on no such clear rational foundations as either the Jewish or the Greek, it evidently—save for all forms of public concubinage—is based on the Jewish tradition.

Obviously this code which society has adopted is not instinctive. Otherwise it would not have varied, unless we maintain that instincts are changeable. But marital conditions, like shame, are social not instinctive attributes of man. In Rome remarriage was deemed adulterous and a third marriage was severely punished.   This had to be the custom among a people who, believing in a physical future incarnation, envisaged the uncomfortable dilemma of a polygamous after-life.   Today the immorality of remarriage has been scrapped and the State goes so far as to recognize, and the Church to asquiesce in, the custom of divorce. Future generations may be puzzled at our present disputes over the collateral problems of grounds for legalizing what was once called adultery, just as today the concept of Athenian wives with faces covered to prevent the excitement of other males seems bizarre to us.   The men of Sparta placed their wives nude in public places to demonstrate their allure.   Yet they would be shocked at New York musical comedy producers who, after selling out their houses at $7.70 a ticket so that men may see a few nude chorus girls, now desert the Spartan methods and increase sex stimulation by covering those same legs with sheer black silks and the breasts with fake jewels.   Thus customs change in more than one direction.   It is a flow that goes forward, backward, in eddies, often redoubling over its own path.

The changing interpretations of obscenity are closely related to procreation.   We need not muse over the possible types of obscenity that may have existed in those primitive days when man's relation to childbirth was unknown.   In many regions obscenity then was a concept attached to eating, and even today there are tribes which make love in public but eat in modest loneliness.   They treat eating as we, exclusive of college boys and soldiers, do the excrementitious.   But from the Age of the Stork to the Age of Twilight Sleep a great deal has happened.

Obscenity has a different meaning since those prehistoric centuries when neither men nor women even dreamed that children resulted from coition. In those simple bygone days the mother, first feeling the thrills of a child inside her body, connected that fact with the tree, stone or flower that was seen along the roadside at the instant of procreative realization. Such blissful ignorance may have caused the fall of Adam but it assuredly limited the area of the obscene. On the other hand it took many generations of the· spread of knowledge, resisted at times by those who placed emotional comfort above truth, before scientists themselves accepted the novel theory that the female was more than a mere incident in the process of procreation. Even Gibbon, the historian, writing in 1790, was astoundingly ignorant of the existence of the ova in the human female.

The world is still fumbling with ideas of more satisfactory relationship between men and women, the crux of obscenity. Histories of prostitution show government sanctions extended to brothels, armies conquering in the name of the Almighty but assisted by *femmes de guerres,* and large religious sects established on systems antagonistic to monogamy, which if it is not the present practice, is at least the modern ideal. Even Jefferson, in his University, it is said, condoned houses of prostitution for the students. There's obscenity for you!

But in modern times variations are no less marked. A contented civilization in Africa existing for ages without even the concept of a life for women based on pre-marital virginity was recently overrun by our ideas of sex and obscenity. After clothing manufacturers covered the natives' bodies, the missionaries translated the Bible. They sought for a synonym for the word "Virgin" and were given the letters "D N U M B A." Later investigation showed that this word, in· the language of the unconverted, meant "fallen woman," thus attesting to the variety of human belief in the degree of elevation caused by sexual experience.

To be sure, no tales of former or foreign habits could or should convince us necessarily to abandon our own peculiar mores. However, the constant memory of changing moralities is an antecedent to an attitude of tolerance to obscenity. Though many situations that are called obscene in New York exist uncriticized in London or Berlin, nevertheless the obscenity of today will be the propriety of tomorrow. Distances are shortened—the printing press, the radio and the airplane give space a function which eventually may destroy altogether differences in the obscene.

VARIABLE OBSCENITY OF THE HUMAN FORM

FOR centuries men and women have bathed together nude in Japan and Russia, and in other vast portions of the world. The custom now spreads quickly. It has been estimated that one-quarter of all the world's men and women accept this, to us, most obscene fashion. In Japan a modest Emperor once decreed that both women and men must wear clothes to cover their genital organs while in bathing. His subjects continued to play around the beaches nude and then, with serious attention to the letter of the law, jumped into trunks just before going into the water. What a shockingly obscene practice! And still it is only within the last ten years that New York City has allowed women to bathe with bare legs or in one-piece bathing suits. The exposure of the knee represents one of the more perplexing of the minor moralities. A decade ago bare legs were obscene and girls wore stockings rolled down below the knees. It is still pertinent to inquire: "At just what point does the leg become obscene?" Bare knees in 1911 could be legally exhibited at bathing places but calves had to be covered by hose. In 1900 the indecency laws, closely akin to obscenity styles, would have been invoked against any female who went on the Coney Island Beach without a long skirt and long sleeves as part of her bathing apparel. There goes perhaps forever one type of obscenity. In 1906 Olga Nethersole acted in *Sappho*, which was suppressed because she was carried upstairs by a man. This in the days when ladies' skirts dragged up the dirt of the streets, and covered not only knees, but shoes. In fact, a knee today is the equivalent of an ankle of 1900, just as a bosom in Dicken's time was no more than a shoulder in 1928. Thus we see that even the obscenity of nudity has no unalterable status.

THE OBSCENE FATHERS

THE peoples of each country look to the Founders of the Nation for precept and guidance in all walks of life. Although the United States of this era has discredited the libertarianism of Jefferson, the eminent Fathers are still quoted with national pride—and to their revolutionary utterances the new interpretations of this century are imparted. Although Jefferson's speeches in support of the people's right to preach revolution has been perverted into a plea for censorship, no such deviation from the Fathers' notion of obscenity can be distorted from an examination of their literary preferences. Here no confusion can develop.

Most of the men who framed our Constitution were lovers of what today is deemed obscenity. The diaries and historical documents of that time record high praise for the favorite authors of our early patriots. Smollett, Fielding, Sterne were the popular writers. All of the early Presidents enjoyed the frankness and vulgarity of fleshly novels, and James Kent, a stern soul, in 1796 wrote: "No writer that ever lived was superior to Fielding. He was a man of wonderful talents and immutable humor. I now own all his works." This is the Kent who, as Chancellor of New York, helped establish the crime of blasphemy in America, the land of religious equalities.

On the other hand, in these days of obscenity hunting our parks and playgrounds are filled with Maypole parties, but none other than Alexander Hamilton, a man singularly noted for his sexual derelictions, protested against the Maypole in America, giving a vivid description of the phallic obscenity of the festival. Now this custom appears obscene to no one. And if we want further evidence of our sexual purification we might look through the writings of the heroes of our Revolution, and fail to find any protest against the delightful old New England practice of "bundling," a sexual game played by fully clothed men and women in bed, but excused on the basis of a perpetual coal shortage.

Obviously the vice societies have a dire choice between patriotism and obscenity. Only by disowning Washington and his associates can they arrive at the new codes of obscenity. They must discredit the signers of the Declaration of Independence for these worldly patriots enjoyed their obscenity.

PROXIMITY OF IMMORAL OBSCENITY

AMPLE illustrations of variety in obscenity between different nations might be given but it is obvious that we in

America have our own aims distinct and apart from the habits even of the British. In France prostitutes walk the streets of all the big cities while respectable maidens go out of evenings only if chaperoned. In New York the streets are clean of so-called street walkers and daughters of all classes go to vaudeville and burlesque shows unattended. England has legalized the spread of contraception and a member of Parliament has boasted that the English birth rate is decreasing. And still it is very doubtful if the extent of virginity, adultery or promiscuity varies much in any of these countries.

But we are no longer so sure of ourselves. Foreign thought seeps through and has the enchantment of distance. We can play with obscenity in foreign forms without the same fear of infection. Lowell in his *Bigelow Papers* wrote:

> "I du believe in Freedoms Cause
> Ez fur away as Paris is."

For this reason, many of us nowadays are willing to tolerate the experiment in Russia. On this theory, a moving picture of beautiful sunburnt nude women playing on the beach of Southern islands, as in *Moana,* can legally be exhibited, whereas similar poses of our heroines of Hollywood would shock the most fastidious. In like manner the protest against the obscene language of our doughboys as depicted in *What Price Glory* would have created no alarm if the actors had dressed as Mexicans or Nicaraguans. A "son of a bitch" sounds different uttered by a Haitian than by a U. S. Marine.

EVEN if we admit the instability of sexual standards we may nevertheless believe that the present customs are better suited to our environment than any practices of other lands or bygone ages. At the same time a belief in constant flux prevents the establishment of ironbound unmoving laws and court decisions. If society's point of view toward sex and obscenity changes, what becomes of those legal injunctions which sent to destruction the poems of Walt Whitman? What of the court mandates against books once thought obscene but now accepted in politest society? The decisions must be reversed or the injunctions nullified. Neither course portends good to the majesty of the law. Courts, the handmaidens of hidebound procedure, should have no place in the fields of intellect. Legal institutions are not suited to changing standards of obscenity. Our judicial system cannot appreciate rapidly enough the significance of changing customs. If our courts were to accept their full responsibility in such matters would they not have to retry each spring all books banned in previous years? Otherwise public opinion must hold in contempt the outworn verdicts of former suppressions.

The newspapers provide a record of contemporary changes in the obscene. Imagine the following colloquy in court. In 1924, the judge addressing a convicted publisher: "I shall send you to the workhouse for ninety days. To mention Lesbianism in a two-penny sheet is to poison the public mind. The home, the foundation of our society, will be destroyed by the spread of such disgusting ideas."

And still in 1928, March 7th, to be precise, *The Daily*

News in New York City ran a picture of a girl in boy's costume with a caption reading:

VELMA WEST IN MALE ATTIRE. This is one of the photos the state had planned to use to prove that Mrs. West slew her husband to prevent him from coming between her and a woman.

In 1927 a jury was shocked by the term "masturbation" in a novel by John Herrman. We predict that the newspapers will use this word before 1930 and will even abandon "bloodlust," employed by the New York *Evening Post* in 1927 as a synonym for sadism. In 1927 the New York *World,* arch instigator of vice societies in their campaign for suppression of art magazines, published, not as part of its moral editorials, a front page story detailing the pride of a husbandless mother. Mere reporting was not enough, the story was commendatory of unmarried parenthood. In 1925 the same paper would have editorialized against such obscenity in newspapers. In Ohio, in 1924, the O. Henry parrot was banned for shrieking, "Give her Hell, Dickey," and in New York, in the same year, it was illegal to quote a child as saying about a spanking: "This hurts you more than it hurts me, but not in the same place." In 1928 no censor would call this obscene.

The courts have allowed the press in Georgia, for example, to report the bloody details of the rape of virgins, and as far back as the Thaw trial a dignified socially minded paper like the New York *Sun* omitted no minutiae of Evelyn's rape or Harry's sadism. And still, less than fifty years ago there was public protest at the newspaper stories detailing the use of the first bathtub—the obscene invention of the middle nineteenth century. In those days the press called a leg a "limb," the only gentlemanly method of describing that part of the body between the ankle and the knee—everything above the knee being non-existent.

The sex standards which create the forbidden also create the obscene. The standards change in type and mood. But destroy one and another takes its place. The variability of public taste can be traced over millenia, centuries, and decades. Within the span of months or single years we shed our old obscenities and cast about for new subjects which will invite *"schmutziges Gelächter"* and "hectic blushes." Any eighteen-year-old girl can trace in her own lifetime definite changes in the fashions of obscenity. As an illustration of this point Rockwell Kent the artist tells a delightful tale. In 1917 he drew for *Vanity Fair,* an ingenious and uninhibited periodical, a picture of an attic scene. The original drawing showed a lady standing nude in a tub, her back toward the reader, with a towel partly covering the buttocks. The owner of *Vanity Fair,* correctly interpreting the mores of sophisticated New York in 1917, was afraid of the obscenity of hidden buttocks and insisted the lady be clothed. Kent brought out a corset, a pair of bloomers, and high laced boots, and thus draped the objectionable parts of the anatomy. The emended picture was printed. In 1924 the editor came across the unpurified version of the drawing. He decided to run it, forgetting the earlier fashion of the obscene. The public meanwhile had changed its attitude toward ladies' rears. The nude maiden, with buttocks partly shielded by the towel, appears unashamed in the issue of May, 1924. Thus in less than seven years the public taste had so varied that a sensitive editor like Mr. Crowninshield could change the standards of the same magazine, published in the same city, distributed to the same type of readers.

This story does more than indicate a public change. It stands as a healthy compliment to a rare ability to interpret and adopt the new in art and morality. In spite of the historical, incontrovertible evidence of rapid change few publishers dare carry out society's new attitudes. The old moralities are still taught by literature and history, because it takes so long to get modernity into books.

That man changes his opinions on obscenity is consistent with all other phases of public development. Joan of Arc was burned for blasphemy in 1431, rehabilitated by the Church in 1456, declared blessed in 1908 and canonized in 1920. Our modern attitude toward sex changes with even greater rapidity.

To discard the ideals and ideas of our day is trying. To admit change to creep in is painful. The acceptance of anything new means the relegation of the old. Society hates the new because cohesion comes from adhering to set and established formulæ. But the pace of this period is increasing and books themselves have indelibly determined for our civilization that obscenity merely means those momentary passing sex fashions, not moralities, which are set up for the sport of being pulled down.

XIV

PORNOGRAPHY AND THE CHILD

Let it alone, 'tis a book of my young days, never intended for yours.—MONTESQUIEU to his daughter.

At the root lies always the desire to maintain morals as they are, and this is shown by the invariable cry that the incriminated book or picture is a danger to the young which conveys the fear that the young will grow up.—W. L. GEORGE.

THE patient reader at this point may no doubt be thinking: You have been writing about obscenity laws but how about the disgusting picture post cards? You have been talking loftily of Literature but how about *A Night in a Turkish Harem, Behind the Curtains of a Female Seminary,* and *Fanny Hill?* Seriously, you really do not intend to sweep away all the safeguards of the obscenity laws, and leave nothing in their place? You may have convinced us that they are confusion worse confounded—but it is perhaps better to struggle along with them than to let down the bars entirely. Certainly you are not so lost to every sense of moral responsibility that you will, for instance, subject schoolchildren to the vilest filth? If you cannot give us some hint at a possible way out of such a dilemma, you have not been very constructive. Is there no distinction between obscenity and pornography? Is there no possibility of writing a new law to take the place of the present absurd one?

Even though history does not indicate that Hercules was called upon to fill up the Augean stables which he had emptied, a search for a cure is always in order. These questions are not only pertinent but they raise most perplexing problems which can be answered only after examining additional facts.

"THE BUSINESS OF SMUT"

IT is true that in large urban centres there is a traffic in dirty post cards and cheap prints of sexual or homosexual material. The pictures are sold for as little as five cents but the market usually supports prices ranging from a quarter to a dollar. It is not unlikely that our censorship laws create the motive for engaging in the sale of this smut. They make it profitable. In the absence of a ban the price of dirty postal cards would have to recede from three for a dollar to three for a nickel. The present risk of prosecution is insured against by increased gross profits. This economic price determinant is in accord with the market fluctuations of illegal liquor, aigrette plumes, or limited editions of sophisticated erotica. The removal of all barriers might conceivably reduce the cost of the pictures to the price of ordinary post cards, thus wiping out that wide margin of profit which always accompanies the distribution of any commodity of taboo. This phase of the situation is of particular importance, as the purveyors of the dirt are not prophets of perversion but merely merchants for profit. The vendors are soda-water dispensers, barbers, news dealers, or clerks in men's shops. Small stationery stores in the neighborhood of schools have been found to be violators of the laws. The publishers of the material are said by the vice societies to be normal business men dealing in smut instead of ships or sealing wax. We had expected to learn that the responsible producers of this vile material were low perverts, but the

affable Secretary of the New York Vice Society assures us that they are quite normal.

Much of the material is little more than reprints of newspaper scandals furtively sold in blind covers. If found in the tabloids many of these composite pictures would pass by with little comment. Moreover, the material itself varies greatly at any one time and particularly from season to season. The fashions change. *September Morn, Paul and Virginia,* and reproductions of old masters still hanging in art museums formerly fetched fancy prices. They were the vile pornography of the schoolboys of a decade ago. Today the girls behold them without a tremor. At present the vogue includes alleged photos of nude women snugly slumbering in crescent moons, partially robed ladies about to enter the bath, the modern versions of Susanna and the Elders, and great quantities of post cards of the same poses as those used in nickelodeon slot machines in all large cities. In addition there are some pictures of a homosexual or Lesbian character. Probably some traffic in photographs of persons in the sexual act itself continues.

Up to 1924 during a half century of its existence the New York Vice Society "confiscated" on an average nearly 65,000 obscene pictures and post cards a year. The total number of cards and pictures in fifty years was three million. It is impossible to examine the standard of obscenity maintained in this era of confiscation. But these pictures included poses of the sort now adorning our theatre entrances and covers of art magazines. The manufactured pictures in the Sunday magazine section of the New York *World* make many of them seem prim and polite in comparison.

In 1923 New York City went pure. The number of such pictures dropped to 907, which is less than one card for each

10,000 readers in the City district. In the following two years the New York Society did a better job for the figures jumped to 13,757 and 12,943 respectively, dropping in 1926 to 7965, and again dropping to an insignificant 3440 in 1927. This included a variety of poses. There is no way of explaining these tides except that since 1922 the New York Society has been more concerned with crusades against slot machines, stag shows, letter pests, night clubs, contraception, racing dope sheets, revues, and the infamous punch card devices. Such activity, which is strictly not the business of the Society and may well be a violation of its charter, may indicate that so little pornography is now on the market that to occupy itself with this alone would leave its agents comparatively idle. It is also possible that the mere threat of the existence of the office on 22nd Street has caused many a peddler to enjoy his own cards without the risk occasioned by "offering for sale."

Such picture cards are known to all male adults, and the rising feminism has brought in women as part of the purchasing public in this traffic. Practically every man, and particularly the crusaders against vice, can recall seeing one or more of these disgusting pictures. In spite of statutes, police, prosecutors, and the large funds of the vice societies the pictures were bandied about in our youth, much as they are today. Nevertheless, that the authorities fail to apprehend every violator of a crime is in itself no reason for the recision of the law.

WOMEN, THE POOR, AND NEGROES

THE layman, perhaps, may not understand that a great deal of the difficulty would be removed if the Law of Persons were extended to the administration of the obscenity laws. When a jurist speaks of the Law of Persons, he has reference to the relaxations and modifications of the general rules of the law so as to recognize the existence of classes of persons according to age, sex, or other conditions. One of the great myths of the law is that all men are equal before it. The fact is that every legal system which presumes to be civilized and intelligent recognizes that it must artificially remove a great many natural inequalities before legal equality begins. The most familiar example is the status of children and minors acknowledged by many special laws. The cry for censorship laws has always been to protect others: the weak, the lowly, the women, the children. No one has ever urged a strict law against obscenity with the statement: "Please pass this statute to protect *me* from this sexually abhorrent material."

It follows that conceit and a feeling of superiority are ingredients of a censor's make-up. He, above pollution, fears for his fellow men. Most censors of intellectual thought possess a cunning which hides sensual emotions beneath a thin veneer of modesty. It is rare that a censor has shown his hand as clearly as did Mary Boyce Temple, a valued presiding officer of the Daughters of the American Revolution, at Knoxville, Tennessee. She is quoted as saying of *Rain,* by Somerset Maugham, at a meeting of equally superior women:

"We do not fear the effect which such a play would have on us. We of the D. A. R. and the United Daughters of the Confederacy have had the advantages of education and travel and have been prepared for such things. Such a play would not injure us; it would only disgust us. But there are other women who have not had these advantages, and there are the young peo-

ple who are inexperienced in the problems of life. It is for their
benefit and protection that we seek to prevent the showing of
such plays in Knoxville. Such a play would not injure me, but
I have seen the world. Nobody knows the world better than I.
No woman has had greater educational advantages, has been
more in social life, or has traveled more than I. I am able to
judge of the temptations that come to the young and the inexperienced. It is the duty of us to protect those who have not
had our advantages."

Such inclination to protect other adults is part of a fading
mode of immaturity. During many centuries the great
moral drive was to protect women. They were restricted in
dress, limited as to hours when they could walk the thorough-
fares and even discouraged from entering into serious discussions. When the stage became a transmitter of public
thought, women were barred for years from the audience
and then, when finally allowed to witness these spectacles,
they were prevented from engaging as actors even in pan-
tomime. But the urge to protect women has been beaten
down by women themselves.

During this period the poor came in for their share of
this protective energy. Knowledge was kept from the poor.
They weren't ready for it. We rich sophisticated people
know how to read obscenity and remain uncorrupted. The
hired hand became a criminal if he read the Bible and the
right to read often rested upon property qualifications.
Those whom we called our poor brothers were to be kept
poor in knowledge, for knowledge is power and we wanted
to retain the power. The high priced limited edition of obscenity today is a remnant of this attitude. But the poor
do not remain politically impoverished. Even public education, so bitterly opposed, was finally grudgingly granted by

the rich. And now obscenity also is democratized. It can no longer be limited to rich adults and denied to the poor.

Our paternalistic concern was also clearly aroused toward the Negroes. Many of our Southern States up to the Civil War made it criminal to sell or exhibit books to colored folk. The Negroes constituted a minority requiring protection. In this realm, as with women and the poor, censorship became synonymous with subjection. In this generation we may still be influenced by atavistic inclinations to censor the reading of these groups, but no one in the community would dare ask publicly for separate obscenity laws to shield special adult classes of the community.

THE CHILDREN

It is obviously absurd to censor adult reading down to the level of the child's intellect. The reading of doctors, lawyers, clergy, and all men or women in scientific pursuits is practically exempt. Such sentiment as still exists in favor of obscenity laws applying to all adults is solely supported by some of the disheartening medical data of man's feeble-mindedness. It has been reported that large percentages of our doughboys tested as morons, that half of our prison population bears the stigmata of insanity and that the rest of us free adults are appreciably below the mythical normal. There follows from such a record a delightful example of "reasoning around the circle." Thus runs the argument: The vice hunter declares that most adults are mentally deficient and need protection, which protection is written into laws and which laws are administered by none other than those very same adults most of whom are mentally deficient. In other words, we who cannot protect our-

selves against ourselves without special laws try to do so by
legislation which we enact.

For society to protect adults against intellectual assaults
converts grown people into children. With a child, however, the protective hypothesis rests on the patent inequalities of forces. The pernicious influence of overt acts on
children is easily defined, but the vicious intellectual influences are so varied and changing that no statute could enu-
merate them. As a result we find that the program of
intellectual protection for minors rests on the idea that
passion is the sole immorality and obscenity the lone danger.
This is obviously untrue. Crime news, emulation of mere
wealth, public applause for victories through cunning and
stealth are probably more hurtful to the child than any
amount of pornography. When we think of censorship
for children we are apt to overlook the vicious effects of inspiring through the press the war spirit of murder, or
the flagrant violation of constitutional amendments. It is
not improbable that the sight of nude statues in the museums
has a less harmful effect on society than the daily image of
parents defiantly drinking bootleg liquor. A distorted view
of life or any phase of life can do more harm than any
amount of disgusting truth, for children are conditioned
not alone by sexual environment. Society is made uncomfortable and meagre more often by deceit than by obscenity, although these other elements are virtually disregarded
by our censors and our law-makers. The admiring stories
of the sexual indiscretions of wealthy persons and the tales
of the success in life of public rogues, lead to more serious
intellectual perversions than do the vilest of pictures. Most
of our high-school boys and girls know about the Censor
of the Movies—the Czar of the Films—Will Hays. He is

a well-known public character. But they may also read the
slimy testimony of the same Will Hays before the United
States Senate Oil Investigation Committees. All the press ac-
claims the fact that this Mr. Hays, a former cabinet minister,
dines with President Coolidge and continues to retain his
high position as an elder of the Presbyterian Church. This
is typical of the morally confused influences to which the
young are subjected. In comparison, pornography is perhaps insignificant.

Before determining the effect of pornography on the child
we really should know a little more about the child himself.
What has Red Riding Hood with its obvious sadism, or
Cinderella with its unreal love imagery, done to the infant's
mind? In the childrens' libraries women once waged war
on the Katzenjammer Kids. Possibly Mutt and Jeff do
more harm than dirty post cards. Boys and girls in New
York high schools may incidentally see a horrible picture of
abnormal sex attitudes, but their ordinary literary diet is
composed of lawful confessional magazines. The uncen-
sored periodicals which are the favorites of the adolescent
carry stories almost any of which could be entitled: "Can
a boy make love to two women at the same time?" The
proclaimed editorial policy of these sheets is: "Let the
shadow of a bed be on every page but never let the bed
appear."

No book or picture can approximate in power the effect
of such publicly condoned obscenity, which no government
would or could prevent. Some years ago the virtue clubs
of Pennsylvania protested against the accuracy of certain
statues which adorned the State Capitol at Harrisburg,
whereupon the stone masons of Ben Franklin's State acknowledged the victory of the prim by a public castration

of those heroic figures. By that one performance, attended
by thousands of children, enough obscenity was embedded
in the young of the Keystone State to keep parents and
teachers of that State busy for a decade eradicating the
effects. Such public demonstrations of so-called morality have an immoral effect on the young. We have been
informed that the Ladies' Auxiliary of a church in
Emporia, Kansas, rented out copies of *The President's
Daughter* at twenty-five cents a week to help pay for a new
chapel!

Obviously no one defends such influences. Every parent prefers to supply to a child a life so true and rich that
dishonest trash is disgusting and unexciting. If our peda-
gogues had not been restrained by the censors, possibly they
would have pondered more over these problems which have
been ineffectively abandoned to the State. Possibly the
reader will agree that in comparison to all such legalized
and prevailing environment of degradation obscenity is a
negligible item. The law acquires disrespect when it strains
after trifles.

Yet a lover of freedom like Professor Chaffee of Harvard
University has declared that obscenity is like poison candy to
children. Here we have an example of a liberal who follows
the Jeffersonian philosophy of the right to preach revolution
but still shies off at the relatively minor danger of obscenity.
Though most elements of the community are united in the
opinion that children often deserve special treatment, there
is nevertheless a twilight zone of disputed control between
parents and government. This contest has its origin in the
ultra-governmental ideology—that petty juries and legislators are better qualified than parents to create standards of
living for children. Our compulsory education laws, the

attempts to abolish parochial schools, the endeavor to ban German from our institutions of learning, all trace a weird course of public thinking in this parent-teacher-legislator struggle for child domination. The arguments for protection of minors rest on recognition of the minor's weaknesses. In the realm of economics the forces against the child are deemed so overwhelming that children are prevented by legislative decree from working ten hours a day in cotton mills. In the crimes of passion, seductions of young girls fall in the category of crimes by physical or emotional duress, although even here the age limits vary with the climate. Some states fix eighteen as the age of consent while in others, particularly in the South, the age has been as low as twelve. The fixing of the age of protection is always a bothersome problem; it will be reduced if modern education accomplishes its aim, liberates the children, and teaches them a greater degree of self-reliance.

In the movies we find the conflict over the child neatly accentuated. In many cities a child may go to the movies only if accompanied by an adult. Thus, here, perhaps, there is bestowed on parents alone the right to corrupt their own children. This is peculiarly interesting since it is in the field of our severest American censorship. Movies are cut by state officeholders to meet their own vague and varied fashions of decency. And still we find it necessary to supplement all this moralization of the films with adult control of minor attendance. There are special laws making it a crime to give or sell cigarettes to minors, yet no one would even jestingly suggest that adult smoking must cease because of the danger of children taking incidental puffs. Similarly the motives of pre-Volstead laws, forbidding the sale of liquor to children, or even prohibiting a child from going to its father's saloon to call him home to dinner, are in no way the reason for our present prohibition legislation.

Although most adults heard dirty words or saw sexual pictures or indecent poetry before or during adolescence, and although no individual ever admits any injury as a result of such contacts, nevertheless the first reaction of every adult is to condemn all such material for children. Almost the only data which can pretend to be scientific on the subject is that which we have analyzed and printed in a previous chapter. But let us assume that the pictures sold are of the worst conceivable sorts, portraying the sex act or perverted or abnormal variations thereof. What is the effect on the child? Obviously, if the pictures or words create intellectual or emotional disgust, if they act as repellants to anti-social practices, the effects are beneficial. The danger, however, lies deeper. Much of the pornography exhibited to children may create morbid emotional distortion. Possibly some of those neurotic adults who fear passion, who dread the sex aspects of life, trace the origin of such complexes to terrifying pictures of sex. Whether pictures and books are the remote or proximate cause is not known. In any case the family, the school, or the church must assume the responsibility of censor. The church for ages admitted its share in the problem by forbidding the reading of Ezekiel to children under thirteen years of age; the schools of late have revised their treatment of the subject of biology and the parents are gradually taking the place of the petty jurors.

The modern point of view toward sex and the child may revolutionize all our standards and tests of the obscene. The civilized school no longer permits the exhibit in physiology classes of charts of the human form with the genital organs removed.   Mystery concerning these organs, not the organs themselves, is obscene.   The schools of today address themselves openly and frankly to the problems of dirty sexual words.   For example, nearly every child in the United States has whispered like a low sneak the word "fuck."   The modern teacher explains the word, its derivation meaning "to plant," its former propriety in English society and its present disrepute which dictates the wisdom of its avoidance by those who do not care to become objectionable to friends and neighbors.   When boys pick up girls' skirts, they are no longer merely rapped on the knuckles.   On the contrary, the teacher talks to the boys and girls together in order to discover whether any abnormality is involved.   A frankness of approach is replacing evasion to questions and dishonesty of replies.

In some modern homes the children see their parents nude.   The nude body as such is not obscene.   Some children see the mother and father nude together.   Thus, much of their intellectual curiosity is satisfied, although obviously only life and living can satisfy the emotional curiosity.   The child of today is not brought up on the stork theory of birth.   "Where did I come from?" is a natural early inquiry addressed to every parent.   Other questions follow, after seeing pregnancy or after children are born in the homes of friends.   All of these questions discuss the material of pornography.   But although the material is usually clean, the ideology of many parents is still so confused that they talk to their children with blushes, shame and hesitancy.   If they do not err on this side they go to the other extreme of telling the child more than he wants to know with precocious stimulation as a result.   In time, however, a proper balance will be struck.

The sources of premature sexual excitement are not definitely known.   Within the life of this passing generation great changes have been effected in this domain.   Colleges and high schools would have been raided thirty years ago if there had been lectures such as are given today on venereal disease, promiscuity of sexual relationship, or effects of excessive masturbation.   In 1919 a consensus of opinion of prominent doctors and psychiatrists was taken to investigate the educative effect upon the public of certain films used in campaigns for the control of venereal diseases.   This report, previously referred to, published by the National Committee for Mental Hygiene, Inc., indicates a strong trend toward complete and frank disclosure of all the truths known to science.   We find leaders in the medical profession, like Dr. Ernest Jones, testifying that maladjustment is always the result of woman's belief in the "obscenity of all sex relations."

Moreover when we consider the advisability of controlling literature for children we can no longer overlook the prevalence of auto-erotic practices.   And although we may not agree with Bernard de Voto that "the acquisition of a sex code takes place along about the time that the individual acquires language," nevertheless the reports of the Society for Social Hygiene indicate the probability that masturbation commences often at the age of five, continues through life, is practised by the majority of women, is continued after marriage, and creates as its greatest danger a feeling of guilt.   The wholesome viewpoint of modern psychiatry is that such practice is normal particularly in a society where sex is considered abnormal and where few, if any, persons are sexually content and satisfied.   How peaceful life would be if all these disturbing factors of adolescent life could be reduced to a calm by legislative enactment.

THE practical answer to all this may still be that although we cannot control all of life's obscenity let us at least forbid, by law, the spread to children of actual pornography in picture form. If pornography, which some declare is "grosser obscenity," could be defined, and if there were a hope of censorship being effective, and if there were no counterbalancing evils, many lovers of freedom and liberty would no doubt subscribe to such a project.

To this end we have tried to frame a statute. We present it not as a legal instrument fully polished but as a basis for considering whether any legislation can provide a way out.

"Sec. 1. Pornography is any matter or thing exhibiting or visually representing persons or animals performing the sexual act, whether normal or abnormal.

"Sec. 2. It shall be criminal for anyone other than a teacher in the course of his employment, or a doctor in the regular practice of his profession, or a parent (of the child in question) to exhibit, sell, rent or offer for exhibition, sale or rent, any such pornographic material to any person under the age of eighteen."

We have heretofore criticized obscenity legislation because of its vagueness. The proposed law at least has the asset of clarity. For this purpose we have limited the banned materials to pictures, statues, or other visual representations. Obviously these are more easily defined than the more subjective images derived from words in books. If this narrow definition cannot stand up under obvious tests, then a broader one including books surely will not.

In general terms such a law recognizes a desire to protect children and defines the material under the ban. It would have the further advantage of preventing the continued nullification of the present law under which material that creates "sexual thoughts" or "libidinous desires" circulates freely although illegally.

Under such a statute, the crime would be the sale or other disposition to a child. Adults' food would no longer be cooked according to a recipe for a child's diet; and those pictures of perversions which are a problem to thinking parents would be proscribed.

But even such legislation has manifold difficulties. Should the age be eighteen? Why not twenty-one? If fixed at any age will not the boy or girl attaining that age grasp eagerly for the adult tabooed material? Will not the law accentuate the quest for the obscene? Will possession of adult material be deemed a token of maturity and the law create a pressure for obtaining it surreptitiously? Will not the child of eighteen years and one day zealously exhibit the filth to his junior of a day or a week or a year? If the statute is limited to pictures or other visual forms of a sex act will it not be circumvented by the sale of nude figures in equally exciting postures, though not actually within the definition? If the law were made broader so as to prevent all portrayals of nudes, would museum statuary and paintings be proscribed? Would not representations of partially clothed humans be so arranged as to appear equally pornographic? If any such law, no matter how defined, were enacted, would not the very bar created thereby raise the price and increase the profit and develop the sales of the tabooed materials?

It will be observed that books are not included in this proposed statute. The infirmity of definition is accentuated when we start to deal with words. Combinations of the alphabet are too elusive to be controlled by any verbal formulæ. The creation of the bounds of words is patently impossible if even a photograph cannot be proscribed for the purposes of obscenity.

It must be apparent that any definition dependent on emotional effects is impossible. Such obstacles are not the usual ones which attend our ordinary criminal law. As we have stated elsewhere there may be much struggle before facts of theft, arson or rape are established. But there the material dealt in is tangible. The identity of the criminal may be in dispute, the taking of the property may be difficult to prove, but the facts do exist somewhere. A photographic film could have been taken of the act. Even the problem of proving premeditation in a murder case, or guilty knowledge in the case of receiving stolen goods, is simple in comparison, for in those instances the jury hears the testimony as it relates to the person who has acted the drama. In determining the effects of pornography under any kind of law we have no child to examine, no effects to scrutinize and no psychiatrist to testify as to previous infections or inoculations. We are in a desert of quandaries having to resort to the myth of an average or subnormal child.

While a minor's pornography law would satisfy many of those who are still exercised over the effects of obscenity on adolescence, we have faith that education, through school and home, will prove the enduring solution. To be sure, the method is slow, but its benefits are lasting. It is easier to form the plastic child mind in the habits of decency than to rely upon censorship legislation. The very existence of any law removes from the parent and the teacher that very pressure which is necessary to spur them on to learn the truth and impart it to the young.

At its best any law will only make distribution of pornography difficult and correspondingly attractive. The censor, like the spy and the *agent provocateur,* must justify his existence by results; he must satisfy his employer. Just so the child must prove his liberation from controls by circumventing the censor. Only the adults close to the child, appreciating that ignorance is not essential to reverence, can treat all life honestly, destroy the real obscenity which lies in taboos, and talk of love and passion as the highest of moralities, placing them on a plane as high even as the adoration of thrift, the sanctity of work, and the adulation of wealth.

IN CONCLUSION

A GREAT variety of personal response to matters of sexual suggestiveness will reflect itself in the reactions to this book. Attitudes toward sex injected into us in childhood cannot be lightly displaced. To the extent that the sex taboo supplies an important comfort, courage is required to destroy it. The human race has not yet learned how to accommodate itself with easy tolerance to all the new. Even Milton, who stirringly urged full freedom for the printed word, demonstrated his blind spot whenever papists were mentioned.

The available literature in support of censorship is based on philosophies of infant damnation and salvation by ignorance. Our approach to the subject was unrelated to such arid attitudes. It might be said that we have steered a course between fatalism on the one hand, free will on the other. A kind of self determination is the mood of this book—for man has bootstraps so that he may be lifted by his ancestry, his environment and his own self. This is our point of deviation from the censors' faith. We find no joy in their creed of man's constant degradation.

We hope we have shown the necessity for a revaluation of obscenity. The objective proof of actual cases should cause a reappraisal of these laws, for vagueness of definition assures their futility and stimulates the hypocrisy of the censors. The stronger jurists flounder in a mirage of illusory tests while the weaker indulge in purely subjective interpretations. The size of any nation further increases the confusion. Uncertainty has converted these laws into whips against new ideas. Political, economic, or religious innovations have been limited by their reckless invocation. This is their native heritage—for legal obscenity is a recently acquired play-toy of man. It was born of the fading suppression by Church and State. The fall of the temporal power of the Church liberated blasphemy and the adoption of civil liberties in written constitutions restricted the charges of sedition. Man had thus won for himself comparative liberty to discuss the rights of the State or the affairs of the Church. But Sex is still in the dark regions where those in power hold a threatening forefinger across the lips. And like censors of old they know no limits—even though the effects of obscenity are subject neither to proof nor gauge.

If we were living with unrecorded history we might be deluded into thinking that obscenity, and all the mores connecting with it, are static. But so constant is its flux that the parent or the teacher, and not the State, are the only agencies capable of ready adjustment.

Since we know that no law is perfect, we have endeavored to weigh the advantages and disadvantages of censorship. The scales weigh heavily in favor of freedom and liberty. On the other side are the deep-rooted desires for conformity, the censor's conviction of his own infallibility, and the obscene idea that sex is filthy and passion immoral.

The losses to civilization from censorship can never be determined quantitatively. No adding machine can tabulate emotional reactions. We have had occasion to mention a few of the books that have been suppressed by public prosecution, or withdrawn under semi-official pressure. The underhand methods of sex censorship make it impossible to ascertain the exact number. But the case is not to be based upon the length of the *Index Librorum Prohibitorum,* whether it contains a hundred, a thousand, or ten thousand volumes. It is rather as an index of our civilization. These restrictive mandates have exercised a pervading influence in the subconscious recesses of individual minds, and have colored the thinking of generations. The spirit of this censorship has so penetrated into the very interstices of our civilization that it has affected almost every kind of human endeavor. Its first effect was simply to bowdlerize literature but soon it was felt also in science; and biology, psychology, history, biography, and finally criticism became subject to its influence. There are instances where anthropologists have approached the study of phallicism with a wry expression upon their faces as if they proceeded to the disagreeable inquiry only from the most solemn sense of duty. One can hardly estimate what the taboos of decency have done to delay the attack upon venereal disease or the scientific discussion of limiting population. Even psychoanalysis is discussed with moral fervor rather than scientific detachment. We will probably never know the extent to which the obsession has distorted our view of history and personality. The great Victorians have fixed perhaps forever in the popular mind a false picture of the decline of Roman grandeur in terms of moral decadence, and we hear much of the orgies of the Emperors, but little of the territorial and military factors in the decline of Rome. Such flattering perversion of history is really obscene.

The final refutation of the criminal obscenity laws lies in their futility. Even if a legal sage arose to define with precision the words "lewd," "lascivious," "filthy," "indecent," "disgusting," and "obscene," the ultimate logic of life would remain. Life itself has deep tendencies both toward elevation and corruption. None can escape such forces from the cradle to the grave. Even if sexual excitement were proved to be a fatally vicious influence we could scarcely hope to eradicate it by law or to establish ideals of asceticism by the suppression of every art. Although the censors are often accused of underestimating æsthetic values and the potency of the arts, their actions belie their words. Each assault on the printed word is a confession of a greater potency in art than in life.

If we lived in a society where men and women led sheltered lives and were never touched by the breath of sin, there might be cogency in the effort to preserve innocence. But today the change in the sexual customs of society can only be directed by a free market for thought. To proceed otherwise justifies the conclusion of Herbert Spencer that "The ultimate effect of shielding man from his own follies is to make a world full of fools."

This logic has always impressed men of letters. Goethe, when asked if he did not regret the writing of *Die Leiden des Jungen Werthers,* which was supposed to have led to many suicides, remarked: "Life displays the most scandalous scenes in abundance"; and Walter Pater noted the paradox that Angelo was tempted to his fall by the sight of the pure-minded Isabella, the incarnation of virtue. George Moore has observed that if the vice societies should succeed, suppress all the arts and destroy the last indecent book, there would still be the seduction of spring days. What will the crusader do, when after a long winter we feel the April breezes and smell the apple blossoms?

The whole case was stated by Lord Macaulay when many respectable people contended that the plays of the Restoration dramatists ought to be suppressed.

"We find it difficult to believe, that in a world so full of temptation as this, any gentleman, whose life would have been virtuous if he had not read Aristophanes and Juvenal, will be made vicious by reading them. A man who, exposed to all the influences of such a state of society as that in which we live, is yet afraid of exposing himself to the influence of a few Greek or Latin verses, acts, we think, much like the felon who begged the sheriffs to let him have an umbrella held over his head from the door of Newgate to the gallows because it was a drizzling morning and he was apt to take cold. The virtue which the world wants is a healthful virtue, a virtue which can expose itself to the risks inseparable from all spirited exertion—not a virtue which keeps out of the common air for fear of infection and eschews the common food as too stimulating. It would be, indeed, absurd to attempt to keep men from acquiring those qualifications which fit them to play their part in life with honor to themselves and advantage to their country, for the sake of preserving a delicacy which cannot be preserved—a delicacy which a walk from Westminster to the Temple is sufficient to destroy."

The yearning for a fuller life has always been thwarted by the passion of the censor. We may speculate that eating and hunger in the early days of the race were the front trenches of suppression. As man attained the right to all foods the taboo shifted to religion. To prevent fresh views on spiritual matters libraries were destroyed and thousands of Brunos burned at the stake. Furthermore the regimentation of the people could not continue if free thought on matters of state was permitted. To whisper about the King became sedition. The censor's ax was swung with violence.

Food, religion, the state—then sex. What next? Will those who want to control the thoughts and emotions of others shift to new unleavened realms of taste and æsthetics? Are we at the dawn of an era when the word "obscene" will be replaced by "unæsthetic," "lewd" by "in poor taste," and "filthy" by "ugly"? Must the tyranny of words proceed forever? Possibly some divine power ordains that intellectual stamina and emotional peace can only be acquired by conquest over censors.

Appendices

APPENDIX I

The indictment in Regina vs. Bedborough (the Havelock Ellis prosecution).

CENTRAL CRIMINAL COURT, TO WIT:

The jurors for our Sovereign Lady the Queen upon their oath present that George Bedborough, being a person of a wicked and depraved mind and disposition, and unlawfully and wickedly devising, contriving, and intending to vitiate and corrupt the morals of the liege subjects of our said Lady the Queen, and to raise and create in them lustful desires, and to bring the said liege subjects into a state of wickedness, lewdness, and debauchery, on the 27th day of May, in the year of our Lord, one thousand eight hundred and ninety eight, at a certain shop, to wit, Number 16 John Street, Bedford Row, in the County of London, and within the jurisdiction of the said Court, unlawfully, wickedly, maliciously, scandalously and wilfully did publish, sell and utter, and cause and procure to be published, sold and uttered, a certain lewd, wicked, bawdy, scandalous, and obscene libel, in the form of a book entitled *Studies in the Psychology of Sex: Vol. I. Sexual Inversion,* by Havelock Ellis, in which said book are contained among other things, divers wicked, lewd, impure, scandalous and obscene libels and matters, which said book is, pursuant to the provisions in that behalf, of the Law of Libel Amendment Act, 1888, deposited with this indictment, together with the particulars showing precisely by reference to pages, columns and lines, in what part of the said book the alleged libel is to be found, to the manifest corruption of the morals and minds of the liege subjects of our said Lady the Queen, in contempt of our said Lady the Queen, and her laws, in violation of common decency, morality and good order, and against the peace of our said Lady the Queen, her Crown and Dignity.

THE INDICTMENT IN THE JURGEN CASE

This is of particular interest because:—

(a) Obscenity is presumably reduced to an exact science by the citation of pages.

(b) The book is described as "offensive, lewd, lascivious, and indecent" without mention of "filthy," "disgusting," or "obscene."

(c) The Grand Jury believed the book too offensive to set forth in detail. (Note: The Court found that the book "contains nothing obscene." See decision which follows.)

January 15th, 1920.

John S. Sumner, Agent New York Society for the Suppression of Vice, being duly sworn, says: That on the 6th day of January, 1920, and prior, and sworn thereto at the City and County aforesaid Robert M. McBride & Company, a corporation, and Guy Holt, manager of said corporation, Book Department, did at No. 31 East 17th Street in the City and County aforesaid, unlawfully print, utter, publish, manufacture and prepare, and did unlawfully sell and offer to sell and have in their possession with intent to sell a certain offensive, lewd, lascivious and indecent book, in violation of Section 1141 of Penal Code of the State of New York. At the time and place aforesaid, the said Robert M. McBride & Company by and through its officers, agents and employees did print, publish, sell and distribute and on information and belief of the said Guy Holt did prepare for publication and cause to be printed, published, sold and distributed a certain book entitled *Jurgen* by one James Branch Cabell, which said book represents and is descriptive of scenes of lewdness and obscenity, particularly upon pages 56, 57, 58, 59, 61, 63, 64, 67, 80, 84, 86, 89, 92, 93, 98, 99, 100, 103, 104, 105, 106, 107, 108, 114, 120, 124, 125, 127, 128, 134, 135, 142, 144, 148, 149, 150, 152, 153, 154, 155, 156, 157, 158, 161, 162, 163, 164, 165, 166, 167, 168, 170, 171, 175, 176, 177, 186, 196, 197, 198, 199, 200, 203, 206, 207, 211, 228, 229, 236, 237, 238, 239, 241, 242, 271, 272, 275, 286, 321, 340, 342, 343, thereof, and which said book is so obscene, lewd, lascivious and indecent that a minute description of the same would be offensive to the Court and improper to be placed upon the records thereof: Wherefore a fuller description of the same is not set forth in the complaint.

THE DECISION IN THE CASE OF
PEOPLE *VS.* HOLT, M^CBRIDE & CO. ET AL.

The defendants herein, at the close of the People's case, have moved for a direction of acquittal and the dismissal of the indictment on the ground that the book *Jurgen* on the possession of which the indictment is based, is not an "obscene, lewd, lascivious, filthy, indecent or disgusting book" within the meaning and intent of section 1141 of the Penal Law, for the alleged violation of which the indictment has been found.

Questions to be Asked by a Layman

I have read and examined the book carefully. It is by Mr. James Branch Cabell, an author of repute and distinction. From the literary point of view its style may fairly be called brilliant. It is based on the mediæval legends of Jurgen and is a highly imaginative and fantastic tale, depicting the adventures of one who has been restored to his first youth but who, being attended by a shadow in the guise of the shadow of his old self, retains the experience and cynicism of age which frustrates a perfect fulfillment of his desire for renewed youth.

Is the author's reputation a factor?

Does a brilliant style overcome the obscene?

Is realism to be penalized?

The adventures consist in wanderings through mediæval and mythological countries and a sojourn in Hell and Heaven. He encounters beings of mediæval folklore and from classical Myth-

ology. The most that can be said against
the book is that certain passages therein
may be considered suggestive in a veiled
and subtle way of immorality, but such *Is immorality moral*
suggestions are delicately conveyed and *if delicately con-*
the whole atmosphere of the story is of *veyed?*
such an unreal and supernatural nature
that even these suggestions are free from
the evils accompanying suggestiveness in
more realistic works. In fact, it is doubt-
ful if the book could be read or understood *Is obscenity related to*
at all by more than a very limited number *scarcity of sales?*
of readers.

In my opinion the book is one of unusual *Is literary merit sub-*
literary merit and contains nothing "ob- *ject to the court's*
scene, lewd, lascivious, filthy, indecent or *analysis?*
disgusting" within the meaning of the
statute and the decisions of the courts of
this state in similar cases. (See Halsey *vs.*
New York Society, 234 N. Y. 1; People
vs. Brainard 192 App. Div. 116; St. Hubert Guild *vs.* Quinn, 64 Misc. 336.)

The motion, therefore, is granted and
the jury is advised to acquit the defendants.

THE DECISION IN THE CASE OF "POWER"
BY LION FEUCHTWANGER

In the Police Court for the City of   *Instructions to*
   Toronto: *Authors, Pub-*
               lishers, and

REX *vs.* JULIUS RAIN   *Bookdealers — to*
               be Read from
Judgment   *This Decision.*

HIS WORSHIP MAGISTRATE JONES:
   This is a prosecution in respect to a
German book by Feuchtwanger, which has *Previous sale is a fac-*
been on the market since October, 1926.   *tor.*

The charge is that the accused knowingly sold an obscene book tending to corrupt morals, contrary to section 207 of the Criminal Code.

It is difficult, if not impossible, to decide whether a book comes under this section by reason of isolated passages which, at first sight, might be offensive against good taste, or worse; but the book must be judged as a whole and the objectionable passages must be read with their context.

A little isolated obscenity is not so dangerous.

There have been many reviews of this particular book; one critic, Rafael Sabatini, writing that "It is a story conceived and written on a level rarely reached." Whether this level is a high one or a low one, the book is of such a character that it could never attract those persons whom the Statute intended to protect. The book contains 425 pages, the chapters are mostly over 100 pages in length, the type set in very solid form without illustrations, and for the most part, without any dialogue.

Quotations from a critic are material.

A long book gathers immunity. Write long chapters. Avoid illustrations. Dialogue has perils. Use solid type.

A reader looking for obscene matter would get tired of reading the book within the first thirty pages, as the subject is only of interest to students of history, who are endowed with brains and application above the ordinary.*

Bored readers are important.

It seems to me futile to prosecute anyone in respect to such a book, such prosecution only resulting in advertising the work and increasing its sale.

The book is in no sense within the class aimed at, which is more aptly illustrated

---

* The publishers inform us that nearly 100,-000 copies of the book had been sold in the English language at the time of this decision.

by certain American magazines which unfortunately have from time to time found entrance to this country, and which all good Canadians should join in banning, *Americans, beware of* whether by process of law or otherwise. *Canada!*

It seems to me that some more workable system of censoring books might be found which might result in less publicity and in more fairness to the retail bookseller, who cannot possibly read all the books upon his shelves and against whom it is difficult and almost impossible to prove that he "knowingly sold" a book containing obscene matter.

To those of us who have confidence in Canadian publishers and booksellers, it seems possible to evolve some plan whereby they themselves, through their various organizations, might assist the police in enforcing this very wise provision of the Criminal Code, which provision however, is of no use unless wisely and fairly administered.

The charge will therefore be dismissed.

(Signed) J. E. JONES

Police Magistrate

Toronto, April 30th, 1928.

APPENDIX II

No complete list of books banned in Boston has ever been officially announced by the public authorities. The following list, which appeared in the Authors' League *Bulletin,* indicates the varied types of works which were deemed obscene in 1927:

The Wayward Man by St. John Ervine, *Dark Laughter* by Sherwood Anderson, *High Winds* by Arthur Train, *Blue Voyage* by Conrad Aiken, *The Irishman* by St. John Ervine, *What I Believe* by Bertrand Russell, *Circus Parade* by Jim Tully, *The American Caravan, Move Over* by E. Pettit, *Oil* by Upton Sinclair, *From Man to Man* by Olive Schreiner, *Mosquitoes* by William Faulkner, *Pilgrims* by Edith Mannin, *Horizon* by Robert Carse, *The Sorrows of Elsie* by André Savignon, *Nigger Heaven* by Carl Van Vechten, *Power* by Lion Feuchtwanger, *Twilight* by Keyserling, *Black April* by Julia Peterkin, *An American Tragedy* by Theodore Dreiser, *The World of William Clissold* by H. G. Wells, *Wine, Women and War, Manhattan Transfer* by John Dos Passos, *Count Bruga* by Ben Hecht, *Ariane* by Claude Anet, *The Captive* by Edouard Bourdet, *Crazy Pavements* by Beverley Nichols, *Young Men in Love* by Michael Arlen, *In Such a Night* by Babette Deutsch, *The Starling* by Doris Leslie, *Pretty Creatures* by William Gerhardi, *The Madonna of the Sleeping Car* by Maurice Dekobra, *Dream's End* by Thorne Smith, *Tomek the Sculptor* by Adelaide Eden Phillpotts, *The Plastic Age* by Percy Marks, *The Hard Boiled Virgin* by Frances Newman, *The Rebel Bird* by Diana Patrick, *The Butcher Shop* by Jean Devanny, *The Ancient Hunger* by Edwin Granberry, *Antennae* by Herbert Footner, *The Marriage Bed* by Ernest Pascal, *The Beadle* by Pauline Smith, *As It Was* by Helen Thomas, *Elmer Gantry* by Sinclair Lewis, *Doomsday* by Warwick Deeping, *The Sun Also Rises* by Ernest Hemingway, *Blinded Kings* by J. Kessel and Hélène Iswolsky, *Spread Circles* by F. J. Ward, *Little Pitchers* by Isa Glenn, *Master of the Microbe* by Robert W. Service, *Evelyn Grainger* by George Frederick Hummel, *Cleopatra's Diary* by Henry Thomas, *The Allinghams* by May Sinclair, and *The Revolt of Modern Youth* by Judge Ben Lindsey.

APPENDIX III

List of Publications Prohibited to Be Imported into Canada*

Official List on March 1, 1914:

PERIODICALS

The American Cottage Home, The American Household Journal, American Fireside and Farm, The American Homestead, The Agents' Guide, The American Agent, The American Nation, The American Farmer, The Agents' Herald, The Advance, The Blue Devil, The Breeze, Chicago Dispatch or the Chicago Journal, The Climax, The Chicago Mascot, Cheerful Moments, Cupid's Columns, Detroit Sunday Sun, Detroit Sunday World, Fantasio, Fox's Weekly, The Gatling Gun, Gil Blas (Illustré), The Household Companion, The Home, The Hearthstone, The Home Circle, The Home and Fireside, Hours at Home, House and Home, Illustrated Police News, Illustrated Monthly Fireside Gem, The Illustrated New York News,

---

*This list is prepared under the Canadian Customs Act of 1907 directed against "immoral," "indecent," "treasonable," or "seditious" material. The Government refused to indicate which objective applies and in many instances has been unwilling to indicate the part of the writing which was objectionable. This list is by no means complete but will nevertheless suggest the breadth of the attack. In many cases the ban is subsequently raised. In the case of *The New Masses* the Government advised that the prohibition would not be lifted until six months after the suppression. Correspondence with the authorities fails to show just why six months—no more, no less—brings absolution to a magazine.

The Illustrated Companion, The Illustrated Record, The Illustrated Sun, Jim Jam Gems, Krums of Kumford, L'Asino, Life, London Illustrated Standard, Le Journal Amusant, La Vie Parisienne, La Calotte, Lapatossu, Les Refractaires, L'Anarchie, Menace, The Merry Maker, Music and Drama, The Metropolitan and Rural Home, Modern Stories, New Photo Fun, Our Country Home, Pages Folles, The People's Journal, The Public Herald, The Police Gazette, The Police News, Photo Bits, Photo Fun, The Rambler, Social Visitor Magazine, The Treasury Home, The Truth Seeker, The Welcome Friend, The Welcome Visitor, Youth and Home, The Yank or The Columbian, Young America, Young's Magazine.

BOOKS

Arabian Nights (unexpurgated edition) by Burton, *Always Lock the Door* by Guy de Maupassant, *After the Pardon* by Matilde Serao, *The Confessions of a Princess* Anonymous, *Cynthia in the Wilderness* by Hubert Wales, *The Diary of a Lost One* by Margaret Bohme, *Diseases of Men* by Bernarr MacFadden, *The Double Pins* by Guy de Maupassant, *Droll Stories* by Balzac, *Her Reason* Anonymous, *Hippolyte's Claim* by Guy de Maupassant, *Jereboam* by Guy de Maupassant, *The Lonely Lovers* by Horace W. C. Newte, *Marriage a Life-Long Honeymoon* Anonymous, *Memoirs of Prince John de Guelph* Anonymous, *A Mistake* by Guy de Maupassant, *Mr. and Mrs. Villiers* by Hubert Wales, *Mrs. Drummond's Vocation* by Mark Ryce, *One Day, a Sequel to "Three Weeks"* Anonymous, *The Rose Door* by Estelle Baker, *A Strange Traffic* by Guy de Maupassant, *Superb Virility of Manhood* by Bernarr MacFadden, *Three Weeks* by Elinor Glyn, *Thrift* by Guy de Maupassant, *The Tree of Knowledge* Anonymous, *The Woman Herself* Anonymous, *The Wedding Night* by Guy de Maupassant, *Woman's Wiles* by Guy de Maupassant, *The Yoke* by Hubert Wales.

Since 1914 no single list has been published but the Canadian Consul's Office in New York City has instructions as to prohibition of the following:

Wecelya Druh ("Jolly Friend")–Ukrainian publication, New York.
Chouquette en Vacances–illustrated magazine, Paris.
Zhalo–Ukrainian newspaper, New York.
Beau–monthly, New York.
The New Masses–monthly, New York.
Laughter–illustrated monthly, Philadelphia.
Studies in Rationalism–by E. Haldeman-Julius, Girard, Kansas.
Dawn–illustrated magazine, published by All Arts Group Inc., Wilmington, Del.
Calgary Eye Opener–illustrated magazine, published monthly, Minneapolis. (Ban lifted Feb. 14, 1927.)
Two Worlds Monthly–New York.
Sex–illustrated monthly, New York.
Art Classics Magazine–monthly, Wilmington, Del.
Smik y Pravda ("Humor and Truth")–Ukrainian publication, New York.
American Beauties–monthly, Philadelphia.
Arts, Fads, Modes Magazine–Wilmington, Del.
Art Studio Life Magazine–monthly, Wilmington, Del.
The Tyranny of God–by Joseph Lewis.
The Truth Seeker–weekly, New York.
Convent Cruelties–by Helen Jackson.
The Bible Unmasked–by Joseph Lewis.
Art Lovers' Magazine–illustrated monthly, New York.
Film Fun—illustrated monthly, New York.
The Rail Splitter–monthly.
The Daily Mirror–illustrated newspaper, New York. (Ban lifted August 16, 1926.)
Liberty–weekly, New York. (Ban lifted March 29, 1928.)
My Life–by Frank Harris.
L'Humeur–weekly, Paris.
Parisiana–weekly, Paris.

Le Merle Blanc–weekly, Paris.

Gens qui Rient–weekly, Paris.

Art and Beauty–monthly, New York.

Paris Nights–monthly, Philadelphia.

Arts Monthly Pictorial–Los Angeles.

Artists and Models Magazine–New York.

Ziffs–monthly, Maywood, Ill.

La Revue Parisienne–Chicago.

Breezy Stories–semi-monthly, New York.

Circular issued by the Allied Book Co., New York, advertising the Chapter Headings and Contents of two books entitled *The Sexual Question* by August Forel, and *Psychopathia Sexualis*, by Krafft-Ebing.

The International of Youth–Sweden.

French Frolics–monthly, Newark, N. J.

The Black Sheep–illustrated monthly, Chicago.

T.N.T.–monthly, Los Angeles.

The Live Wire–monthly, Chicago.

Red Pepper–monthly, Newark, N. J.

Peretz–periodical, New York.

I Confess–semi-monthly, New York.

Le Sourire–illustrated weekly, Paris.

Droll Stories–monthly, New York.

Young's Magazine–monthly, New York.

Telling Tales–semi-monthly, New York.

Contraception–by Marie Carmichael Stopes, London.

The Black Prophet–by Guy Fitch Phelps, Cincinnati.

Home Brew–monthly, Brooklyn, N. Y.

Ulysses–by James Joyce, published for the Egoist Press, London, by John Rodker, Paris, 1922.

Gloom, the Devil's Book–monthly, Los Angeles.

The Flapper–monthly, Chicago.

Midnight–weekly, New York.

True Confessions–Minneapolis.

Hot Dog–weekly, Cleveland.

The Sinn Feiner–New York.   (Issue of Saturday, Oct. 30, 1920.)

The Police Gazette–weekly, New York.

Bovha–monthly, published in Russian by Anarchist Federated Commune Soviets of America.

Gosudarstro I Revolyutzia ("State and Revolution")– booklet by N. Lenin, New York.

Pilsni Rabotchykh ("Songs of the Workers")–booklet, author and place of publication unknown.

Molot–Ukrainian semi-monthly newspaper, New York.

L'endehors–semi-monthly newspaper, Orleans, France.

Follies–illustrated magazine, New York.

True Romances–monthly, New York.

Whiz Bang–Robbinsdale, Minn.

Radiant Motherhood–by Dr. Marie Stopes.

Married Love–by Dr. Marie Stopes.

Wise Parenthood–by Dr. Marie Stopes.

Real Life Stories–monthly, Cooperstown, N. Y. (Ban lifted Jan. 1, 1928.)

Experience–monthly, Chicago.

The Sunday Star–weekly newspaper, Detroit, Mich.

Simplicissimus–illustrated magazine, Munich, Germany.

Secrets–monthly, Cleveland.

Woman and the New Race–by Margaret Sanger.

Snappy Stories–semi-monthly, New York.

Hollywood Confessions–monthly, Los Angeles.

Naye Welt ("The New World")–weekly Yiddish newspaper, New York.

Allgemeiner Bücher–Katalog–New York.

Glos Robotnicezy ("The Voice of the Workers")–daily Polish newspaper, Detroit, Mich.

Molot ("The Hammer")–semi-monthly Ukrainian newspaper, New York.

Indystriyalish–monthly, Ukrainian, New York.

Bielgi Terror ("The White Terror")–Russian booklet, Chicago.

Die Arbeitslosigkeit ("Unemployment")–booklet by Dr. M. Goldfarb, New York.

Der Sozializmus, Seine Ursachen, Ziehlen und Wegen– ("Socialism, Its Causes, Objects, and Paths")–booklet, Chicago.

Der Klassenkampf ("The Class Struggle")–booklet, Philadelphia.

Golos Truzhenika–weekly newspaper, Chicago.

Uroky Revolyoutzi ("Lessons of the Revolution")–by N. Lenin, New York.

Branda–weekly newspaper, Stockholm, Sweden.

Soviet Russia–weekly, New York.

Valon Tiella ("The Lighted Road")–printed in Finnish, Fitchburg, Mass.

The Proletarian Revolution in Russia–by N. Lenin and Trotsky.

Kuryfo Polski–Polish newspaper, Milwaukee, Wis.

Khlieb I Volia ("Bread and Freedom")–weekly newspaper, New York.

APPENDIX IV

SHORTLY after the famous trial of Annie Besant for obscene libel, she prepared a pamphlet entitled *Is the Bible Indictable?* The passages referred to in the pamphlet are:

GENESIS: IV, 1, 17, 25; VI, 4; IX, 20-25; XVI, 1-5; XVII, 10-14, 23-27; XIX, 4-9, 30-38; XXV, 21-26; XXVI, 8; XXIX, 21-35; XXX; XXXIV; XXXV, 22; XXXVIII, 8-10, 13-26, 27-30; XXXIX, 7-18.

EXODUS: I, 15-19; IV, 24-26; XXII, 16, 17, 19.

LEVITICUS: V, 3; XII; XV; XVIII, 6-23; XX, 20-21; XXII, 3-5.

NUMBERS: V, 12-29; XXV, 6-8; XXXI, 17, 18.

DEUTERONOMY: XXI, 10-14; XXII, 13-21; XXIII, 1, 10, 11; XXV, 11, 12; XXVII, 20, 22, 23; XXVIII, 57.

JOSHUA: V, 2-8.

JUDGES: III, 15-25; XIX.

RUTH: III, 3-14.

1 SAMUEL: II, 22; V, 9; XVIII, 25-27; XXI, 4, 5; XXV, 22, 34.

2 SAMUEL: VI, 14, 16, 20; X, 4; XI, 2-13; XII, 11, 12; XVI, 21, 22; XIII, 1-22.

1 KINGS: I, 1-4; XIV, 10, 24.

2 KINGS: IX, 8; XVIII, 27.

1 CHRONICLES: XIX, 4.

ESTHER: I, 11; II, 2, 4, 12-17; VII, 8.

JOB: III, 2.

PSALMS: XXXVIII, 5, 7.

PROVERBS: V, 17-20; VI, 24-32; VII, 5-23.

ECCLESIASTES: XI, 5.

SONG OF SOLOMON: I, 2, 13; II, 4-6, 17; III, 1-4; IV,

5, 6, 11; V, 2-4, 8, 14-16; VII, 2, 3, 6-10, 12; VIII, 1-3, 8-10.

ISAIAH: III, 17; XX, 2, 4; XXVI, 17, 18; XXXII, 11, 12; XXXVI, 12; LVII, 8, 9; LXVI, 7-12.

JEREMIAH: I, 5; II, 20; III, 1-3, 6-9; V, 7-8; XI, 15; XIII, 26, 27; XX, 17-18.

LAMENTATIONS: I, 8, 9, 17.

EZEKIEL: IV, 12-15; VI, 9; XVI, 4-9, 16, 17, 25, 26, 33, 34, 37, 39; XVIII, 6, 11, 15; XXII, 9-11; XXIII; XVI, 6-9, 14-21, 29, 41-44.

HOSEA: I, 2; II, 2-13; III, 1-3; IV, 10-18; V, 3, 4, 7; VI, 9-10; VII, 4; VIII, 9; IX, 1-10, 11, 14, 16; XII, 3; XIII, 13.

MATTHEW: I, 18-25.

ROMANS: I, 24-27.

1 CORINTHIANS: V, 1; VI, 9, 15, 16, 18; VII.

1 THESSALONIANS: IV, 3-7.

HEBREWS: XIII, 4.

2 PETER: II, 10-18.

REVELATION: II, 20-22; XVII, 1-4.

APPENDIX V

In 1888, at the time of the charges against Vizetelly, he prepared a memorial addressed to the Solicitor of the Treasury indicating the inconsistency of suppressing Zola's works (since then legalized in England by nullification) while permitting the circulation of the most famous English classics which are full of so-called obscene passages. This 86-page book is in the Congressional Library, Washington, D. C., and, through the courtesy of government officials, was photostated and mailed to the authors. The following list is a condensation of that famous pamphlet.

Extracts Principally from the English Classics, showing that the Legal Supression of M. Zola's novels would logically involve the Bowdlerizing of some of the greatest works in English literature.

SHAKESPEARE. *Troilus and Cressida:* Act I, sc. 2; Act III, sc. 2; Act IV, sc. 1, sc. 2; Act V, sc. 1. *Romeo and Juliet:* Act I, sc. 3; Act II, sc. 4. *King Lear:* Act IV, sc. 6. *Anthony and Cleopatra:* Act II, sc. 5. *Two Gentlemen of Verona:* Act II, sc. 7. *Measure for Measure:* Act II, sc. 1; Act III, sc. 1. *Much Ado About Nothing:* Act III, sc. 3. *Taming of the Shrew:* Act II, sc. 1. *As You Like It:* Act III, sc. 2. *Winter's Tale:* Act I, sc. 2; Act IV, sc. 3. *Henry VIII:* Act V, sc. 3. *Pericles:* Act IV, sc. 6. *Venus and Adonis:* entire.

BEAUMONT AND FLETCHER. (Eleven volumes, edited by
Rev. Alex Dyce. London, Moxon, 1843.) *The
Maid's Tragedy:* Vol. I, pp. 342-3, 349, 352, 353, 356,
361, 363, 364, 365. *Thierry and Theodoret:* Vol. I, pp.
115, 143. *The Knight of the Burning Pestle:* Vol. II,
p. 222. *A King and No King:* Vol. II, pp. 325, 328.
Cupid's Revenge: Vol. II, pp. 403, 440. *The Custom
of the Country:* Vol. IV, pp. 408, 441, 443, 465, 472.
Valentinian: Vol. V, p. 273. *The Wild Goose Chase:*
Vol. VIII, pp. 137-8. *The Sea Voyage:* Vol. VIII,
pp. 318-9. *The Spanish Curate:* Vol. VIII, p. 464. *The
Night Walker:* Vol. XI, pp. 151, 152, 212. *The Two
Noble Kinsmen:* Vol. XI, pp. 368-9, 405.

BEN JONSON. (The Works of Ben Jonson, with a biographical Memoir by Wm. Gifford. London, Moxon,
1846.) *The Alchemist:* Act II, sc. 1, p. 245; Act III,
sc. 2, p. 254; Act V, sc. 1, p. 266.

PHILIP MASSINGER. (Edited by Lieut. Col. F. Cunning-
ham. Chatto & Windus.) *A New Way to Pay Old
Debts:* Act II, sc. 1; Act III, sc. 2; Act IV, sc. 3. *The
Maid of Honor:* Act III, sc. 1; Act IV, sc. 1. *The City
Madam:* Act II, sc. 2; Act IV, sc. 2.

JOHN FORD. *'Tis Pity She's a Whore:* Act II, sc. 1;
Act IV, sc. 3.

THOMAS CAREWE. *Poems, Songs and Sonnets.* (London, 1772.) "A Rapture": pp. 75-9. "On the Marriage
of T. K. and C. C.": p. 130. "The Compliment": p.
167. "The Second Rapture": pp. 173, 174. "Love's
Courtship": p. 184.

SIR G. ETHEREDGE. (Plays and Poems, edited by A. W.
Veriteg. London, Nimms, 1888.) *Love in a Tub:*
Act II, sc. 3, pp. 39, 40; Act IV, sc. 4, p. 108; Act V,
sc. 5, p. 116. *She Would If She Could:* Act II, sc.
2, p. 155, 156; Act III, sc. 2, pp. 180, 185. *The Man of
Mode:* Act I, sc. 1, p. 259. *The Imperfect Enjoyment:*
pp. 398-9.

JOHN DRYDEN. (Dramatic Works. Edited by Sir Walter
Scott and George Saintsbury. Edinburgh, 1882.) *Sir*

Martin Morall: Vol. III, p. 43. *The Mock Astrologer:* Vol. III, pp. 267, 292.

WILLIAM WYCHERLEY. (The Dramatic Works of Wycherley, Congreve, Vanbrugh, and Farquhar, with biographical and critical notes by Leigh Hunt. London, Moxon, 1840, and Routledge & Sons.) *The Country Wife:* Act I, sc. 1, pp. 70, 71, 72, 73; Act II, sc. 1, pp. 74, 77, 78, 79; Act III, sc. 2, p. 80; Act IV, sc. 2, p. 88; sc. 3, p. 90; sc. 4, p. 94; Act V, sc. 1, p. 95; sc. 4, p. 98.

WILLIAM CONGREVE. *The Old Bachelor:* Act III, sc. 10, p. 159; Act IV, sc. 18, p. 165; sc. 19, p. 165; sc. 21, pp. 165-6; sc. 22, pp. 166-7; Act V, sc. 7, p. 169; sc. 8, p. 170. *The Double Dealer:* Act II, sc. 5, p. 181; Act III, sc. 4, p. 184; Act IV, sc. 9, p. 192. *Love for Love:* Act I, sc. 5, p. 205; Act II, sc. 3, p. 210; sc. 5, p. 211; sc. 11, p. 215; Act III, sc. 9, p. 219; sc. 15, p. 222; Act V, sc. 6, p. 232. *The Way of the World:* Act I, sc. 9, p. 263.

SIR JOHN VANBRUGH. *The Provoked Wife:* Act I, sc. 1, p. 337; Act II, sc. 1, pp. 341, 342; Act III, sc. 1, p. 349; sc. 3, p. 351; Act IV, sc. 3, p. 353; Act V, sc. 6, p. 361. *The Confederacy:* Act III, sc. 2, p. 429. *The Relapse:* Prologue on the Third Day, p. 302; Act I, sc. 3, p. 306; Act II, sc. 1, pp. 311-2; Act IV, sc. 1, p. 319; sc. 3, p. 322; Act V, sc. 1, pp. 326-7; sc. 3, p. 329; Epilogue, p. 355.

THOMAS OTWAY. (Plays and Letters. Edited by Thornton.) *The Soldier's Fortune:* Act I, sc. 1; Act II, sc. 1; Act IV, sc. 2.

THOMAS HEYWOOD. (Dramatic Works of Thomas Heywood. Vol. V. London, 1874.) *The Rape of Lucrece:* Act III, sc. 5, p. 215; Act IV, sc. 6, pp. 232-3.

DANIEL DEFOE. (In Bohn's British Classics, Bell & Sons, 1887. Vol. III of Novels, etc., of Daniel Defoe.) *Moll Flanders:* Title page and pp. 15, 19, 21, 29, 42, 44, 68, 73, 74, 89, 90, 91, 94, 130, 135, 136, 147, 165, 183, 184, 185.

MATTHEW PRIOR. (Poetical Works of Matthew Prior.

London, 1779.) *Paulo Purganti and His Wife:* Vol. I,
pp. 131-4. *Hans Carvel:* Vol. I, pp. 126-7. *A True
Maid:* Vol. I, p. 290. *A Sailor's Wife:* Vol. II, p. 193.
Chaste Florimel: Vol. II, pp. 211-2.

DEAN SWIFT. (A Complete Edition of the Poets of Great
Britain. Volume the Ninth. London and Edinburgh.)
The Problem: p. 8. *Corinna:* p. 20. *The Lady's Dress-
ing Room:* p. 135. *Strephon and Chloe:* p. 137.

HENRY FIELDING. (The Works of Henry Fielding with
Memoir of the Author by Thomas Roscoe. London,
printed for Henry Washbourne, 1840.) *Tom Jones:*
pp. 44, 55, 73, 76, 77, 85, 86, 96, 97, 130, 139, 140, 147,
173, 218, 219, 220, 244, 255, 268, 272, 373. *Jonathan
Wilde:* pp. 541, 545, 570, 571, 585.

TOBIAS SMOLLETT. (The Miscellaneous Works of Tobias
Smollett with Memoir of the Author, by Thomas Roscoe.
London, Henry G. Bohn, 1858.) *Roderick Random:*
pp. 12, 13, 21, 37, 39, 48, 82, 89, 101, 106. *Peregrine
Pickle:* 227, 229, 246, 258, 261.

REV. LAWRENCE STERNE. (Works of Lawrence Sterne.
London, Routledge & Sons.) *Tristram Shandy:* pp.
1, 2, 30, 46, 90, 91, 107, 109, 145, 165, 175, 183,
185, 186. *A Sentimental Journey:* pp. 21, 28, 31, 42.

LORD BYRON. (Poetical Works. People's edition. 1884.)
Don Juan: Canto I, pp. 310-3; Canto II, p. 332; Canto
V, pp. 361-2; Canto VI, pp. 367-72; Canto VIII, pp.
391-2.

DANTE GABRIEL ROSSETTI. (Poems. London, F. S.
Ellis, 1870.) *Eden Bower:* pp. 32, 40. *Jenny:* p. 115.
The House of Life: Sonnet 2, p. 190; Sonnet 4, p. 192;
Sonnet 5, p. 193; Sonnet 39, p. 227.

ALGERNON CHARLES SWINBURNE. (London, Chatto &
Windus, 1878.) *Poems and Ballads:* pp. 21, 26, 34,
172, 191, 310, 197.

Bibliography

BIBLIOGRAPHY

THE material on which this book is based consists not only of the books, pamphlets and documents which are listed below but scores of magazine articles, both in general and legal periodicals, and newspaper reports. In addition we have had personal interviews with various officials. As a rule, books mentioned in the bibliographies of works cited below have not been included in this list.

CENSORSHIP BIBLIOGRAPHIES

Schroeder, Theodore: *Free Speech Bibliography.* N. Y., H. W. Wilson, 1922.

Young, Kimball, and Lawrence, Raymond D.: *Bibliography on Censorship and Propaganda.* University of Oregon Publication, Journalism Series, Vol. I, No. 1.

GENERAL WORKS ON CENSORSHIP, POLITICAL, THEOLOGICAL AND SEXUAL

Putnam, George Haven: *The Censorship of the Church of Rome.* Two Volumes, 1906.

Putnam, George Haven: *Authors and their Public in Ancient Times.* Third Edition, 1923.

Ditchfield, P. H.: *Books Fatal to their Authors.* 1895.

Forrest, James Anson: *Books Condemned to be Burnt.* 1892.

Vickers, R. H.: *Martyrdoms of Literature.*

Bury, J. B.: *History of Freedom of Thought.* 1913.

Chaffee, Zechariah, Jr.: *Freedom of Speech.* 1920.

Courtney, Janet E.: *Freethinkers of the Nineteenth Century.* 1920.

Houben, H. H.: *Verbotene Literatur von der klassischen Zeit bis zur Gegenwart.* Berlin, 1924.

Houben, H. H.: *Hier Zensur—wer dort?* Leipzig, 1918.

Houben, H. H.: *Polizei und Zensur.* Berlin, 1926.

Bell, Clive: *On British Freedom.* 1923.

Milton, John: *Areopagitica*, with a Commentary by Sir Richard Webb. Cambridge University Press, 1918.

WORKS RELATING PARTICULARLY TO SEX CENSORSHIP

Schroeder, Theodore: *"Obscene Literature" and Constitutional Law.* 1911.

Schroeder, Theodore: *Free Press Anthology.* 1909.

Broun, Heywood and Leech, Margaret: *Anthony Comstock: Roundsman of the Lord.* 1927.

Calverton, V. F.: *Sex Expression in Literature.* 1926.

English, Paul: *Geschichte der erotischer Literatur.* Stuttgart, 1927.

Dennett, Mary Ware: *Birth Control Laws.* 1926.

Proal, Louis: *Criminality and Passion.*

Vizetelly, Ernst: *Emile Zola, Novelist and Reformist.* 1904. Chaps. IX and X.

Gosse, Edmund: *The Life of Algernon Charles Swinburne.* 1917. Chap. V.

Peterson, Houston: *Havelock Ellis, Philosopher of Love.* 1928. Chaps. XI and XII.

Putnam, George P. (editor): *Nonsenseorships.* 1922.

Ford, John: *Commercial Obscenity.* 1926.

Kittredge, D. W. (editor): *All the World Loves a Quarrel.* Cincinnati, Marwick Co., 1911.

O'Connor, William Douglas: *The Good, Gray Poet.* N. Y., Bruce & Huntington, 1886.

GENERAL WORKS CONSULTED

Malinowski, Bronislaw: *Sexual Repression in Savage Society.* 1927.

Langdon-Davies, John: *A Short History of Women.* 1927.

Richards, I. A.: *Principles of Literary Criticism.* 1924.

Ogden and Richards: *The Meaning of Meaning.* 1927.

Summers, Montague: *History of Witchcraft and Demonology.* 1926.

Murray, M. H.: *The Witch Cult in Western Europe.* 1921.

Barnes, Harry Elmer: *History and Social Intelligence.* 1926.

Russell, Phillips: *Benjamin Franklin, First Civilized American.* 1926.

Whyte, Fred: *The Life of W. T. Stead.*

Blanchard, Fred T.: *Fielding, the Novelist.* 1927.

Forsyth, William: *Novels and Novelists of the 18th Century.* 1871.

Sawyer, Harriet Price: *The Library and Its Contents.* 1925. See Chapter by Corinne Bacon: "What Makes a Novel Immoral?"

Rye, R. A.: *Guide to the Libraries of London.* 1927.

Bostwick, Arthur E.: *The American Public Library.* 1923.

Baker, J. A.: *The Public Library.* 1922.

Graves, Charles L.: *Mr. Punch's History of Modern England.* Four Volumes, 1921-22.

Bell, Mackenzie (editor): *Representative Novelists of the 19th Century.* Four Volumes, 1927.

Dreiser, Theodore: *Hey Rub-a-dub-dub.*

Davidson, J. Morrison: *Eminent Radicals.*

Mahaffy, J. P.: *Social Life in Greece.*

Disraeli, Isaac: *History of Printing.*

Mordell, Albert: *The Erotic Motive in Literature.* 1919.

WORKS ON THE BRITISH STAGE CENSORSHIP

Fowell, Frank, and Palmer, Frank: *Censorship in England.* 1913.

G. M. G.: *The Stage Censor.* 1908.

Shaw, George Bernard: *The Shewing Up of Blanco Posnet.* With a Preface on the Censorship. 1909.

Great Britain: *Stage Plays.* Committee Report from the Joint Select Committee of the House of Lords and the House of Commons, together with the proceedings of the Committee, Two Volumes, 1909. London, Wyman & Sons, Ltd. For His Majesty's Stationery Office.

Krutch, Joseph Wood: *Comedy and Conscience After the Restoration.* 1924.

Thompson, Albert M.: *The Controversy between the Puritans and the Stage.* 1903.

Collier, Jeremy: *A Short View of the Immorality and Profaneness of the English Stage.* London, 1698.

ON MOVIE CENSORSHIP

Rutland, James R.: *State Censorship of Motion Pictures.* N. Y., H. W. Wilson Co., 1923. Reference shelf, Vol. II, No. 1.

Oberholzer, Ellis P.: *Morals of the Movie.* Philadelphia, Penn Pub. Co., 1922.

FEDERAL CENSORSHIP

In addition to "Obscene Literature" and Constitutional Law *and* Birth Control Laws, *already cited, see:*

Atkinson, Wilmer: *Freedom of the Press and the Mails.* Philadelphia, 1907.

Flower, O. B.: *The Story of "The Menace" Trial.* Aurora, Mo., U. S. Pub. Co., 1916.

Bakewell, Paul: *An Open Letter to W. H. Lanoir, Solici-*

tor to the Post Office. "The Menace" and the Post Office. The Catholic Mind. Vol. XIII. No. 2, Jan. 22, 1915.

Phife, Robert S.: *Free Speech and Constitutional Law.* Brief filed in Supreme Court of Mississippi, 1922. Official Opinions of the Assistant Attorney General for the Post Office Department from Oct. 25, 1905, to June, 26, 1908. Washington, Government Printing Office.

Post Master General: Reports.

Rogers, Lindsay: *The Postal Power of Congress.* John Hopkins University Press, 1916. Pr. 34, No. 2.

Clemens, G. C.: The United States *vs.* Harmon. Argument for defendant.

Hearing before Committee on Judiciary: House of Representatives, 69th Congress (1st session), on H. R. 10989, Apr. 27, 1926. To amend Sec. 245 of the Penal Laws. Serial 19. Also May 17, 1926, serial 19, Post. 2.

Hearing on the 3rd session of the 63rd Congress: Committee on Post Office and Post Roads. House of Representatives. "Exclusion of Certain Publication from the Mails."

LORD CAMPBELL'S ACT

Hansard: *Parliamentary Debates.* Volumes 145, 146, 147.

Campbell, Lord John: *The Lives of the Lord Chancellors of England.* 1849.

Hardcastle, Mrs. M. S.: *Life of John, Lord Campbell, consisting of a selection from his autobiography, diary and letters.* London, John Murray, 1881. Two Volumes.

Lord Brougham: On Lord Campbell's Act in *Law Magazine and Review* (1857). Pp. 283 *et seq.*

WORKS CONTAINING GENERAL ESSAYS ON
LITERARY DECENCY

Mordell, Albert: *Notorious Literary Attacks.* 1926.

Mencken, H. L.: *A Book of Prefaces.* 1917.

Moore, George: *Avowals.* 1919.

Moore, George: *Memoirs of My Dead Life.* Introduction, 1907.

Bourne, Randolph: *The History of a Literary Radical.* 1920.

Graves, Robert: *Lars Porsena, or The Future of Swearing and Improper Language.* 1927.

Whibley, Charles: *Studies in Frankness.*

Bowman, James Cloyd (editor): *Contemporary American Criticism.* 1926.

Macaulay, T. B.: *Critical, Historical and Miscellaneous Essays.* See Essay on Leigh Hunt.

Harris, Frank: *Contemporary Portraits.*

George, W. L.: *Literary Chapters.* 1918.

George, W. L.: *Eddies of the Day.*

Lippman, Walter: *Men of Destiny.* 1927.

Canby, Henry Seidel: *Definitions, Second Series.* 1924.

Erskine, John: *The Literary Discipline.* 1923.

Howells, William D.: *Criticism in Fiction.*

Drew, Elizabeth: *The Modern Novel.* 1926.

Sherman, Stuart P.: *Points of View.* 1924.

Twelve American Writers: *The Novel of To-morrow and the Scope of Fiction.* 1922.

Johnson, R. Brimley: *Moral Poison in Modern Fiction.*

THE ENGLISH CIRCULATING LIBRARIES

The University Magazine and Free Review: Vol. 5, pp. 337-51. Jan. 1, 1896. "Smith, the Censor."

The Book Monthly: Vol. 14 (1919). "Mudie's Seventy-Five–Not Out."

Moore, George: "Apologia pro Scriptis Meis" in the *Fortnightly Review*, n. s. Vol. 112, p. 529.

Alexander, Mary: "The Rise and Decline of the Three-Volume Novel" in *The Libraries Association Record*, n. s. Vol. II, p. 150. London, 1924.

Lodge, Sir Oliver: "The Responsibility of Authors" in the *Fortnightly Review*, Vol. 93, p. 257, Feb. 1910.

Gosse, Sir Edmund: "The Censorship of Books" in the *Living Age*, Apr. 16, 1910.

Tennyson, Charles: "The Libraries Censorship" in the *Contemporary Review*, Vol. 97, p. 476 (1910).

Moore, George: "The Freedom of the Pen: A Conversation with John L. Balderston" in the *Fortnightly Review*, Vol. 108, p. 539, Oct. 1917.

George Moore: *Circulating Morality*. Vizetelly & Co., 1885.

Saintsbury, George: *The English Novel*. Pp. 263 *et seq.* with reference to circulating libraries.

THE SEX CENSORSHIP ON THE CONTINENT

In addition to the German works already cited, see the following articles:

Slavonic Review: Vol. 4, p. 725. "The Index of the Soviet Inquisition."

Devane, Rev. R. S., S. J.: "The Committee on Printed Matter" in *The Irish Ecclesiastical Record:* Oct., Nov., Dec., 1926.

Dufay, Pierre: "Le Procès de Fleurs du Mal" in *Mercure de France*, Apr. 1, 1921, Vol. 147.

Banville, Théodore de: "Fleurs du Mal" in *Annales Politiques*, March 8, 1925.

Boyd, Ernest: "Adult or Infantile Censorship" in *The Dial*, Vol. 70, p. 381-5, Apr. 1921.

Coffin, Victor: "Censorship and Literature under Napoleon I" in the *American Historical Review*, Vol. 22, p. 288 (1917).

American Journal of International Law: Vol. 5, supplement July 1911, pp. 167 *et seq.*; Vol. 20, supplement, pp. 179-91, Oct. 1926: "International Conference for Suppression of Traffic in Obscene Literature."

Lang, Andrew: "The Evolution of Literary Decency" in *The Book Lover*, Number 5, Autumn 1900.

PAMPHLETS RELATING TO TRIALS

Talfourd, T. N.: Speech for the Defendant in the Queen *vs.* Moxon. 1841.

Schroeder, Theodore: *Constitutional Free Speech Defined and Defended in an Unfinished Argument in a Case of Blasphemy.*   Free Speech League, N. Y., 1919.

Report of the Emergency Committee Organized to Protest against the Suppression of James Branch Cabell's Jurgen: *Jurgen and the Censor.*   N. Y.   1919.

Holt, Guy (editor): *Jurgen and the Law.*   A statement, including the Court's opinion, and the brief for the defendants on motion to direct an acquittal.

Auerbach, Joseph S.: Oral Argument Against the Suppression of *The "Genius"* before the Appellate Division of the New York Supreme Court—First Department. Reprinted in "Essays and Miscellanies." Harper's, 1922, pp. 130-65.

Singer, George Astor: *Judicial Scandals and Errors.* London, University Press, Ltd., 1899.

Besant, Annie: *Is the Bible Indictable?*   London, 187?.

Vizetelly, Henry: *Extracts Principally from the English Classics, showing that the Legal Suppression of M. Zola's novels would logically involve the Bowdlerization of some of the greatest works in English Literature.* London, 1888.

Buchanan, Robert Wm.: "On Descending into Hell." A letter addressed to the Rt. Hon. Henry Matthews, Q. C., Home Secretary, concerning the proposed suppression of literature.   London, G. Redway, 1889.

The Queen *vs.* Edward Truelove. Trial for publishing the Hon. Robert Dale Owen's *Moral Psychology.* 1878.

Rosenthal, Elias: "Theodore Dreiser's *'Genius'* banned."

Mencken, H. L.: "To the Friends of *The American Mercury*: A Statement by the Editor." April 16, 1926.

The Case against the Graphic. Brief. Prosecution instituted by the New York Society for the Suppression of Vice under Section 2 of Section 1141 which prohibits papers undiscriminatingly made up of reports of crime, police reports, lust, etc. Joseph Schultz, counsel. Max D. Steuer, of counsel.

Current Opinion: Judge Hand's opinion in full in the *Hagar Revelly* case. Nov. 1913, p. 353.

ADDITIONAL PAMPHLETS AND .DOCUMENTS

Comstock, Anthony: *Morals, not Art or Literature.* 1914.

Wakeman, T. B.: *Liberty and Purity.* An address before the Committee on Charitable and Religious Societies of the Assembly of the State of New York in opposition to a bill to largely increase the criminal jurisdiction and powers of the Society for the Suppression of Vice. March 23, 1881.

Joint Public Hearing before the Senate Committee on Codes and the Assembly Committee on Codes, March 16, 1926, relating to the Clean Books Bill. In Columbia University Law Library.

John S. Sumner *vs.* Ernest Boyd: Debate on the Clean Books League Bill. The League for Public Discussion, 1924.

Rosenberg, James N.: *Censorship in the United States.* An address before the Association of the Bar of the City of New York on March 15th, 1928.

Blakeman, C. E.: *Thoughts on Books to Read and Books to Burn.* 1906.

Coote, William Alexander: *A Romance of Philanthropy.* Being a Record of Some of the Principal Incidents Con-

nected with the Exceptionally Successful Thirty Years'
Work of the National Vigilance Association. 1916.

International Agreement for the Suppression of Obscene
Publications. Signed at Paris, May 4, 1910. Published
by His Majesty's Stationery Office. Treaty Series 1911,
No. 11.

Shearman, Montague, and Raynor, O. T. (editors): *The
Press Laws of Foreign Countries.* London, His Majesty's Stationery Office, 1926.

Report and Special Report from the Select Committee on
the Matrimonial Causes (Regulation of Reports Bill)
Changed to: Judicial Proceedings (Regulation of Reports Bill). London, His Majesty's Stationery Office,
1923.

Cole, Virginia Lee: *The Newspaper and Crime.* The
University of Missouri Bulletin, Volume 28, No. 4,
Journalism Series No. 44, 1927.

Dannenbaum, Max: *Unzüchtige Schriften, Abbildungen,
und Gegenstände in der Gesamten Rechtssprechung des
Reichsgerichts.* Universität Rostock, 1917.

Egan, Rose Francis: *The Genesis of the Theory of Art
for Art's Sake in Germany and England.* Northamp-
ton, Mass. Smith College.

New York Clean Books League: *Criminal Obscenity
Rampant.*

Mark Twain: *Conversation at the Fireside of Queen
Elizabeth.*

Journal of Social Science: Articles in Vol. IX, Nos. 1,
2, 3.

Bierhoff, Frederick, M. D.: *Control of Prostitution and
Venereal Diseases in this Country and Abroad.*

*American Journal of Obstretics and Diseases of Women
and Children:* Vol. LXVI, No. 3.

New York Medical Journal: Sept., 1907; April, 1911.

Reports of the Gideon and American Bible Societies.

Publications of U. S. Public Health Service.

Publications of National Committee for Mental Hygiene,
Inc.

Reports of American Social Hygiene Association.
Statutes of the United States and separate States and
foreign countries.
Decisions of Law Courts in the United States, separate
States, and foreign countries.

REPORTS OF THE SOCIETIES

Reports of the English Society for the Suppression of Vice.
Reports of the New York Society for the Suppression of
Vice.
Reports of the New England Watch and Ward Society.
Reports of the National Vigilance Association.
Miscellaneous Reports of Drama and other Vice Organi-
zations.

Index

INDEX